S0-BBP-728

This Storyteller's Illustrated Dictionary belongs to:

....

Mrs Wordsmith

Storyteller's

Illustrated Dictionary™

Made with ♥ by word warriors
in London and Los Angeles.

Words hand-picked by our brilliantly
clever data science engine.

mrswordsmith.com

 USNJ5D01E

This is the only dictionary you will read cover to cover and laugh!

Mrs Wordsmith is on a mission to teach every child in the world the 10,000 words they need to succeed.

Founded in London and expanding globally, we won't rest until every child, young storyteller, and family has the words they need to reach their full potential. This is Hollywood creativity, from six rising star illustrators and the artist behind Madagascar's unforgettable characters, combined with world-leading data science. It's literacy at near-light speed.

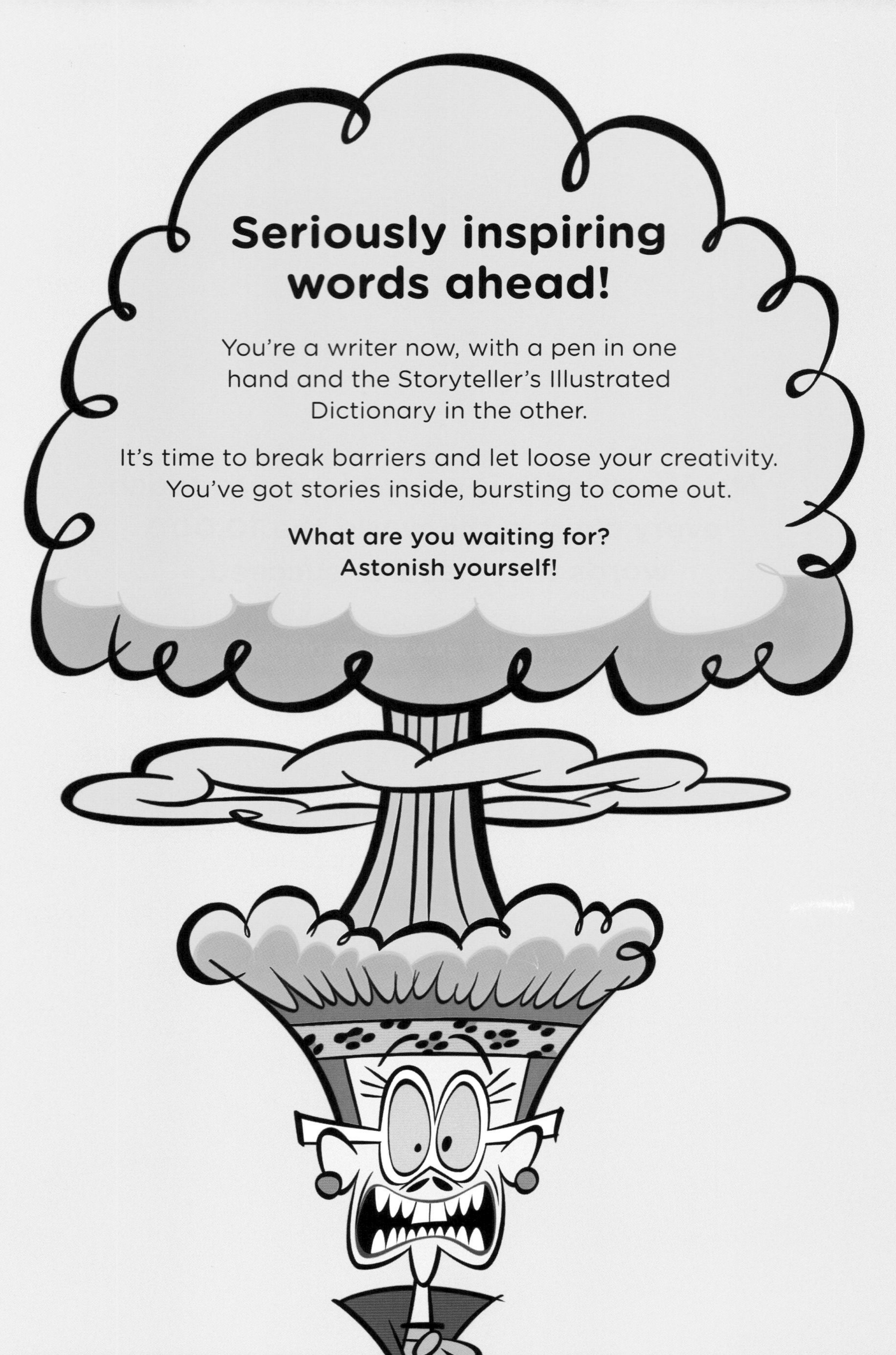
Seriously inspiring words ahead!
You're a writer now, with a pen in one hand and the Storyteller's Illustrated Dictionary in the other.
It's time to break barriers and let loose your creativity. You've got stories inside, bursting to come out.
What are you waiting for? Astonish yourself!

conquer

v. to defeat or get control over; like an army taking over new land

Action

Write a story with...

TOPICS

romance
p. 45

1

sports
p. 50

technology
p. 49

war
p. 41

Character

Write a story with...

gargantuan
adj. huge or enormous; like a giant who towers above you

TOPICS

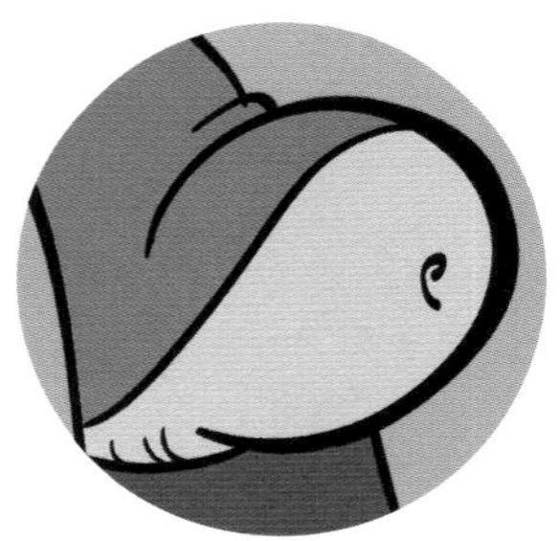

body parts
p. 74

clothing
p. 78

creatures
p. 80

unique features
p. 77

Emotion

Write a story with...

RunningMate 5000

determined

adj. driven or completely set on; like working extra hard to get what you want

Setting

Write a story with...

secluded

adj. quiet or remote; like a place where you can be completely alone

TOPICS

cities
p. 125

countryside
p. 137

mountains
p. 139

space
p. 146

Taste & Smell

Write a story with...

savor

v. to enjoy or appreciate; when you eat very slowly so you can enjoy every bite

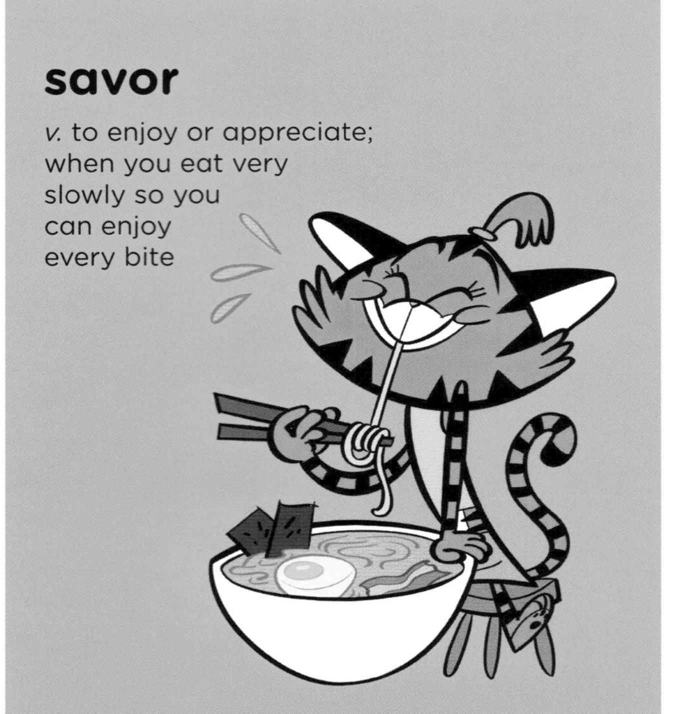

TOPICS

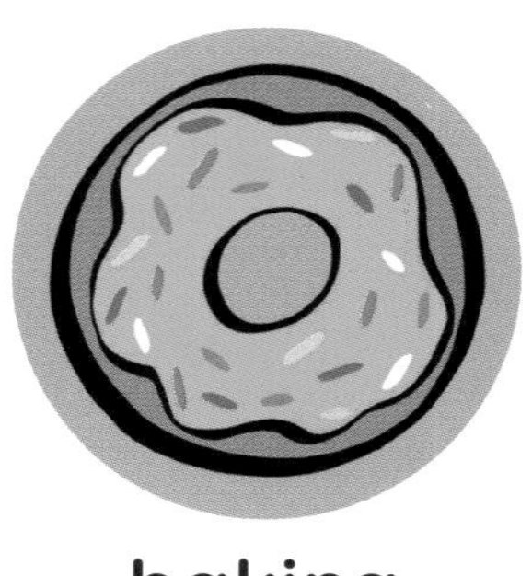

baking
p. 169

drinks
p. 172

W

fast food
p. 178

ingredients
p. 175

flurry

n. a short, swirling gust; like a burst of whirling snow that flies around your head

Weather

Write a story with...

TOPICS

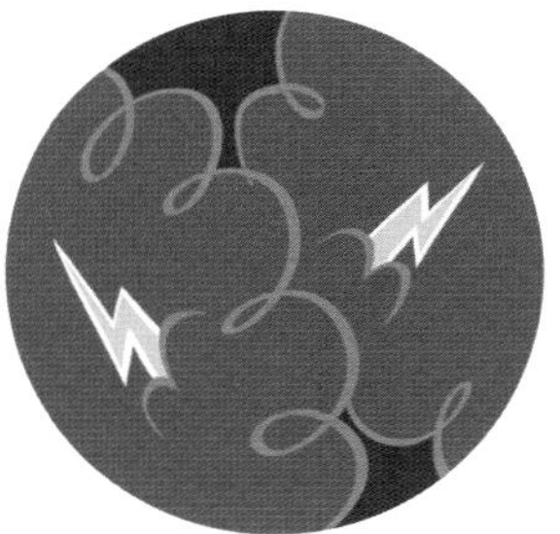

extreme
p. 203

forecast
p. 199

sunny
p. 205

windy
p. 205

Get to know your illustrated dictionary

It holds the answers.

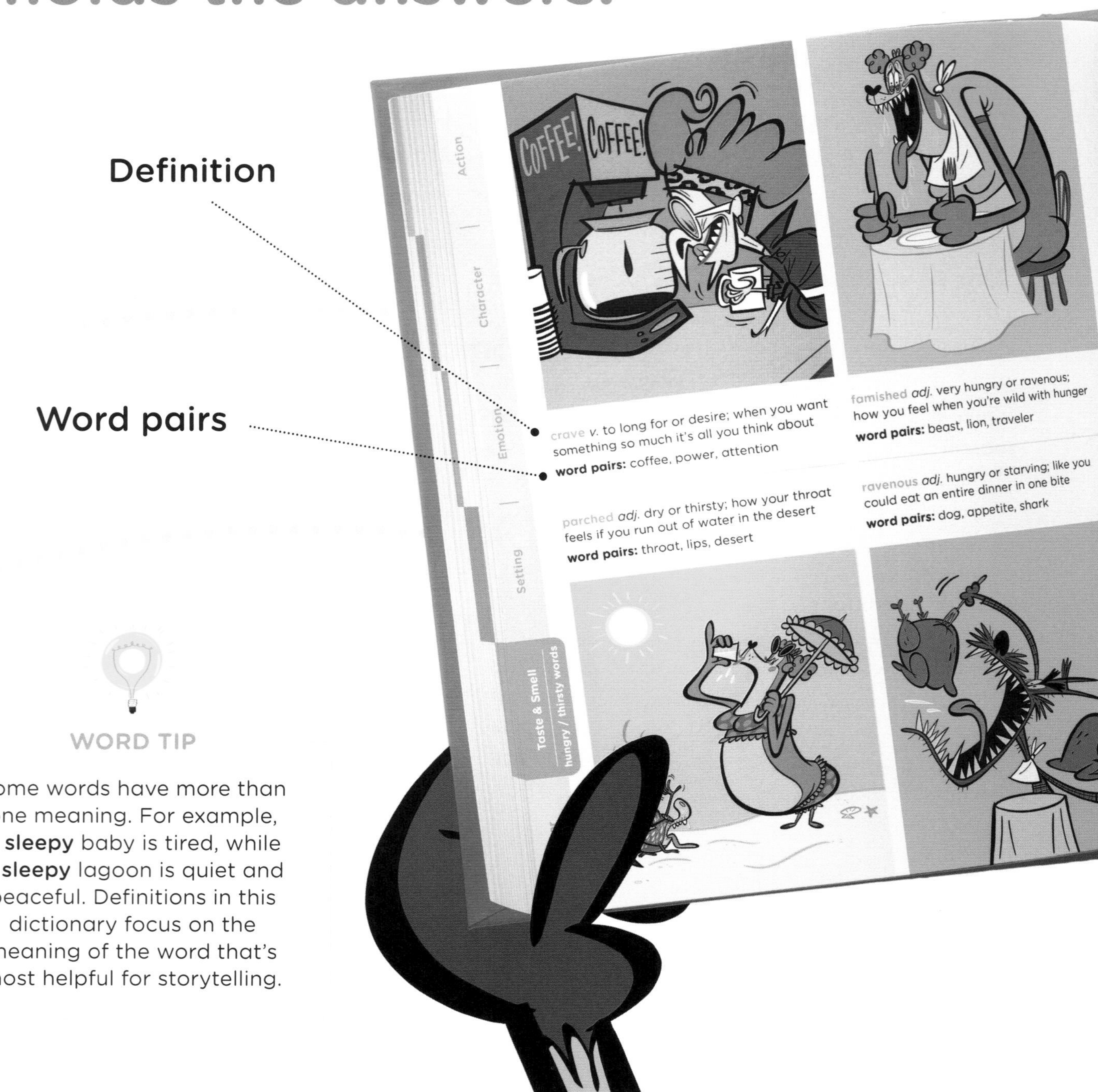

Definition
Word pairs
Action
Character
Emotion
Setting
Taste & Smell
hungry / thirsty words
COFFEE!
COFFEE!
crave v. to long for or desire; when you want something so much it's all you think about
word pairs: coffee, power, attention
famished adj. very hungry or ravenous; how you feel when you're wild with hunger
word pairs: beast, lion, traveler
parched adj. dry or thirsty; how your throat feels if you run out of water in the desert
word pairs: throat, lips, desert
ravenous adj. hungry or starving; like you could eat an entire dinner in one bite
word pairs: dog, appetite, shark

WORD TIP

Some words have more than one meaning. For example, a **sleepy** baby is tired, while a **sleepy** lagoon is quiet and peaceful. Definitions in this dictionary focus on the meaning of the word that's most helpful for storytelling.

WORD TIP

Some word pairs go before the main word, and some go after. If you aren't sure how to use the word pairs, just check the examples on the right side of the page.

insatiable *adj.* greedy or impossible to satisfy; so hungry you never fill up
word pairs: appetite, greed, curiosity

voracious *adj.* greedy or very hungry; like having a never-ending hunger for hamburgers
word pairs: appetite, predator, reader

hungry or thirsty words

word pair after:

crave coffee
famished beast
insatiable appetite
parched throat
ravenous dog
voracious appetite

Action | Character | Emotion | Setting | Taste & Sme... | hungry / thirsty w...

161

Category tabs

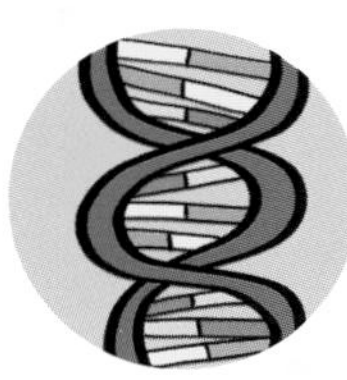

Express your originality

Shake up your stories and inject some originality to create your own sporty little number. Find the word you need here, and use the word pairs around the edge to kick your creativity into overdrive.

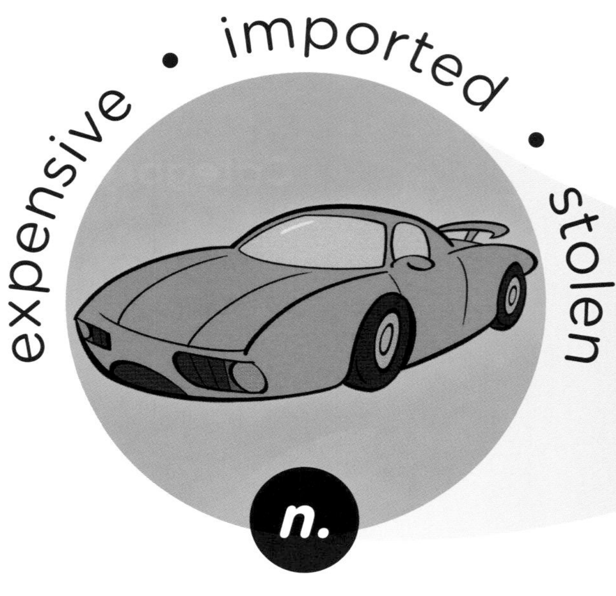

expensive • imported • stolen
n.

ACTION AND ADVENTU
Action
nouns
Character
Emotion
Setting
Taste & Smell
Weather
rented • two-person • powerful
jet ski
private • luxurious • bulletproof
limousine
fast • noisy
motor
electric • folding • compact
scooter
bouncy • plush • ejectable
seats
pirate • sinking
ship
expensive • imported • stolen
sports car
heated • crooked • leather-clad
steering wheel
spare • screeching
tire
crowded • superfast • derailed
train
giant • wobbly • lopsided
unicycle
dirty • smashed • bulletproof
windshield
38

sports car

Oz parked her **expensive sports car** next to her diamond-encrusted swimming pool.

Oz's **imported sports car** gave her a real air of Italian chic.

Oz raced away from the police in the **stolen sports car**.

HASE
charged
torn · built-in · billowing
n.
parachute
powerful · elegant · military
n.
speedboat
urned-out · clanking
n.
railer
ising · palatial
t
N AND ADVENTURE > CRIME
Action
nouns
Character
Emotion
Setting
Taste & Smell
Weather
skilled · dim-witted · suspected
n.
accomplice
masked · desperate · bumbling
n.
burglar
photographic · solid · forensic
n.
evidence
something that proves what really happened; like a doughnut left behind by a criminal during a robbery
single · important · hidden
n.
clue
gruesome · contaminated
n.
crime scene
private · bumbling · cynical
n.
detective
clever · ridiculous · ingenious
n.
disguise
powerful · dim · rechargeable
n.
flashlight
covert · botched · clandestine
n.
operation
deadly · corrosive · radioactive
n.
poison
retired · undercover · corrupt
n.
police officer
locked · fireproof · impenetrable
n.
safe
hidden · digital · hacked
n.
security camera
39

WHAT TYPE OF WORD?

n.

A *noun* or naming word

adj.

An *adjective* or describing word

v.

A *verb* or doing word

conquer

Action

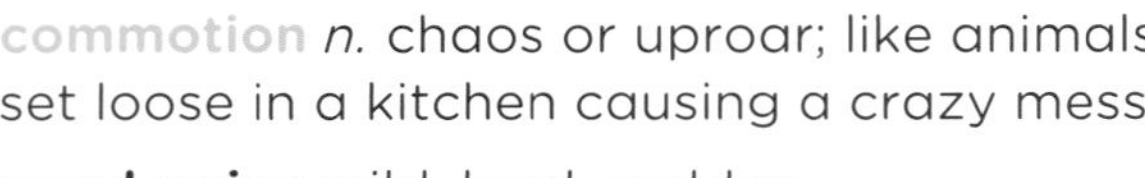

commotion *n.* chaos or uproar; like animals set loose in a kitchen causing a crazy mess

word pairs: wild, loud, sudden

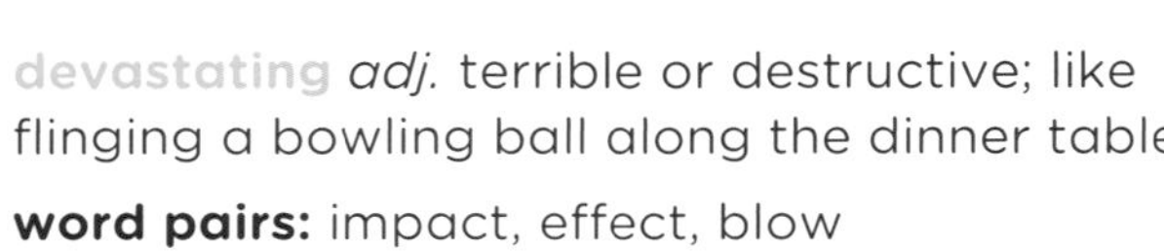

devastating *adj.* terrible or destructive; like flinging a bowling ball along the dinner table

word pairs: impact, effect, blow

rebellious *adj.* naughty or disobedient; like a giraffe who draws on the walls

word pairs: artist, attitude, teenager

turbulent *adj.* violent and unstable; like a plane that gets knocked around by heavy clouds

word pairs: flight, water, history

DOGZ
SMEL

havoc *n.* damage or chaos; like the mess caused by a giant bear smashing through a city

word pairs: cause, wreak, unleash

unruly *adj.* wild, rowdy, and rebellious; like long, frizzy hair at the beach

word pairs: hair, mob, teenager

chaotic words

word pair before:

wild commotion
cause havoc

word pair after:

devastating effect
rebellious artist
turbulent flight
unruly hair

ambush *v.* to make a surprise attack; like a soldier leaping out suddenly from a hiding place

word pairs: enemy, prey, troops

bicker *v.* to argue over silly things; like sisters arguing about nothing

word pairs: constantly, playfully, childishly

conquer *v.* to defeat or get control over; like an army taking over new land

word pairs: country, world, fears

feud *n.* a conflict that is never settled; like people fighting about the same thing for years

word pairs: bitter, long-running, vicious

bombard *v.* to attack or overwhelm; like showering someone with gifts on their birthday

word pairs: enemy, town, castle

siege *n.* a blockade or assault; when soldiers surround the enemy until they surrender

word pairs: brutal, long, bloody

fight or battle words

word pair before:

bitter feud
brutal siege

word pair after:

ambush the enemy
bicker constantly
bombard the enemy
conquer a country

backbreaking *adj.* exhausting or crushing; like lifting something so heavy it hurts your spine

word pairs: work, effort, burden

exhausted *adj.* worn out or very tired; when you are so tired you sleep deeply for hours

word pairs: sleep, voice, troops

laborious *adj.* difficult or exhausting; like the job of pushing big, heavy boulders uphill

word pairs: chore, process, undertaking

overwhelming *adj.* overpowering or immense; like carrying a ton of stuff on your shoulders

word pairs: pressure, majority, urge

grueling *adj.* difficult or draining; like the effort of carrying a huge bear

word pairs: work, climb, schedule

tedious *adj.* boring or dull; like having to work through an endless pile of homework

word pairs: paperwork, task, process

hard-working words

word pair after:

backbreaking work
exhausted sleep
grueling work
laborious chore
overwhelming pressure
tedious paperwork

gawk *v.* to gape or goggle; to look at someone with your eyes popping out of your head

word pairs: stupidly, openly, awkwardly

gaze *v.* to stare or look deep in thought; like looking longingly at an ice cream

word pairs: lovingly, longingly, blankly

peer *v.* to peek or stare; like looking over your shoulder to see what's going on

word pairs: down, inside, curiously

scrutinize *v.* to inspect or study; like when you look at something up close and in detail

word pairs: detail, face, evidence

The Word
BURGER BANDIT STRIKES!

glimpse *v.* to spot or get a quick look; like just seeing a mouse out of the corner of your eye

word pairs: mouse, sea, truth

squint *v.* to look through half-closed eyes; like when you shield your eyes from the sun

word pairs: slightly, curiously, suspiciously

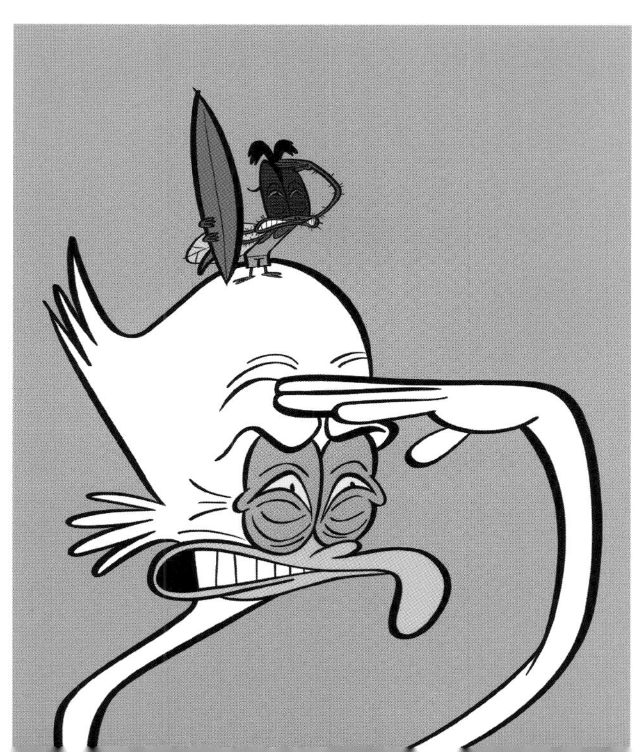

looking words

word pair after:

gawk stupidly
gaze lovingly
glimpse a mouse
peer down
scrutinize the detail
squint slightly

drowsy *adj.* sleepy or dopey; how you feel when your alarm clock goes off

word pairs: driver, voice, afternoon

sluggish *adj.* slow, lazy, or lifeless; how you feel when you get up too early in the morning

word pairs: start, river, pace

MORNI
PERSO

lounge *v.* to lie around or laze; like someone lying in the sun sipping a cool drink

word pairs: comfortably, luxuriously, lazily

soothing *adj.* calming or comforting; like a sweet song that makes you feel peaceful

word pairs: lullaby, voice, ointment

pampered *adj.* spoiled or coddled; like having an indulgent mud bath at a fancy hotel

word pairs: body, guest, lifestyle

unwind *v.* to rest or relax; like when you stretch out on the sofa after a long day at work

word pairs: completely, finally, mentally

relaxing words

word pair after:

drowsy driver
lounge comfortably
pampered body
sluggish start
soothing lullaby
unwind completely

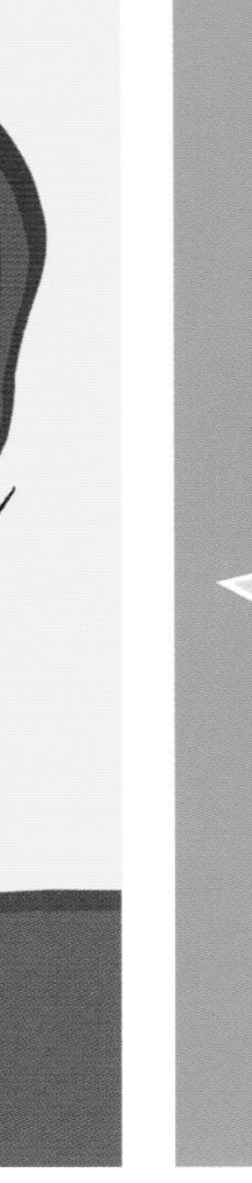

charge *v.* to run or lunge toward; rushing toward a target as fast as you can

word pairs: suddenly, furiously, headlong

dart *v.* to sprint or bolt; running somewhere suddenly and rapidly

word pairs: forward, ahead, away

hurtle *v.* to rush or move very quickly; like a big asteroid plunging toward Earth

word pairs: asteroid, train, spaceship

scamper *v.* to scurry or dash; how you would run if you were very excited

word pairs: away, inside, hurriedly

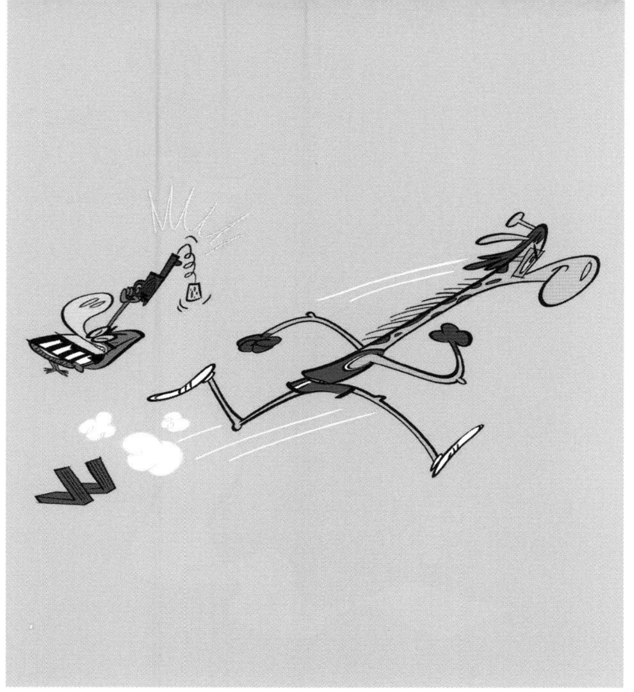

dash *n.* a race or rush; like a sprinter running at full speed toward the finish line

word pairs: sudden, wild, frantic

scurry *v.* to scamper or scuttle; like a scared armadillo trying to outrun a huge wave

word pairs: quickly, away, frantically

running words

word pair before:

sudden dash
the asteroid hurtled

word pair after:

charge suddenly
dart forward
scamper away
scurry quickly

ARMIE
PLATO

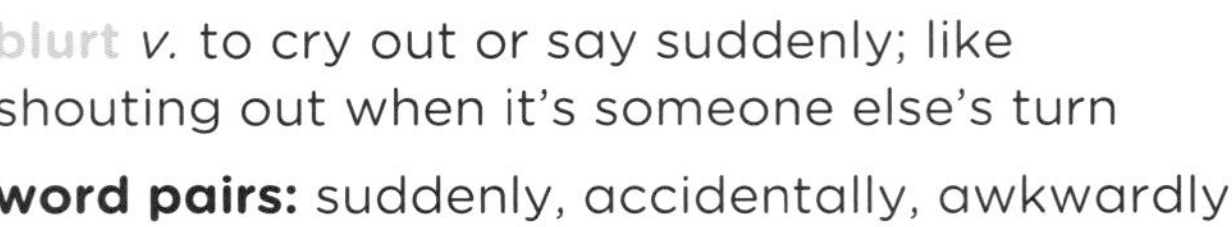

blurt *v.* to cry out or say suddenly; like shouting out when it's someone else's turn

word pairs: suddenly, accidentally, awkwardly

sneer *v.* to smirk or smile nastily; like a mean smile when others make mistakes

word pairs: openly, bitterly, sarcastically

drone *v.* to hum or make a continuous dull sound; like someone reading out a boring list

word pairs: away, endlessly, monotonously

squeal *v.* to wail or yelp; the high-pitched sound someone makes when they're surprised

word pairs: loudly, excitedly, shrilly

protest *v.* to disagree or challenge; like refusing to work until someone listens to you

word pairs: strongly, peacefully, vehemently

whimper *v.* to whine or sniffle; like the soft crying sound when someone is sad or in pain

word pairs: softly, sadly, feebly

FIRST
AID

speaking words

word pair before:

strongly protest

word pair after:

blurt suddenly
drone endlessly
sneer openly
squeal loudly
whimper softly

meander *v.* to wander or follow a winding path; like a sailor roaming across the sea

word pairs: slowly, sluggishly, aimlessly

skulk *v.* to creep or prowl; when you lie low or move carefully to avoid being seen

word pairs: around, behind, sneakily

swagger *v.* to strut or stride; how you walk when you are feeling on top of the world

word pairs: confidently, arrogantly, boisterously

traverse *v.* to cross or travel through; like a hiker making their way across steep hills

word pairs: mountain, globe, desert

stagger *v.* to stumble or walk unsteadily; how you walk after a coconut falls on your head

word pairs: about, downstairs, blindly

trudge *v.* to plod or walk slowly with heavy steps; like a tired dog walking out of the sea

word pairs: slowly, wearily, reluctantly

walking words

word pair after:

meander slowly
skulk around
stagger about
swagger confidently
traverse a mountain
trudge slowly

douse *v.* to drench or put out with water; like pouring a bucket of water over a bonfire

word pairs: flames, blaze, embers

drenched *adj.* very wet or soaked; like when you've had a bucket of water thrown over you

word pairs: hair, clothes, earth

plunge *v.* to dive or plummet; like when you jump off the highest rock into deep water

word pairs: down, headlong, recklessly

squirt *v.* to spray or splatter; like firing a water blaster in all directions

word pairs: water, ketchup, venom

DUNK the DOG!
$1 for 3 Balls

immerse *v.* to dunk or plunge; like pushing someone right to the bottom of a tank of water

word pairs: fully, partly, quickly

submerged *adj.* completely underwater; like a diver at the bottom of the sea

word pairs: diver, feet, shipwreck

wet words

word pair before:

fully immerse

word pair after:

douse flames
drenched hair
plunge down
squirt water
submerged diver

210 astonishing action nouns

Look out below! Drop these nouns and word pairs into your stories with a crash to make your characters panic, investigate, and maybe even fall in love.

missing • private • crashed
n.
airplane
parked • rickety • abandoned
n.
bicycle
giant • airborne • deflated
n.
blimp
magical • runaway • splintered
n.
broomstick
protective • dented • scuffed
n.
bumper
packed • double-decker • jolting
n.
bus
leaky • drifting • capsized
n.
canoe
classic • electric • driverless
n.
car
digital • futuristic • intuitive
n.
dashboard
powerful • purring • turbocharged
n.
engine
overnight • sunken • overloaded
n.
ferry
amazing • enchanted • driverless
n.
flying car
lightweight • crude • motorized
n.
hang glider
dim • blinding • distant
n.
headlights
circling • low-flying • whirring
n.
helicopter
huge • rising • breathtaking
n.
hot air balloon

rented • two-person • powerful
n.
jet ski
private • luxurious • bulletproof
n.
limousine
fast • noisy • turbocharged
n.
motorcycle
torn • built-in • billowing
n.
parachute
electric • folding • compact
n.
scooter
bouncy • plush • ejectable
n.
seats
pirate • sinking • derelict
n.
ship
powerful • elegant • military
n.
speedboat
expensive • imported • stolen
n.
sports car
heated • crooked • leather-clad
n.
steering wheel
spare • screeching • punctured
n.
tire
large • burned-out • clanking
n.
trailer
crowded • superfast • derailed
n.
train
giant • wobbly • lopsided
n.
unicycle
dirty • smashed • bulletproof
n.
windshield
private • cruising • palatial
n.
yacht

skilled • dim-witted • suspected

n.

accomplice

masked • desperate • bumbling

n.

burglar

photographic • solid • forensic

n.

evidence

something that proves what really happened; like a doughnut left behind by a criminal during a robbery

single • important • hidden

n.

clue

gruesome • contaminated

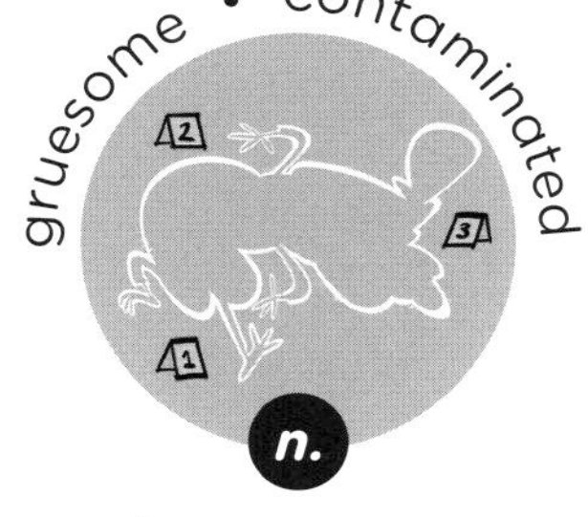

n.

crime scene

private • bumbling • cynical

n.

detective

clever • ridiculous • ingenious

n.

disguise

powerful • dim • rechargeable

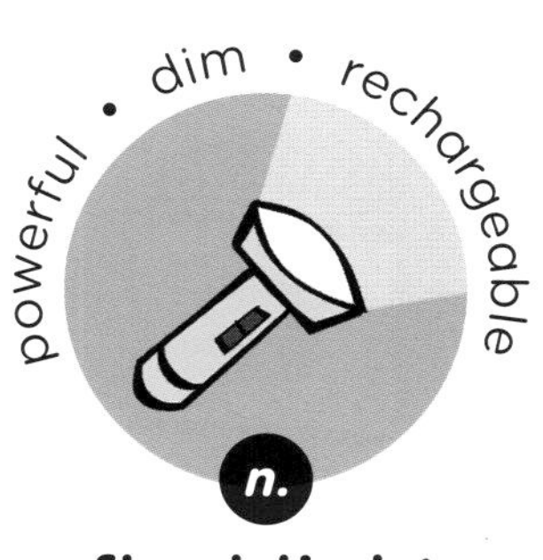

n.

flashlight

covert • botched • clandestine

n.

operation

deadly • corrosive • radioactive

n.

poison

retired • undercover • corrupt

n.

police officer

locked • fireproof • impenetrable

n.

safe

hidden • digital • hacked

n.

security camera

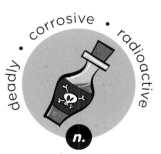

ACTION AND ADVENTURE > CRIME

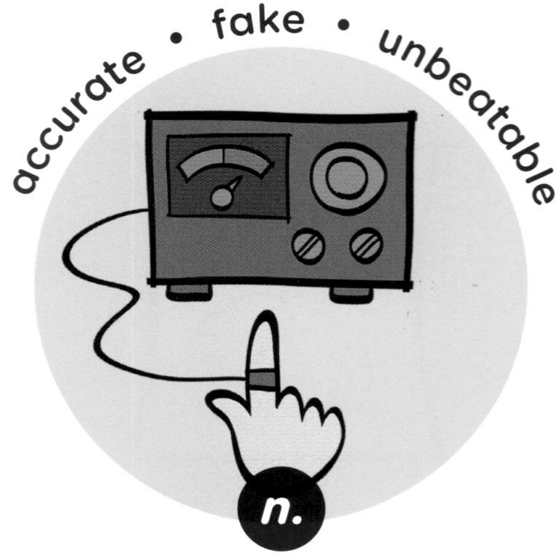
accurate • fake • unbeatable
n.

lie detector

a machine that shows if you're lying;
like a thing connected to you that flashes and beeps when you don't tell the truth

mysterious • alleged • captured
n.
spy
armed • fleeing • unidentified
n.
suspect
deadly • cunning • elaborate
n.
trap
key • credible • hostile
n.
witness

ACTION AND ADVENTURE > CRISIS

empty • automatic • portable
n.
fire extinguisher
basic • complete • essential
n.
first aid kit
bright • intense • sudden
n.
flare
electric • back-up • solar
n.
generator
cramped • capsized • unsinkable
n.
lifeboat
floating • tethered • uninflated
n.
life preserver
distant • approaching • blaring
n.
siren
sharp • shrill • ear-splitting
n.
whistle

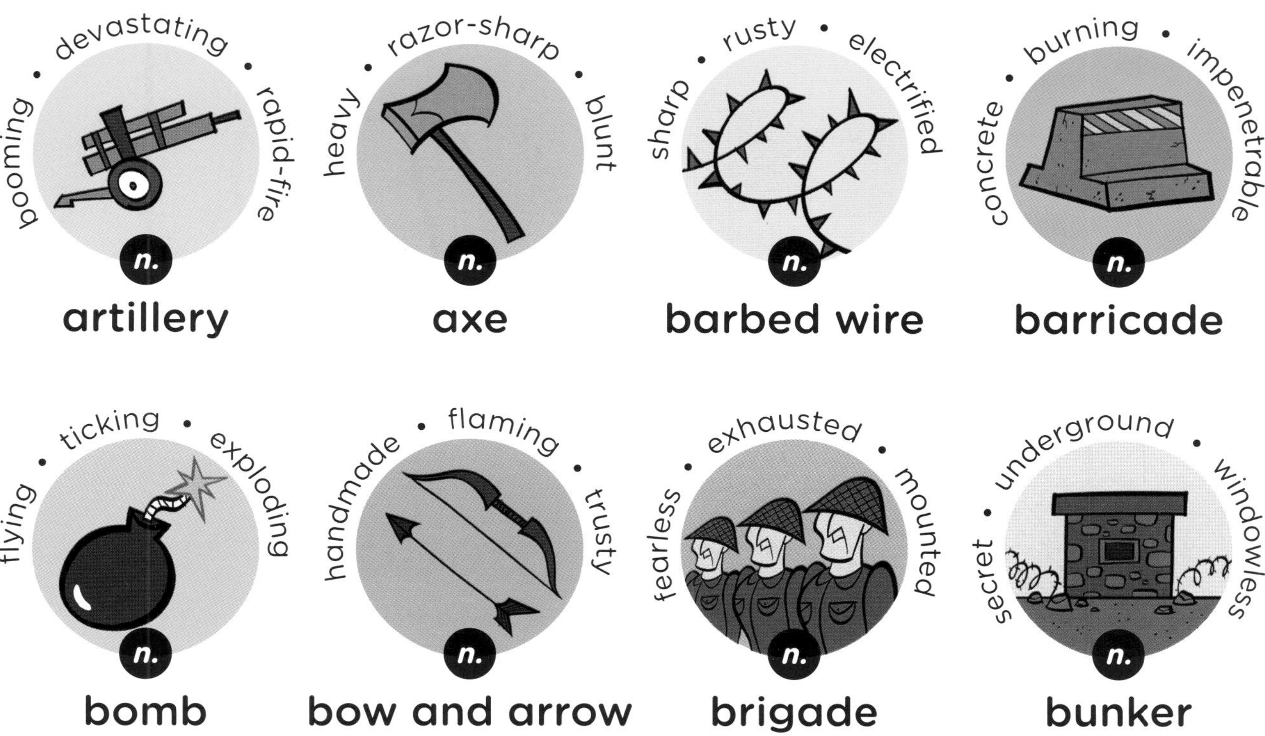
booming • devastating • rapid-fire
n.
artillery
heavy • razor-sharp • blunt
n.
axe
sharp • rusty • electrified
n.
barbed wire
concrete • burning • impenetrable
n.
barricade
flying • ticking • exploding
n.
bomb
handmade • flaming • trusty
n.
bow and arrow
fearless • exhausted • mounted
n.
brigade
secret • underground • windowless
n.
bunker

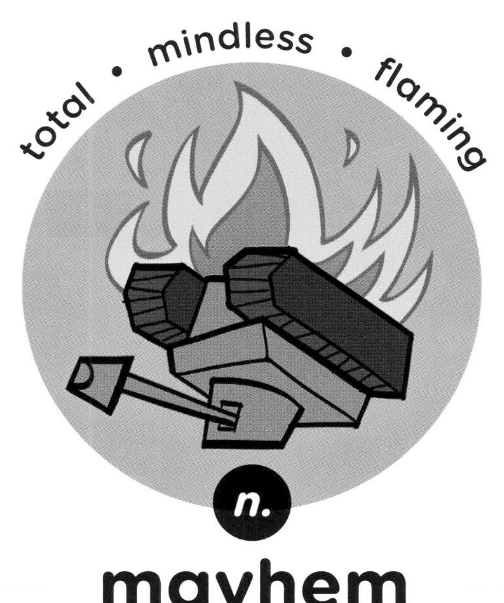
total • mindless • flaming
n.

mayhem

confusion and violent chaos; like a situation so crazy that everything is destroyed

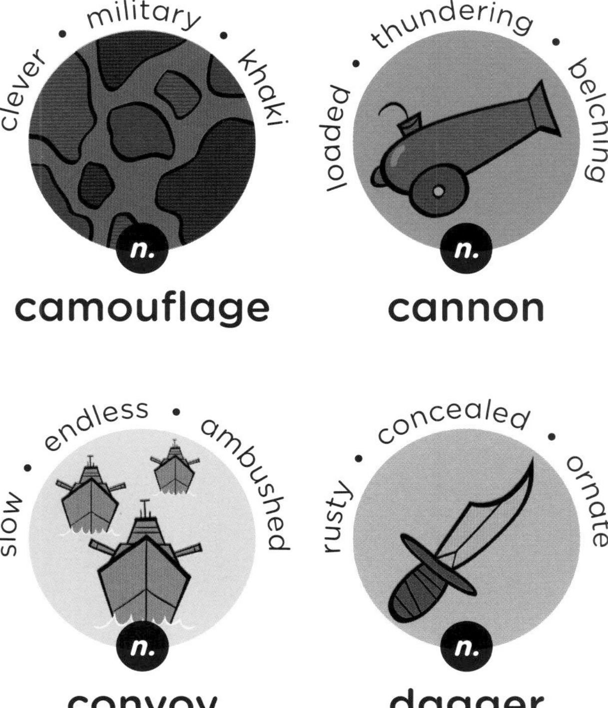
clever • military • khaki
n.
camouflage
loaded • thundering • belching
n.
cannon
slow • endless • ambushed
n.
convoy
rusty • concealed • ornate
n.
dagger

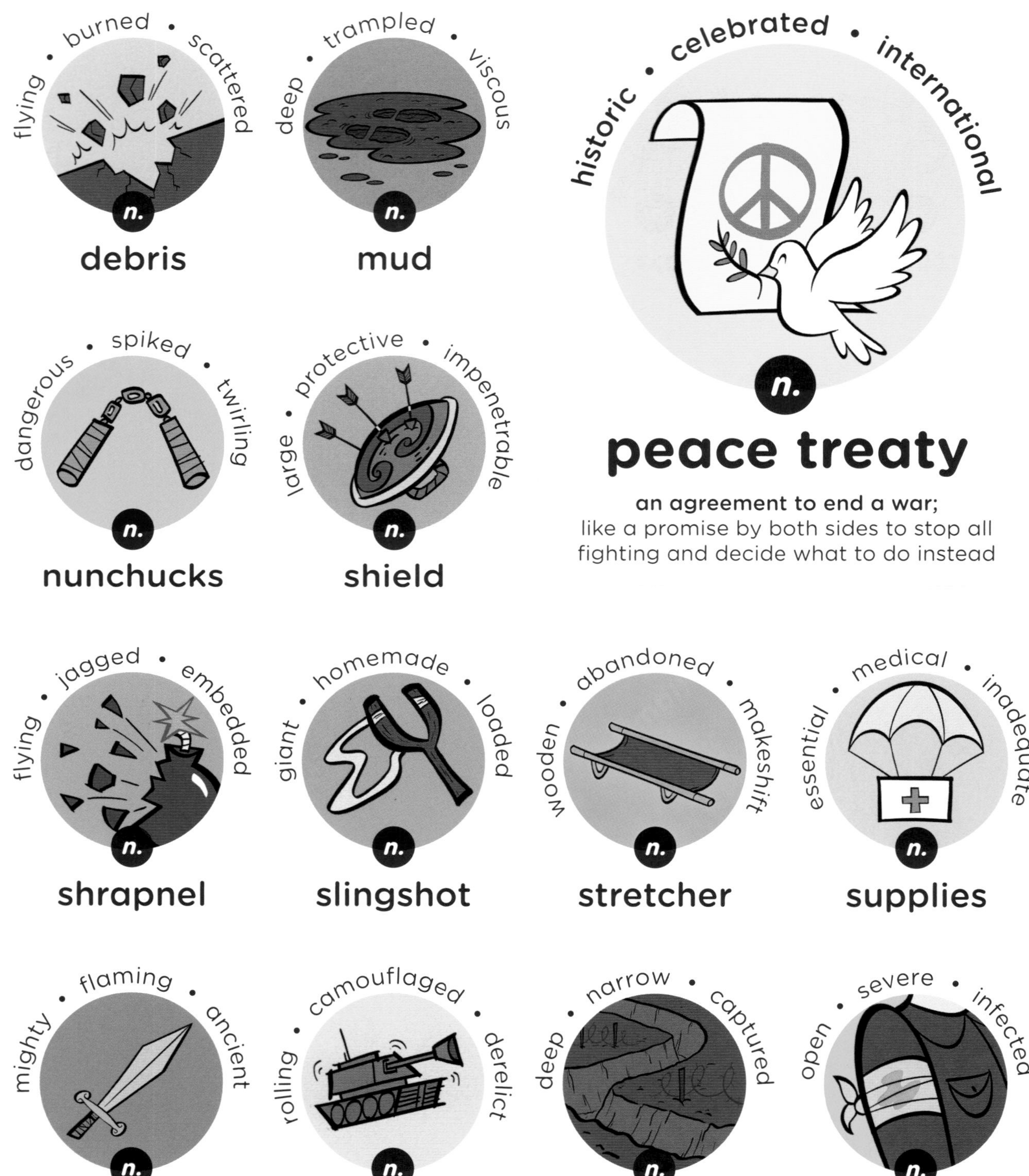
flying • burned • scattered
n.
debris
deep • trampled • viscous
n.
mud
historic • celebrated • international
n.
peace treaty
an agreement to end a war;
like a promise by both sides to stop all fighting and decide what to do instead
dangerous • spiked • twirling
n.
nunchucks
large • protective • impenetrable
n.
shield
flying • jagged • embedded
n.
shrapnel
giant • homemade • loaded
n.
slingshot
wooden • abandoned • makeshift
n.
stretcher
essential • medical • inadequate
n.
supplies
mighty • flaming • ancient
n.
sword
rolling • camouflaged • derelict
n.
tank
deep • narrow • captured
n.
trenches
open • severe • infected
n.
wound

blank • painted • stretched 
n.
canvas

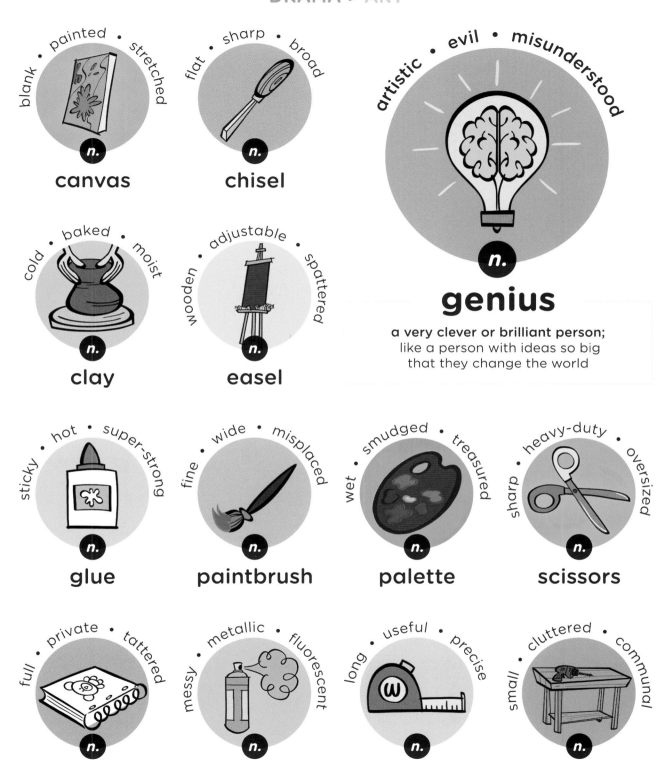

flat • sharp • broad 
n.
chisel

artistic • evil • misunderstood 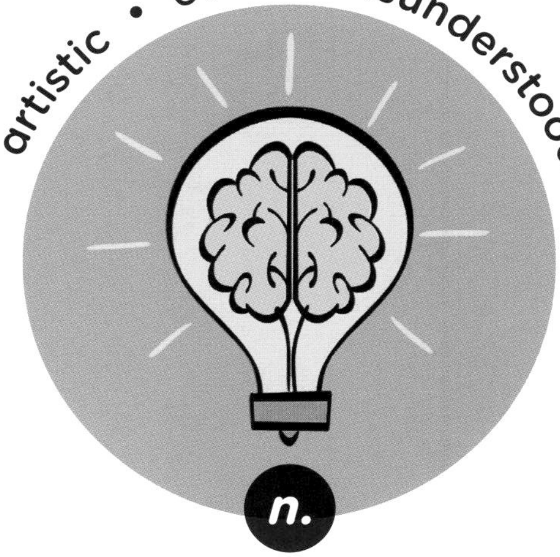
n.
genius

a very clever or brilliant person;
like a person with ideas so big
that they change the world

cold • baked • moist 
n.
clay

wooden • adjustable • spattered 
n.
easel

sticky • hot • super-strong 
n.
glue

fine • wide • misplaced 
n.
paintbrush

wet • smudged • treasured 
n.
palette

sharp • heavy-duty • oversized 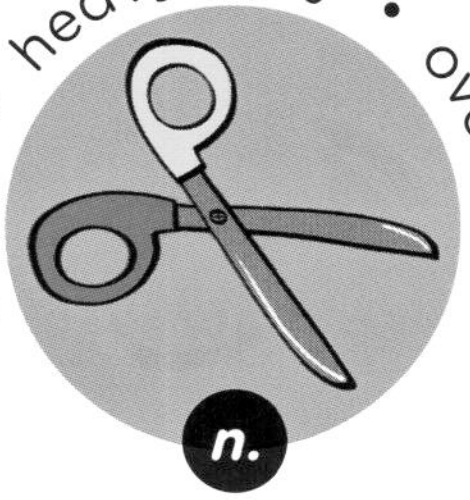
n.
scissors

full • private • tattered 
n.
sketchbook

messy • metallic • fluorescent 
n.
spray paint

long • useful • precise 
n.
tape measure

small • cluttered • communal 
n.
worktable

harsh • chaotic • deafening

n.

cacophony

lots of horrible, loud noises; like terrible singing that's so loud you can't ignore it

famous • strict • expressive

n.

conductor

cool • aspiring • legendary

n.

DJ

beating • muffled • thunderous

n.

drums

soft • gentle • shrill

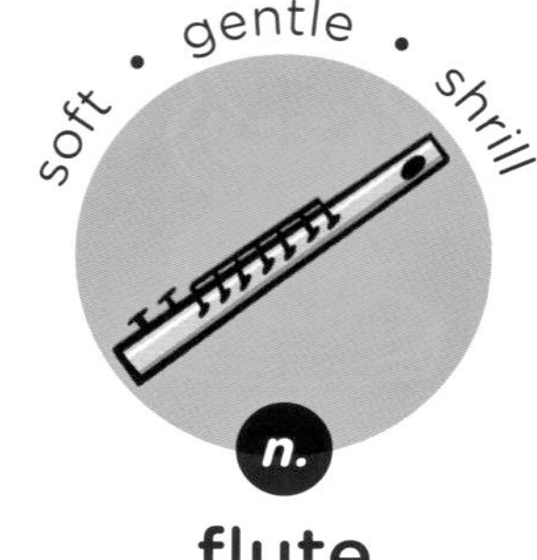

n.

flute

loud • mellow • somber

n.

French horn

wailing • battered • distorted

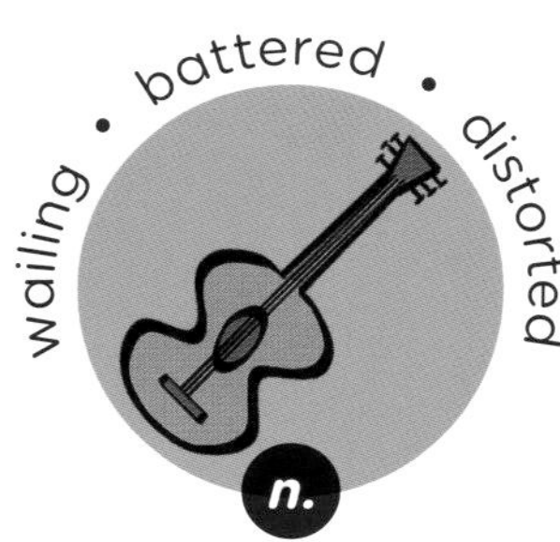

n.

guitar

wireless • hidden • crackly

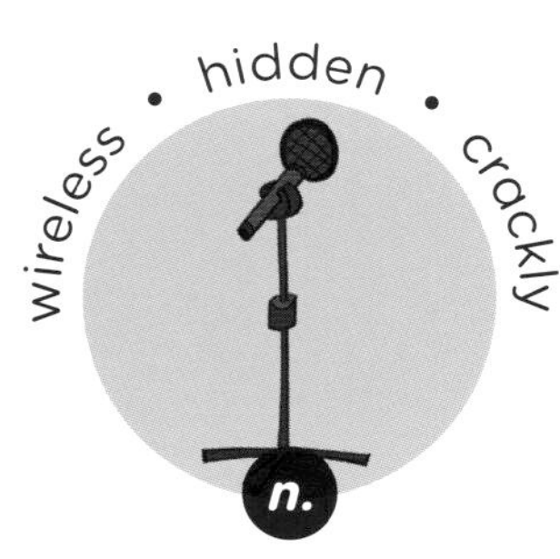

n.

microphone

electric • untuned • beloved

n.

piano

talented • inspiring • versatile

n.

singer

futuristic • hypnotic • droning

n.

synthesizer

clear • shrill • mournful

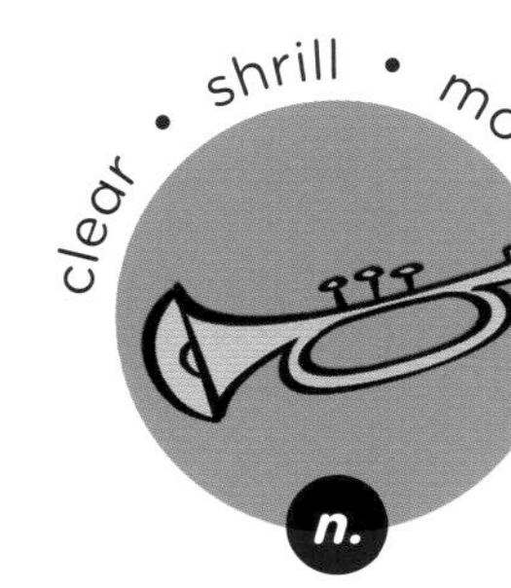

n.

trumpet

sad • screeching • soaring

n.

violin

DRAMA > RELAXATION

giant • billowing • comfortable
n.
blanket fort
thick • rumpled • luxurious
n.
duvet
padded • soothing • scented
n.
eye mask
bubbling • steamy • moonlit
n.
hot tub
deep • ticklish • rejuvenating
n.
massage
daytime • brief • much-needed
n.
nap
outdoor • rustic • sweltering
n.
sauna
exclusive • therapeutic • indulgent
n.
spa

DRAMA > ROMANCE

special • strong • unbreakable
n.
bond
golden • flickering • flattering
n.
candlelight
close • trusted • sympathetic
n.
confidant
secret • undeciphered • gossipy
n.
diary
terrible • devastating • visceral
n.
heartbreak
celebrity • teen • brooding
n.
heartthrob
first • stolen • lingering
n.
kiss
long • handwritten • bittersweet
n.
love letter

DRAMA > ROMANCE

strong • mysterious • magic

n.

love potion

painful • precious • fond

n.

memories

sweet • subtle • intoxicating

n.

perfume

romantic • bold • unexpected

n.

proposal

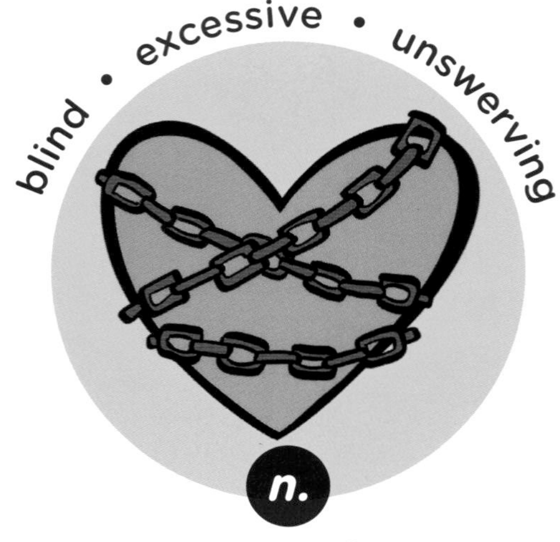

blind • excessive • unswerving

n.

devotion

deep love and commitment;
when you promise your whole heart to something or someone

FANTASY

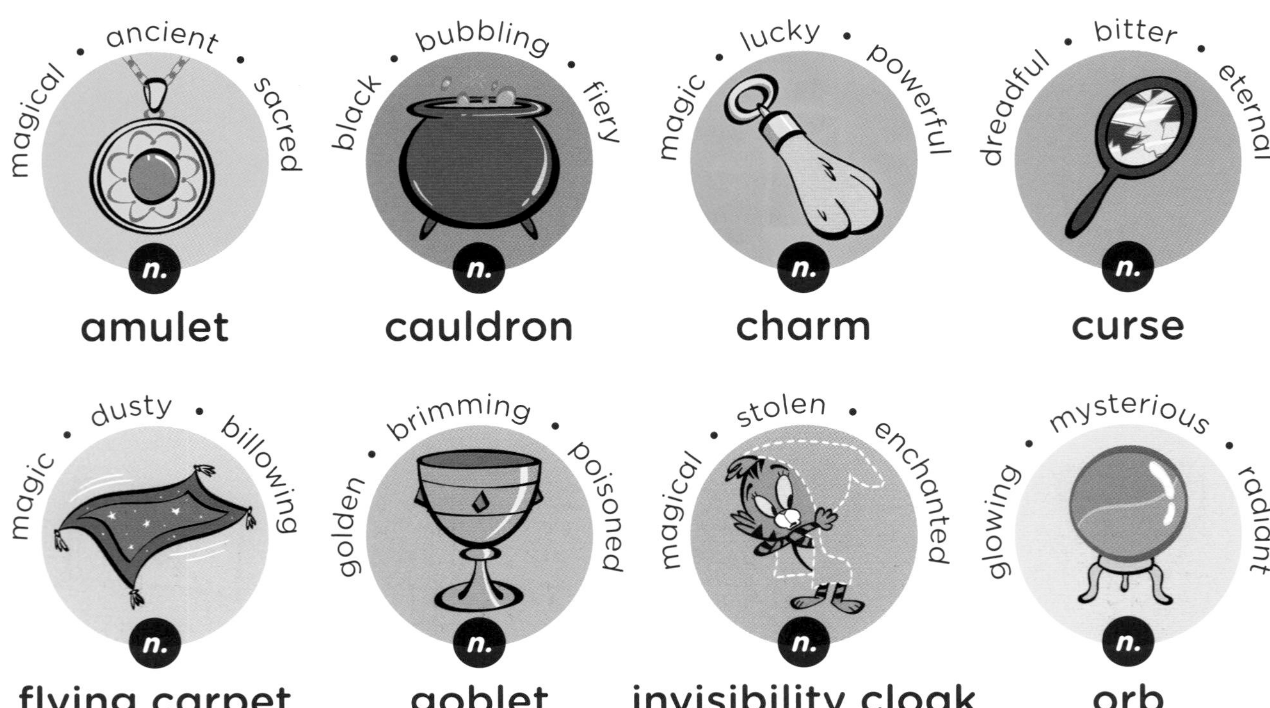

magical • ancient • sacred

n.

amulet

black • bubbling • fiery

n.

cauldron

magic • lucky • powerful

n.

charm

dreadful • bitter • eternal

n.

curse

magic • dusty • billowing

n.

flying carpet

golden • brimming • poisoned

n.

goblet

magical • stolen • enchanted

n.

invisibility cloak

glowing • mysterious • radiant

n.

orb

FANTASY

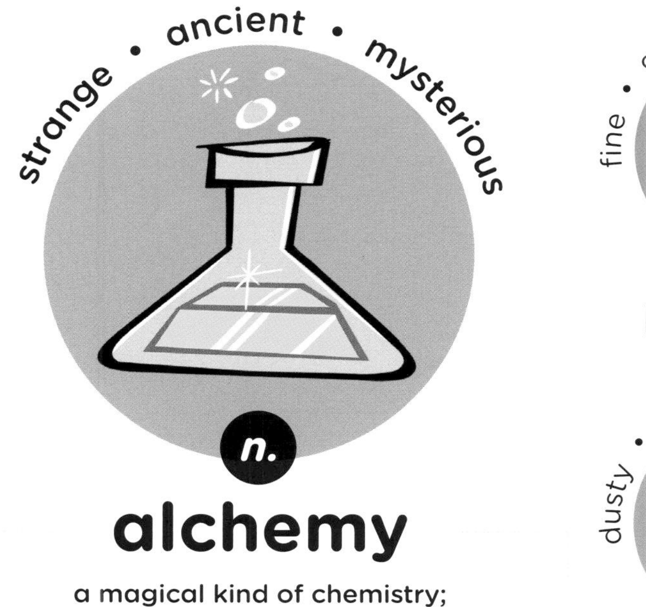
strange • ancient • mysterious
n.

alchemy

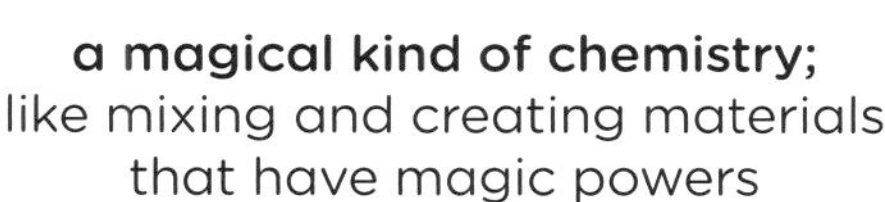

a magical kind of chemistry;
like mixing and creating materials
that have magic powers

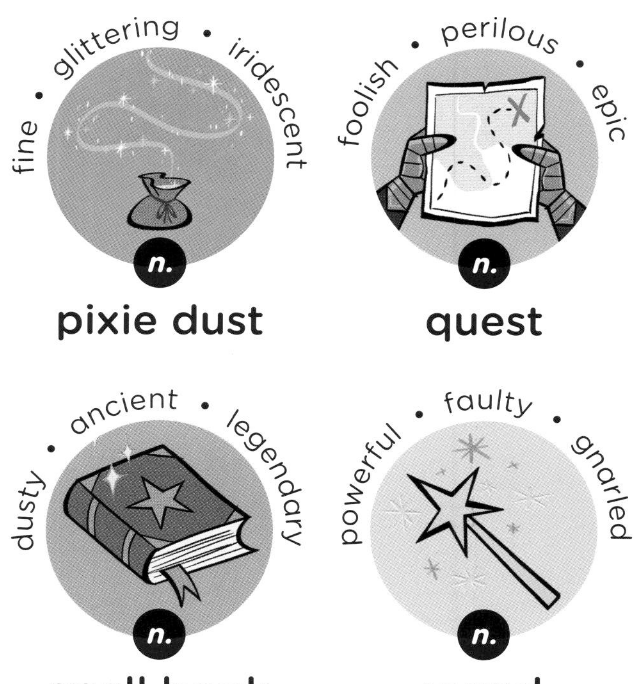
fine • glittering • iridescent
n.
pixie dust
foolish • perilous • epic
n.
quest
dusty • ancient • legendary
n.
spell book
powerful • faulty • gnarled
n.
wand

SCIENCE AND TECHNOLOGY > BUILDING

clear • detailed • architectural
n.
blueprints
gigantic • towering • overhead
n.
crane
noisy • monstrous • devastating
n.
jackhammer
high-tech • robotic • precise
n.
laser cutter
tiled • solar • corrugated
n.
roofing
temporary • flimsy • lofty
n.
scaffolding
dirty • heavy • bent
n.
shovel
handheld • secure • intrusive
n.
walkie-talkie

lit • unattended • corroded

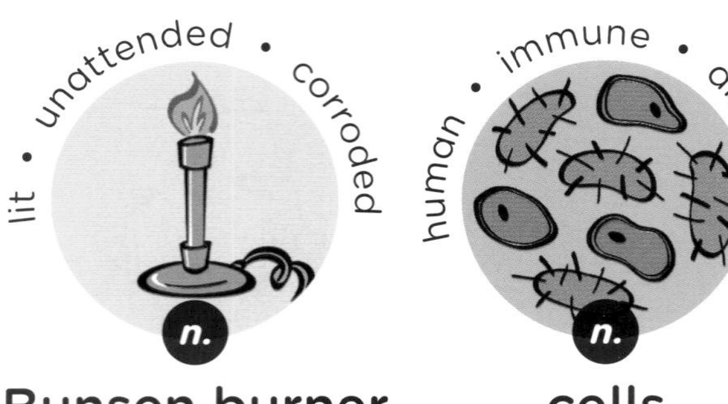

n.

Bunsen burner

human • immune • abnormal

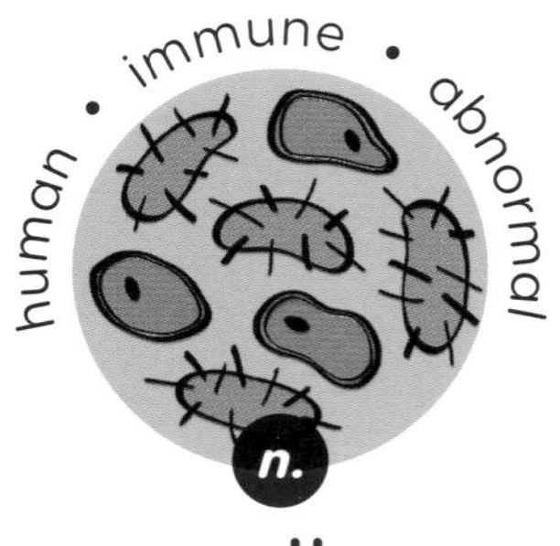

n.

cells

scientific • daring • unsuccessful

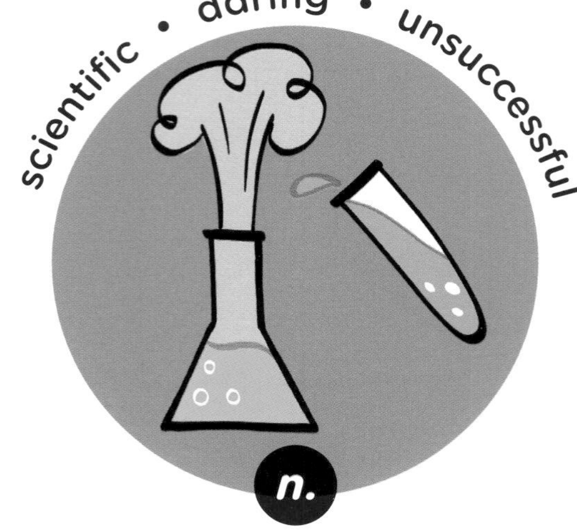

n.

experiment

a test, trial, or investigation;
like mixing two things to find out what happens

speedy • alleged • miraculous

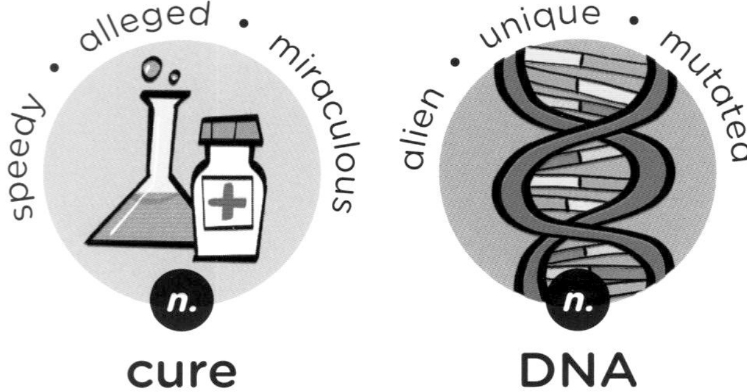

n.

cure

alien • unique • mutated

n.

DNA

clear • grubby • protective

n.

goggles

blinding • surgical • infrared

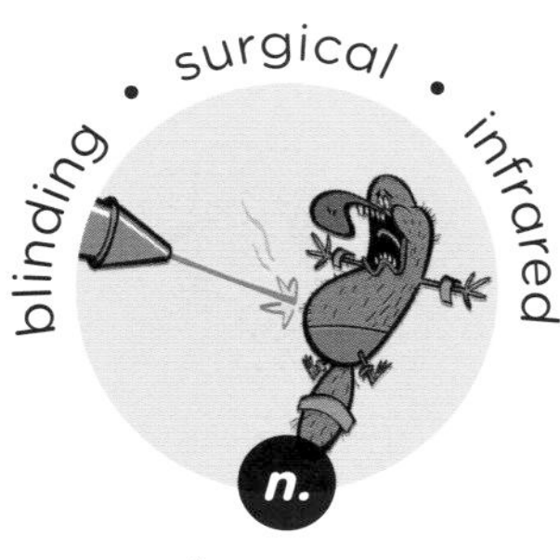

n.

laser

powerful • optical • atomic

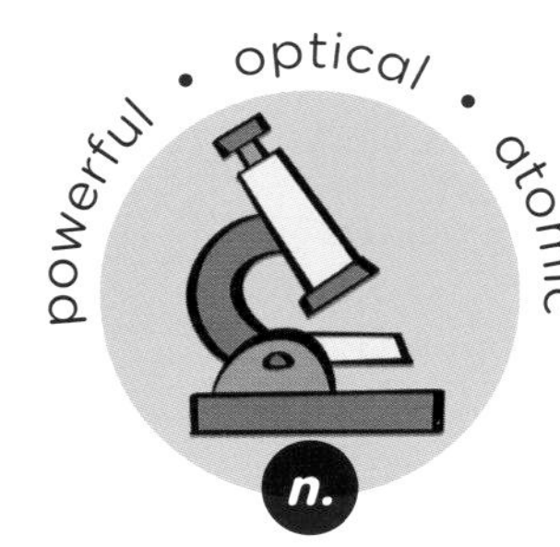

n.

microscope

harmful • random • genetic

n.

mutation

collected • random • tainted

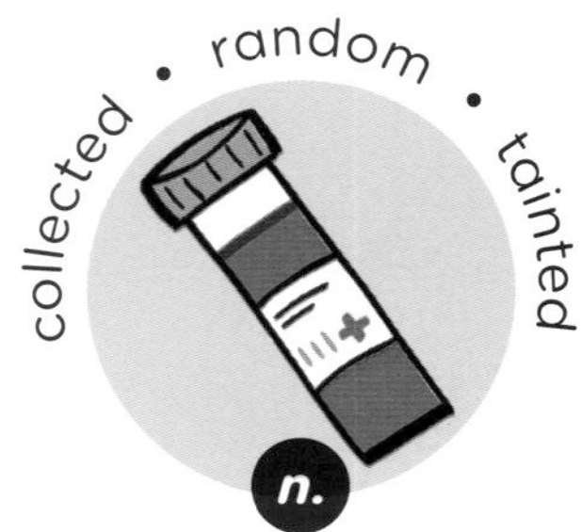

n.

sample

escaped • willing • unwitting

n.

test subject

clean • sealed • sterile

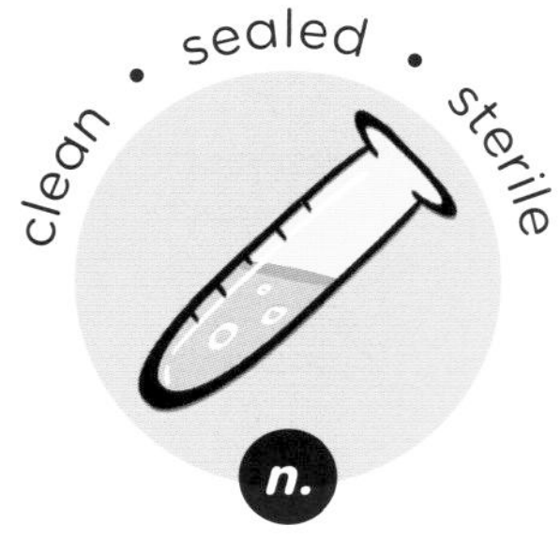

n.

test tube

free • experimental • life-saving

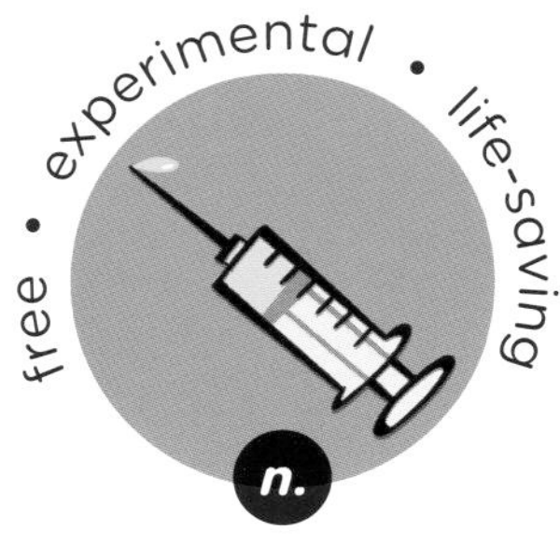

n.

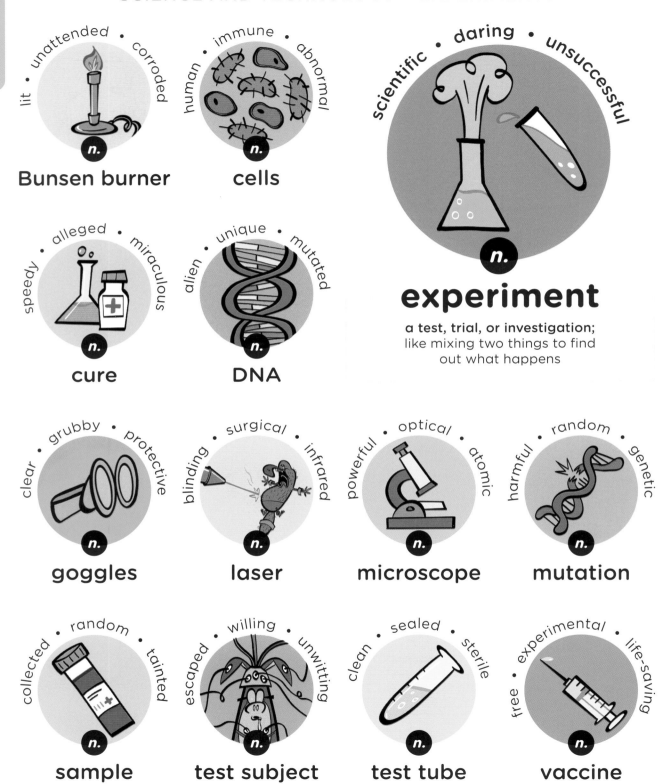

vaccine

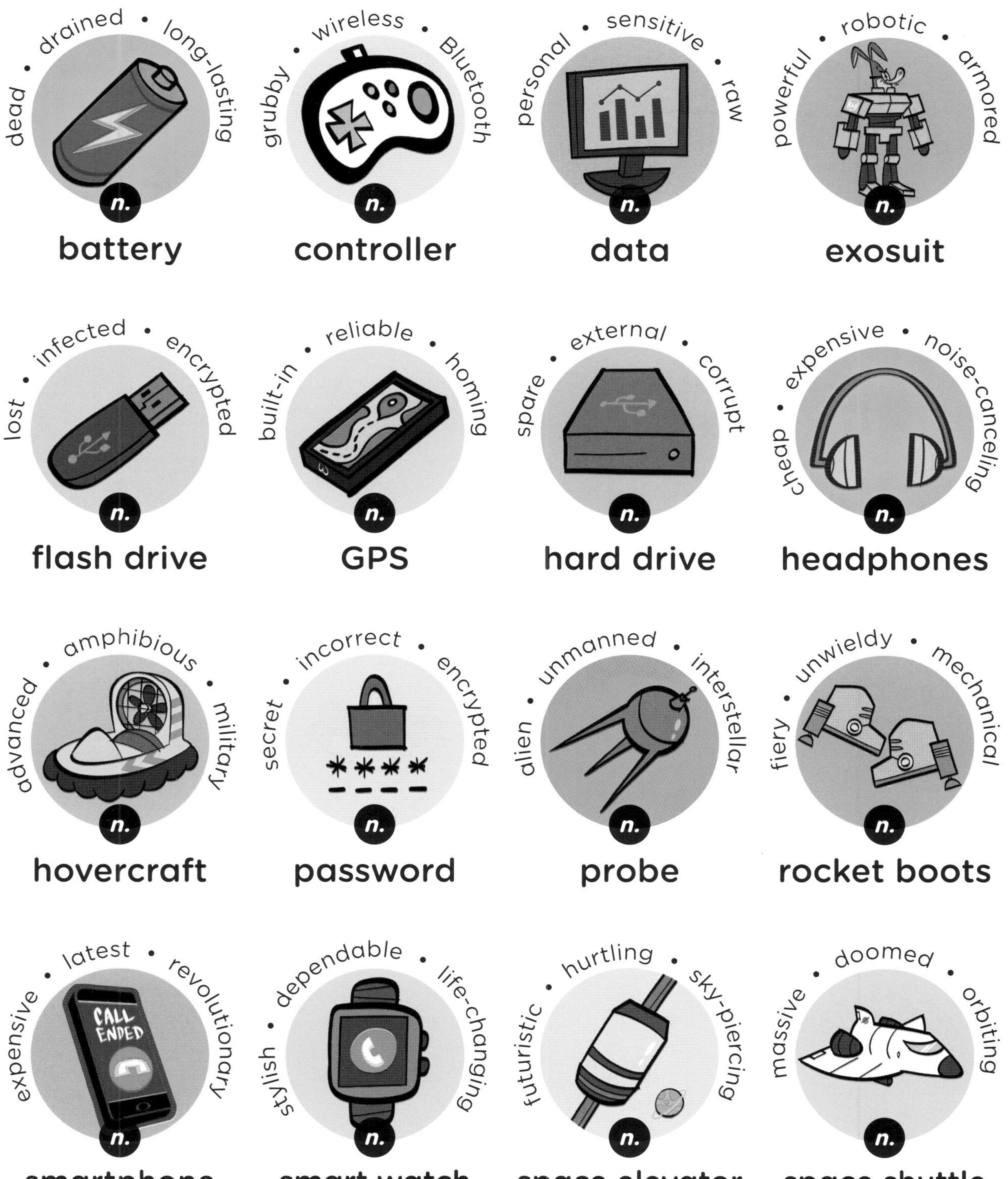
CALL ENDED

battery (n.): dead • drained • long-lasting

controller (n.): grubby • wireless • Bluetooth

data (n.): personal • sensitive • raw

exosuit (n.): powerful • robotic • armored

flash drive (n.): lost • infected • encrypted

GPS (n.): built-in • reliable • homing

hard drive (n.): spare • external • corrupt

headphones (n.): cheap • expensive • noise-canceling

hovercraft (n.): advanced • amphibious • military

password (n.): secret • incorrect • encrypted

probe (n.): alien • unmanned • interstellar

rocket boots (n.): fiery • unwieldy • mechanical

smartphone (n.): expensive • latest • revolutionary

smart watch (n.): stylish • dependable • life-changing

space elevator (n.): futuristic • hurtling • sky-piercing

space shuttle (n.): massive • doomed • orbiting

SCIENCE AND TECHNOLOGY > TECHNOLOGY

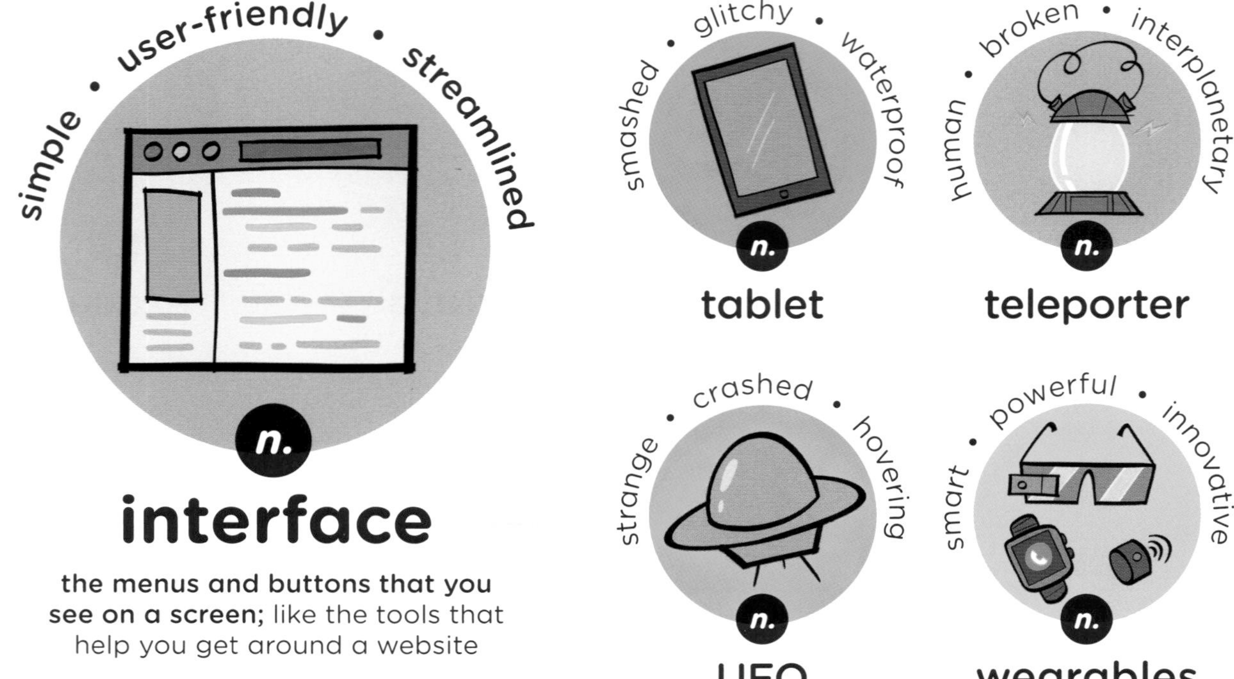
simple • user-friendly • streamlined
n.
interface
smashed • glitchy • waterproof
n.
tablet
human • broken • interplanetary
n.
teleporter
strange • crashed • hovering
n.
UFO
smart • powerful • innovative
n.
wearables

the menus and buttons that you see on a screen; like the tools that help you get around a website

SPORTS > COMPETITION

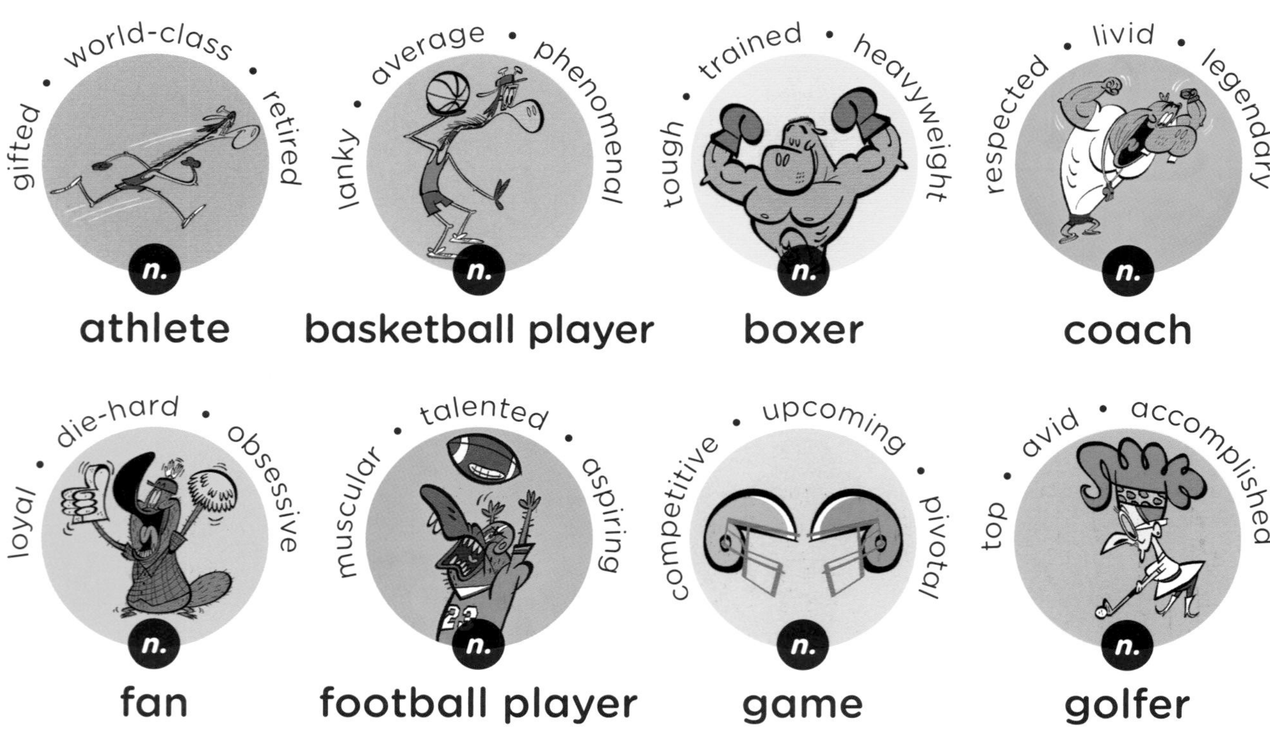
gifted • world-class • retired
n.
athlete
lanky • average • phenomenal
n.
basketball player
tough • trained • heavyweight
n.
boxer
respected • livid • legendary
n.
coach
loyal • die-hard • obsessive
n.
fan
muscular • talented • aspiring
n.
football player
competitive • upcoming • pivotal
n.
game
top • avid • accomplished
n.
golfer

SPORTS > COMPETITION

graceful • powerful • agile
n.
gymnast
unlucky • sore • gracious
n.
loser
close • hard-fought • televised
n.
match
strong • worthy • formidable
n.
opponent
winning • dedicated • undefeated
n.
team
number one • competitive • avid
n.
tennis player
glorious • coveted • prestigious
1ST
n.
trophy
two-time • worthy • unexpected
1
n.
winner

SPORTS > EQUIPMENT

high • slippery • daunting
n.
diving board
smart • accurate • waterproof
n.
fitness tracker
loose • secure • adjustable
n.
harness
protective • flexible • fitted
n.
mouthguard
huge • portable • ruptured
n.
oxygen tank
bubbling • faulty • retractable
n.
snorkel
baggy • comfortable • garish
n.
tracksuit
tight • protective • buoyant
n.
wetsuit

gargantuan

Character

chiseled *adj.* perfectly carved or sculpted; like the square jaw of a handsome superhero

word pairs: jaw, marble, cheekbones

dazzling *adj.* sparkling or amazing; like the glittering lights of a hundred cameras

word pairs: lights, smile, beauty

impeccable *adj.* elegant and perfect; like a well-groomed dog

word pairs: style, reputation, manners

mesmerizing *adj.* very attractive or bewitching; like something that hypnotizes and distracts you

word pairs: effect, music, spell

flawless *adj.* perfect or impeccable; like a ballet dancer who never makes a single mistake

word pairs: performance, skin, logic

statuesque *adj.* tall, beautiful, and dignified; like someone who looks as impressive as a statue

word pairs: figure, model, goddess

beautiful words

word pair after:

chiseled jaw
dazzling lights
flawless performance
impeccable style
mesmerizing effect
statuesque figure

bulky *adj.* large, heavily built, or stocky; like a big body with chunky muscles

word pairs: sweater, camera, body

colossal *adj.* massive or gigantic; like a huge statue that makes you feel tiny in comparison

word pairs: statue, mistake, waste

gargantuan *adj.* huge or enormous; like a giant who towers above you

word pairs: monster, appetite, laughter

pot-bellied *adj.* having a round stomach; like someone with a belly that would fit in a pot

word pairs: appearance, piglet, policeman

big or fat words

flabby *adj.* droopy, soft, and floppy; like the wobbly flesh on a hippo's stomach

word pairs: belly, arms, muscles

robust *adj.* strong and tough; like something so hardy it can't be hurt or broken

word pairs: frame, appetite, health

word pair after:

bulky sweater
colossal statue
flabby belly
gargantuan monster
pot-bellied appearance
robust frame

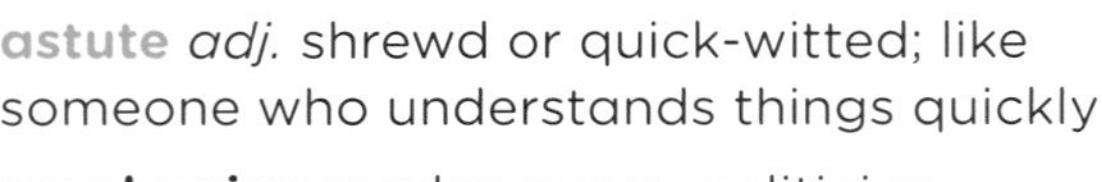

astute *adj.* shrewd or quick-witted; like someone who understands things quickly

word pairs: reader, move, politician

cunning *adj.* sly and crafty; like someone who cleverly gets out of doing their chores

word pairs: plan, fox, disguise

discerning *adj.* clear-sighted or selective; like a judge who can decide on the best cupcake

word pairs: judge, eye, taste

innovative *adj.* creative or inventive; like the genius who carved the first wheel out of stone

word pairs: design, idea, technology

10th Annual
Cupcake Contest
JUDGE

EVIL PLAN

devious *adj.* cheating or sly; like someone who is busy making evil plans

word pairs: villain, trick, plan

shrewd *adj.* clever or sharp-witted; like someone who comes up with a plan to get rich

word pairs: businesswoman, question, politician

$2.00

clever or sly words

word pair after:

astute reader
cunning plan
devious villain
discerning judge
innovative design
shrewd businesswoman

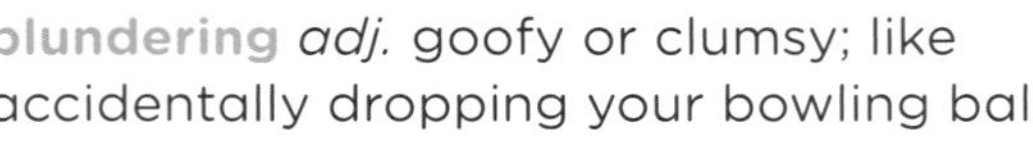

blundering *adj.* goofy or clumsy; like accidentally dropping your bowling ball

word pairs: fool, politician, buffoon

bumbling *adj.* awkward, clumsy, or useless; like a fisherman who gets tangled up in his rod

word pairs: fool, detective, burglar

crude *adj.* rude or savage; like a cavewoman who picks her nose in public

word pairs: cavewoman, manners, joke

daft *adj.* silly or foolish; like having the idea to catapult a stone into a beehive

word pairs: idea, question, movie

butterfingered *adj.* clumsy or accident-prone; like someone who constantly drops things

word pairs: cook, waiter, catcher

tongue-tied *adj.* speechless or lost for words; when you feel shy and can't think of what to say

word pairs: fool, actor, contestant

clumsy or silly words

word pair after:

blundering fool
bumbling fool
butterfingered cook
crude cavewoman
daft idea
tongue-tied fool

CONTRACT

assertive *adj.* forceful or self-confident; like someone who always manages to get their way

word pairs: salesperson, personality, stance

audacious *adj.* bold and daring; like someone brave enough to dive into a pool full of sharks

word pairs: stunt, move, attempt

conceited *adj.* vain or proud; like someone who is constantly taking selfies

word pairs: attitude, snob, oaf

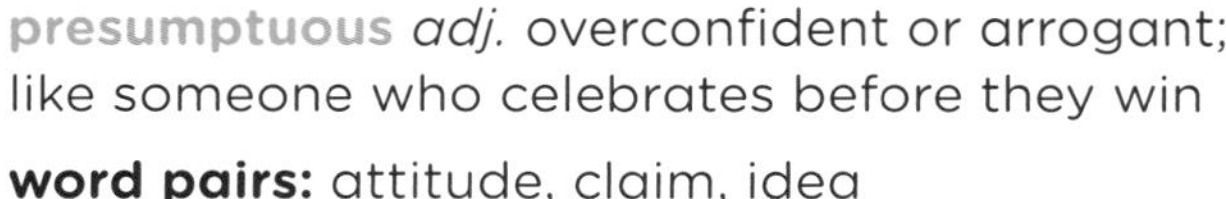

presumptuous *adj.* overconfident or arrogant; like someone who celebrates before they win

word pairs: attitude, claim, idea

1

STOP
POLICE

brazen *adj.* bold and shameless; like stealing a police officer's wallet in plain sight

word pairs: thief, lie, defiance

unflappable *adj.* cool, calm, or unworried; when you're so chilled out that nothing can upset you

word pairs: calm, confidence, poise

confident words

word pair after:

assertive salesperson
audacious stunt
brazen thief
conceited attitude
presumptuous attitude
unflappable calm

3:00AM

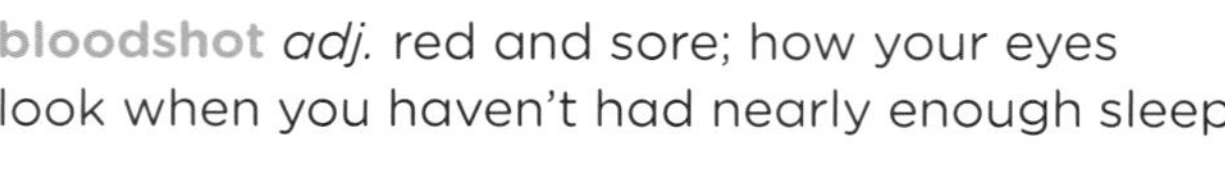

bloodshot *adj.* red and sore; how your eyes look when you haven't had nearly enough sleep

word pairs: eyes, appearance, glare

bulging *adj.* swollen or sticking out; how your eyes look when you stare at something

word pairs: eyes, biceps, wallet

fiery *adj.* hot-tempered or furious; like someone who has lost their temper

word pairs: temper, eyes, debate

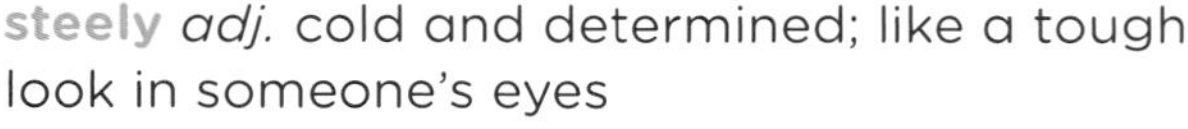

steely *adj.* cold and determined; like a tough look in someone's eyes

word pairs: expression, sky, determination

eye words

expressive *adj.* showing your feelings; like an emotional look in someone's eyes

word pairs: eyes, face, language

vacant *adj.* empty or without emotion; like eyes that have a blank and lifeless look

word pairs: stare, streets, expression

word pair after:

bloodshot eyes
bulging eyes
expressive face
fiery temper
steely expression
vacant stare

diffident *adj.* modest or shy; like someone who doesn't expect to be noticed

word pairs: manner, smile, voice

hesitant *adj.* nervous or uncertain; like someone afraid to jump off a diving board

word pairs: step, start, glance

introverted *adj.* shy or reserved; like someone who dreads parties and hides in the corner

word pairs: mood, artist, personality

sheepish *adj.* shy, ashamed, or uncomfortable; the way you feel when you do something silly

word pairs: grin, laugh, apology

insecure *adj.* anxious or self-conscious; like someone who feels exposed in public

word pairs: person, teenager, password

wary *adj.* careful or cautious; like a fly who is afraid of getting zapped

word pairs: distance, glance, animal

FLY TRAP 9000

shy or uncertain words

word pair after:

diffident manner
hesitant step
insecure person
introverted mood
sheepish grin
wary distance

emaciated *adj.* skeletal or very thin; like a prisoner who is being starved in a dungeon

word pairs: prisoner, corpse, limbs

lanky *adj.* tall, thin, and ungraceful; like a giraffe trying to roller skate for the first time

word pairs: body, teenager, athlete

shriveled *adj.* wrinkled or shrunken; like hippo skin that has been in the bath too long

word pairs: skin, apple, flower

squat *adj.* short and stubby; like a body that looks as if it has been squashed down

word pairs: man, building, hut

scrawny *adj.* thin and bony; like a wet dog who is all skin and bones

word pairs: dog, chicken, neck

willowy *adj.* tall, slender, and graceful; like the branches of a drooping willow tree

word pairs: limbs, dancer, branches

small or thin words

word pair after:

emaciated prisoner
lanky body
scrawny dog
shriveled skin
squat man
willowy limbs

abrasive *adj.* harsh and grating; like a horrible noise that makes your hair stand on end

word pairs: voice, personality, siren

gruff *adj.* rough or husky; like a growling cowboy

word pairs: voice, manner, exterior

nasal *adj.* whiny or from your nose; a voice that sounds like it comes from your nose

word pairs: voice, twang, accent

shrill *adj.* sharp or high-pitched; like the sound of a giant whistle

word pairs: whistle, scream, laugh

hollow *adj.* empty or not solid; like the sound when you shout into an empty tree trunk

word pairs: sound, voice, tree

velvety *adj.* smooth and silky; a voice so lovely it feels like velvet on your ears

word pairs: voice, texture, darkness

voice words

word pair after:

abrasive voice
gruff manner
hollow sound
nasal twang
shrill whistle
velvety voice

164 clever character nouns

Use these nouns and word pairs to give your characters glamorous gowns and slippery slime.

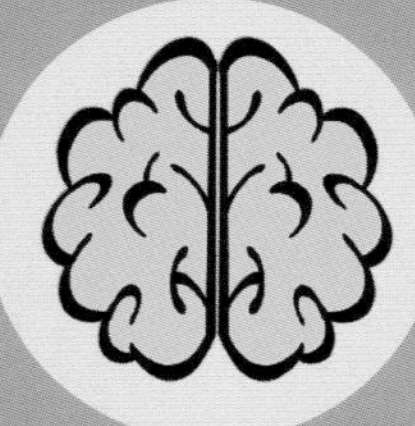

ARCHETYPES - HERO OR VILLAIN?

unlikely • unsung • valiant 
n.
hero

secret • jealous • faithful 
n.
lover

wise • lifelong • spiritual 
n.
mentor

old • arch • vengeful 
n.
nemesis

bitter • longtime • formidable 
n.
rival

sly • charming • lovable 
n.
rogue

mighty • corrupt • oppressive 
n.
ruler

young • loyal • annoying 
n.
sidekick

cowardly • suspected • filthy
n.
traitor

professional • cunning • devious
n.
trickster

frightened • innocent • unsuspecting
n.
victim

evil • scheming • treacherous
n.
villain

clear • scrappy • lovable
n.
underdog

someone who isn't expected to win;
like a tiny boxer facing the heavyweight champion

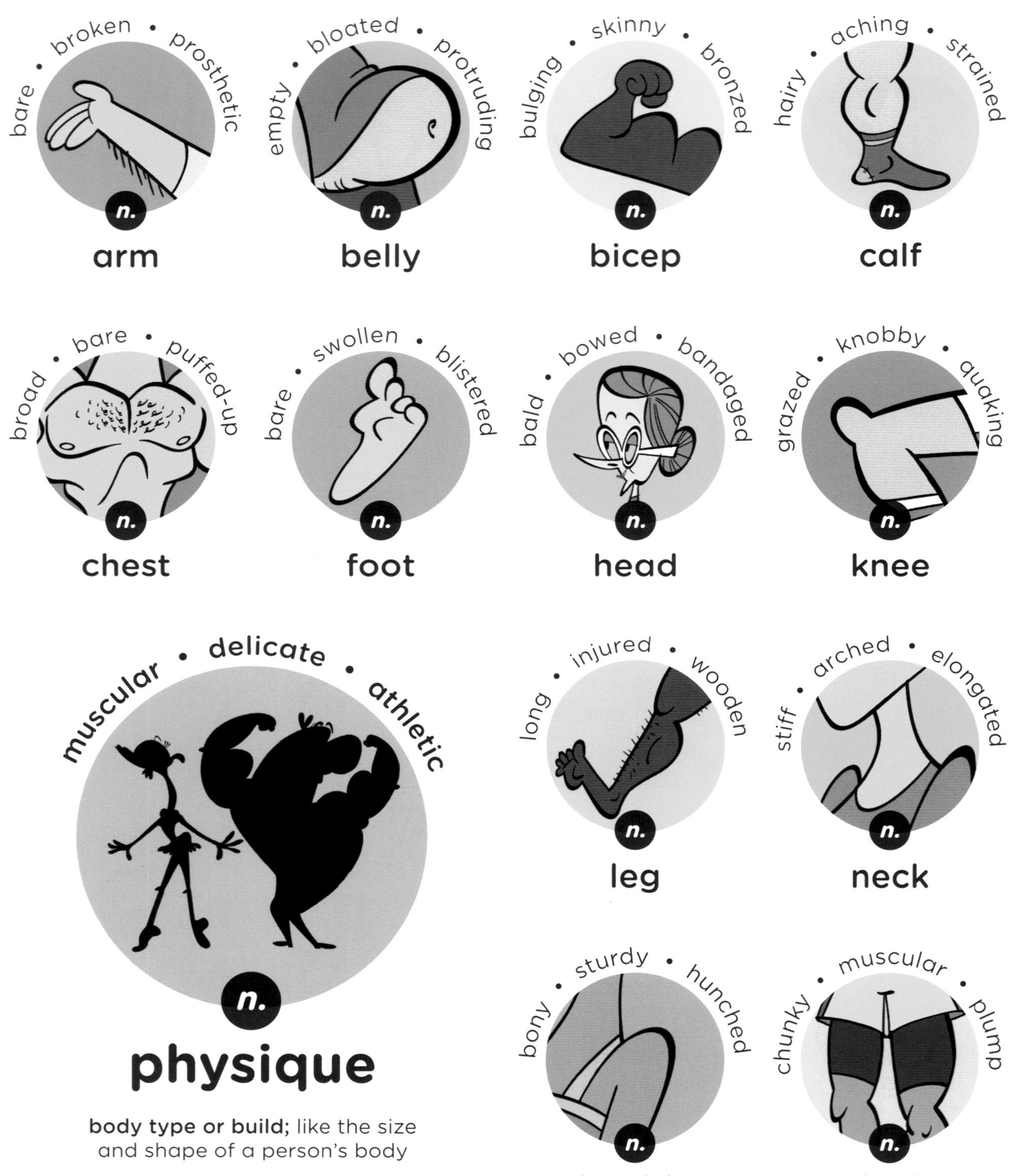
bare • broken • prosthetic
n.
arm
empty • bloated • protruding
n.
belly
bulging • skinny • bronzed
n.
bicep
hairy • aching • strained
n.
calf
broad • bare • puffed-up
n.
chest
bare • swollen • blistered
n.
foot
bald • bowed • bandaged
n.
head
grazed • knobby • quaking
n.
knee
muscular • delicate • athletic
n.
physique
long • injured • wooden
n.
leg
stiff • arched • elongated
n.
neck
bony • sturdy • hunched
n.
shoulder
chunky • muscular • plump
n.
thigh

body type or build; like the size and shape of a person's body

THE BODY > GROSS STUFF

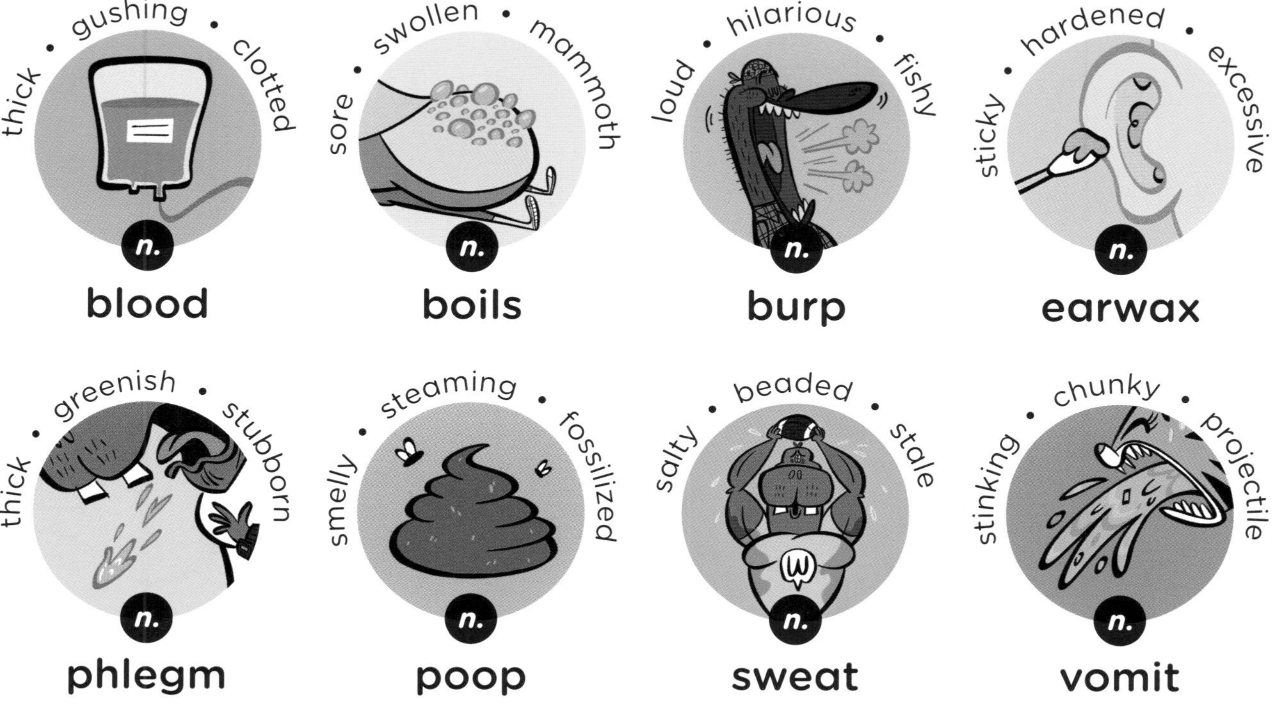
thick • gushing • clotted
n.
blood
sore • swollen • mammoth
n.
boils
loud • hilarious • fishy
n.
burp
sticky • hardened • excessive
n.
earwax
thick • greenish • stubborn
n.
phlegm
smelly • steaming • fossilized
n.
poop
salty • beaded • stale
n.
sweat
stinking • chunky • projectile
n.
vomit

THE BODY > HAIRSTYLES

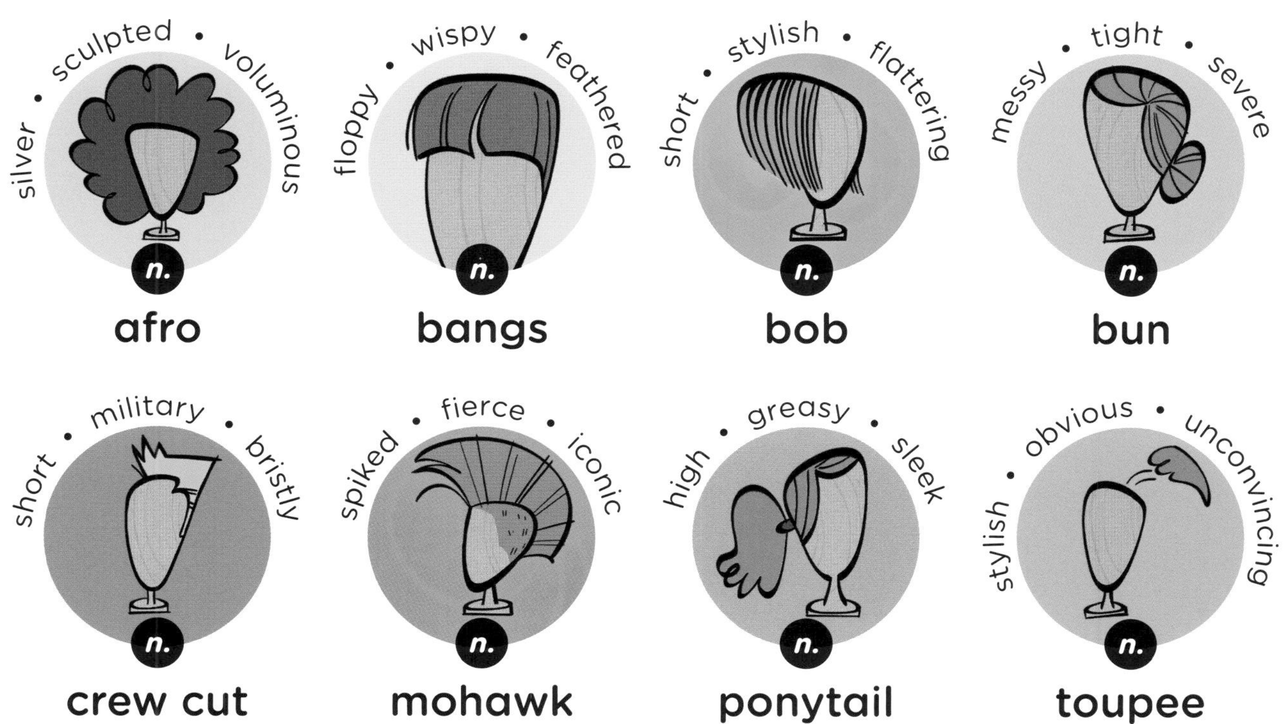
silver • sculpted • voluminous
n.
afro
floppy • wispy • feathered
n.
bangs
short • stylish • flattering
n.
bob
messy • tight • severe
n.
bun
short • military • bristly
n.
crew cut
spiked • fierce • iconic
n.
mohawk
high • greasy • sleek
n.
ponytail
stylish • obvious • unconvincing
n.
toupee

THE BODY > HANDS

THE BODY > INSIDES

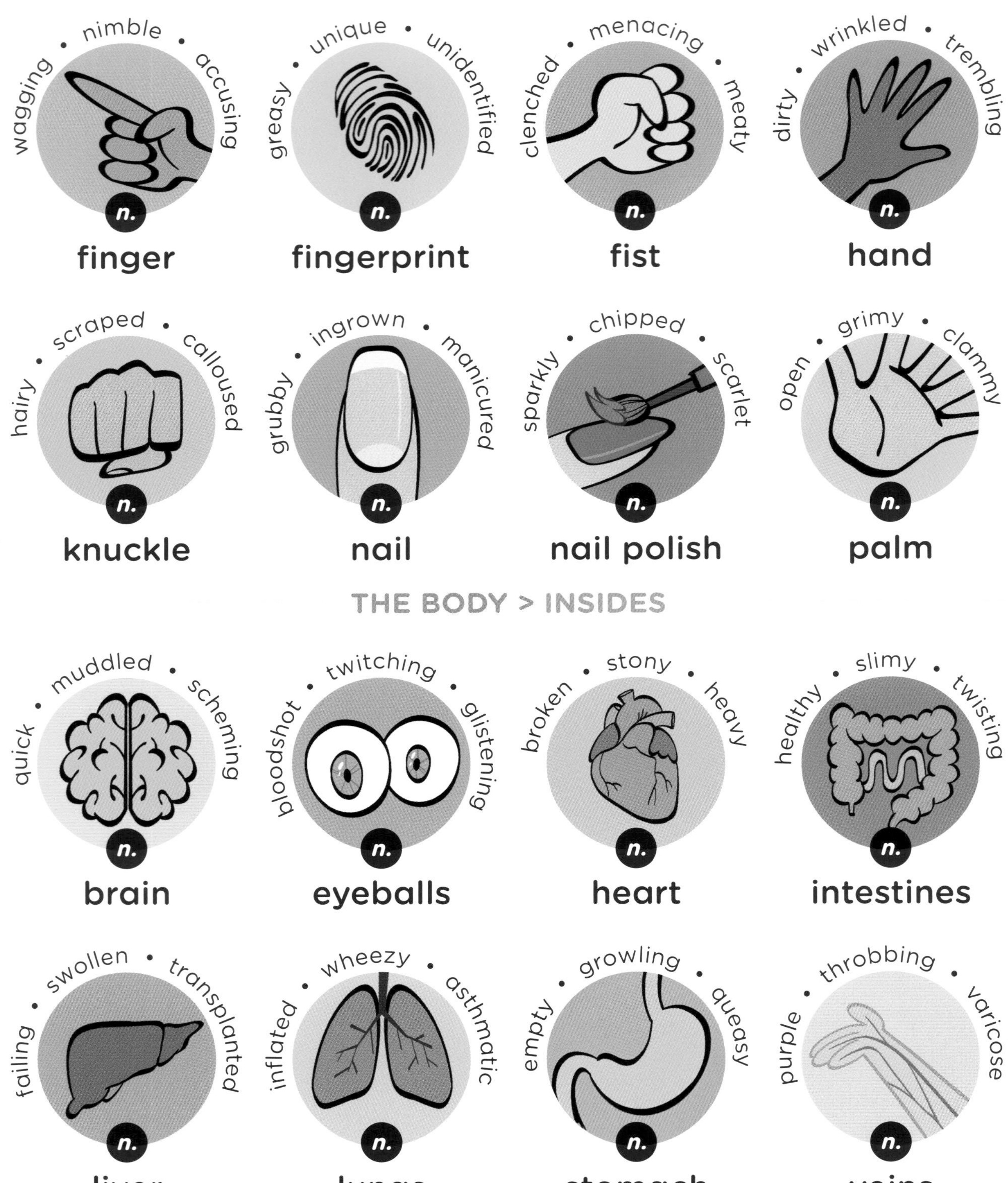

wagging • nimble • accusing
n.
finger
greasy • unique • unidentified
n.
fingerprint
clenched • menacing • meaty
n.
fist
dirty • wrinkled • trembling
n.
hand
hairy • scraped • calloused
n.
knuckle
grubby • ingrown • manicured
n.
nail
sparkly • chipped • scarlet
n.
nail polish
open • grimy • clammy
n.
palm
quick • muddled • scheming
n.
brain
bloodshot • twitching • glistening
n.
eyeballs
broken • stony • heavy
n.
heart
healthy • slimy • twisting
n.
intestines
failing • swollen • transplanted
n.
liver
inflated • wheezy • asthmatic
n.
lungs
empty • growling • queasy
n.
stomach
purple • throbbing • varicose
n.
veins

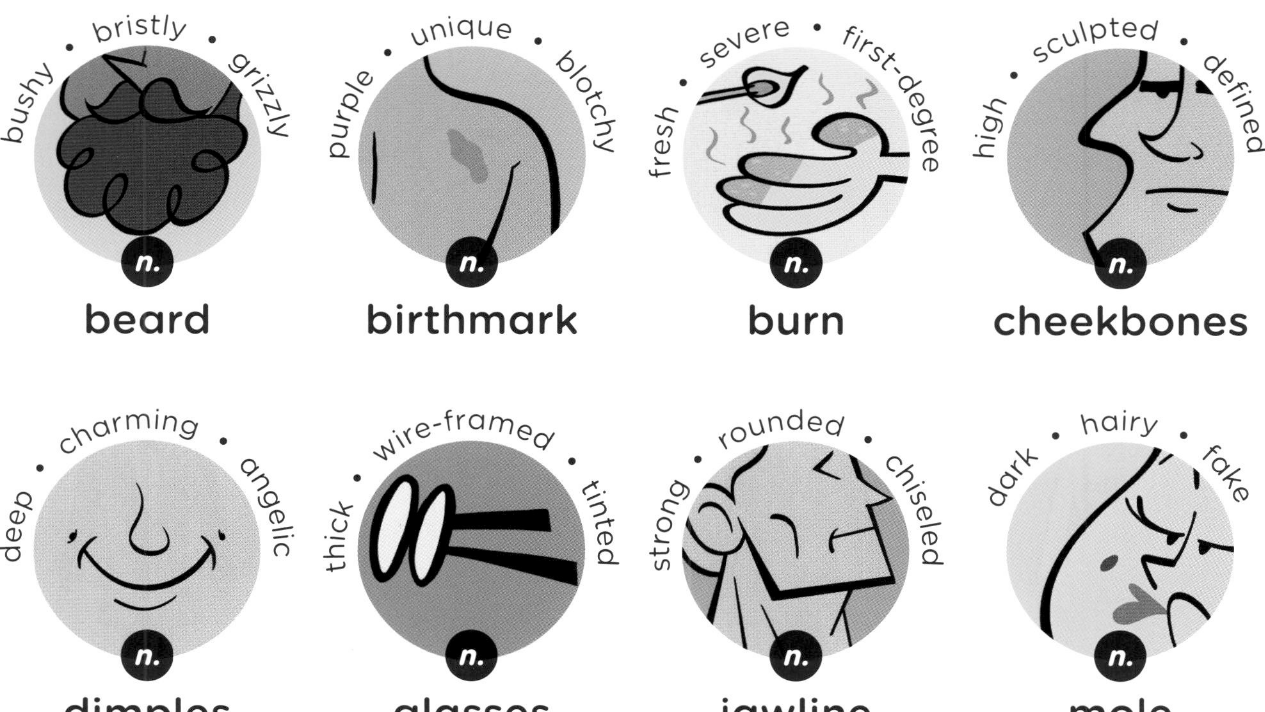
bushy • bristly • grizzly
n.
beard
purple • unique • blotchy
n.
birthmark
fresh • severe • first-degree
n.
burn
high • sculpted • defined
n.
cheekbones
deep • charming • angelic
n.
dimples
thick • wire-framed • tinted
n.
glasses
strong • rounded • chiseled
n.
jawline
dark • hairy • fake
n.
mole

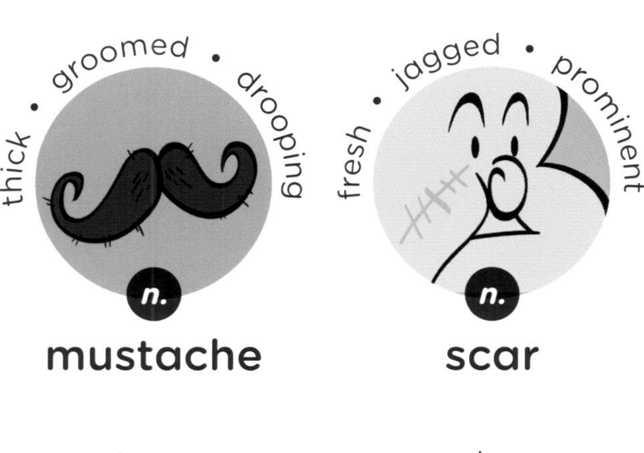
thick • groomed • drooping
n.
mustache
fresh • jagged • prominent
n.
scar

huge • hairy • unsightly
n.
wart
kind • faint • deep-set
n.
wrinkles

stiff • upright • correct
n.

posture

position or stance; like the way a person holds themselves when they're standing or sitting

CLOTHING > DRESSING UP

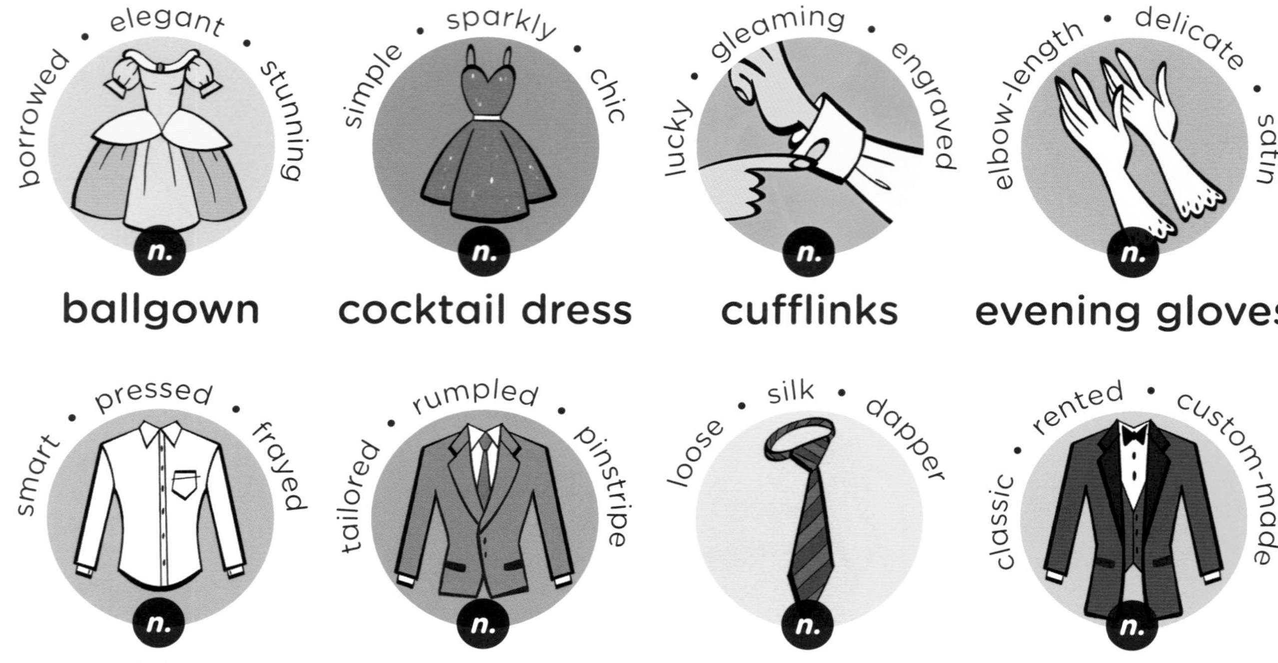
borrowed • elegant • stunning
n.
ballgown
simple • sparkly • chic
n.
cocktail dress
lucky • gleaming • engraved
n.
cufflinks
elbow-length • delicate • satin
n.
evening gloves
smart • pressed • frayed
n.
shirt
tailored • rumpled • pinstripe
n.
suit
loose • silk • dapper
n.
tie
classic • rented • custom-made
n.
tuxedo

CLOTHING > SHOES

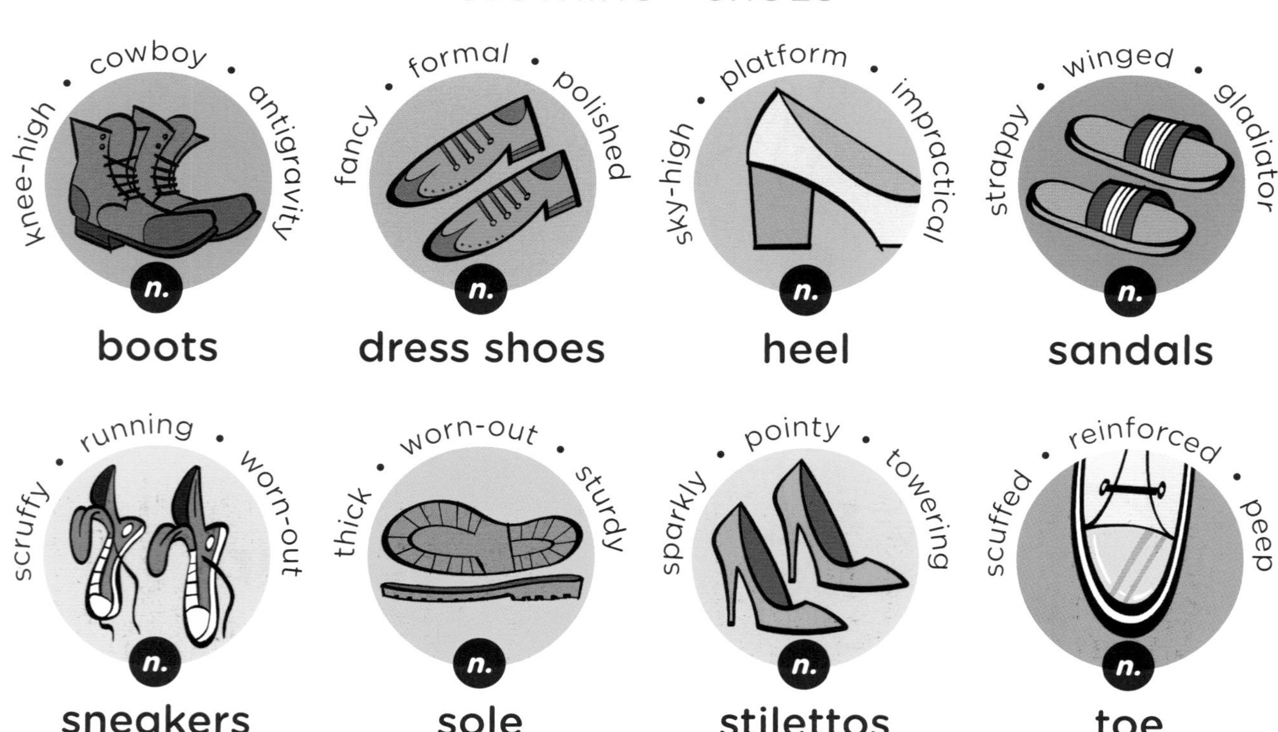
knee-high • cowboy • antigravity
n.
boots
fancy • formal • polished
n.
dress shoes
sky-high • platform • impractical
n.
heel
strappy • winged • gladiator
n.
sandals
scruffy • running • worn-out
n.
sneakers
thick • worn-out • sturdy
n.
sole
sparkly • pointy • towering
n.
stilettos
scuffed • reinforced • peep
n.
toe

CLOTHING > SUMMER CLOTHES

wet • baggy • faded
n.
bathing suit
bright • skimpy • bejeweled
n.
bikini
comfy • squeaky • durable
n.
flip flops
colorful • unbuttoned • garish
n.
Hawaiian shirt
loose • flowing • tie-dyed
n.
sarong
baggy • tailored • khaki
n.
shorts
simple • floral • strapless
n.
sundress
cheap • mirrored • branded
n.
sunglasses

CLOTHING > WINTER CLOTHES

fluffy • knitted • moth-eaten
n.
cardigan
favorite • tattered • faded
n.
denim jacket
comfy • fuzzy • protective
n.
earmuffs
leather • fur-lined • protective
n.
gloves
toasty • activated • robust
n.
hand warmer
dark • quilted • concealing
n.
hood
ripped • skinny • well-worn
n.
jeans
cracked • studded • vintage
n.
leather jacket

CLOTHING > WINTER CLOTHES

wooly • waterproof • heavy-duty
n.
mittens
warm • comfy • unicorn
n.
onesie
short • dripping • lightweight
n.
raincoat
furry • bulky • quilted
n.
snowsuit
knee-high • holey • mismatched
n.
socks
wooly • baggy • bulky
n.
sweater
oversized • well-cut • nondescript
n.
trench coat
heavy • itchy • double-breasted
n.
winter coat

CREATURES > CREATURE FEATURES

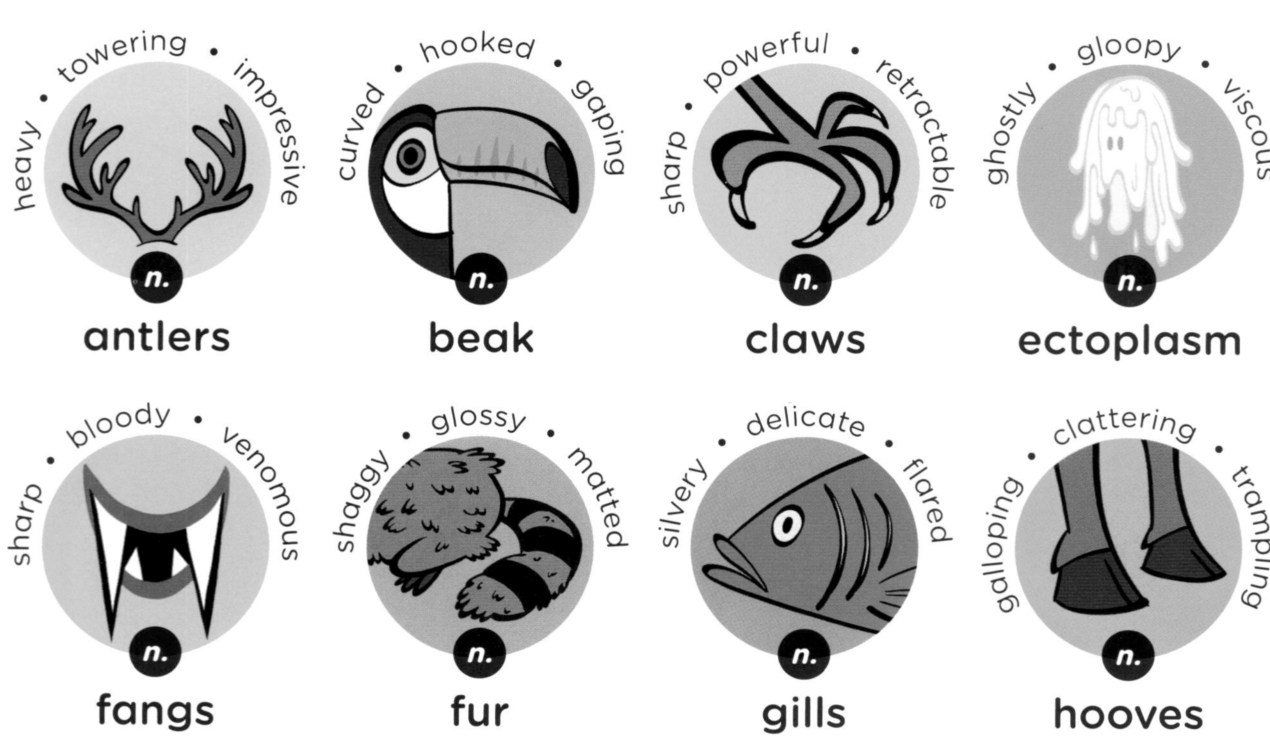
heavy • towering • impressive
n.
antlers
curved • hooked • gaping
n.
beak
sharp • powerful • retractable
n.
claws
ghostly • gloopy • viscous
n.
ectoplasm
sharp • bloody • venomous
n.
fangs
shaggy • glossy • matted
n.
fur
silvery • delicate • flared
n.
gills
galloping • clattering • trampling
n.
hooves

sharp • stubby • spiraling
n.
horns
mighty • clenched • gaping
n.
jaws
broad • pointed • velvety
n.
muzzle
muddy • nimble • oversized
n.
paws
huge • crushing • unforgiving
n.
pincer
slimy • coarse • glistening
n.
scales
protective • outer • fragile
n.
shell
rubbery • greasy • shriveled
n.
skin
slippery • toxic • oozing
n.
slime
sharp • bristly • bony
n.
spines
striped • deadly • fearsome
n.
stinger
bushy • stumpy • curly
n.
tail
powerful • menacing • fierce
n.
talons
long • writhing • venomous
n.
tentacle
sensitive • bristly • twitching
n.
whiskers
flapping • outspread • clipped
n.
wings

CREATURES > MONSTERS

wounded • savage • ravenous
n.
beast
greedy • beastly • leering
n.
cyclops
evil • ancient • vengeful
n.
demon
scaly • hulking • snarling
n.
dinosaur
flying • two-headed • fiery
n.
dragon
howling • headless • vengeful
n.
ghost
sleeping • gentle • towering
n.
giant
sneaky • angry • cunning
n.
goblin
ugly • slobbering • savage
n.
ogre
golden • reborn • immortal
n.
phoenix
rare • beached • mythical
n.
sea creature
wicked • alluring • mesmerizing
n.
siren
lonely • beady-eyed • loathsome
n.
troll
bloodsucking • charming • rogue
n.
vampire
howling • prowling • rabid
n.
werewolf
drooling • mindless • flesh-eating
n.
zombie

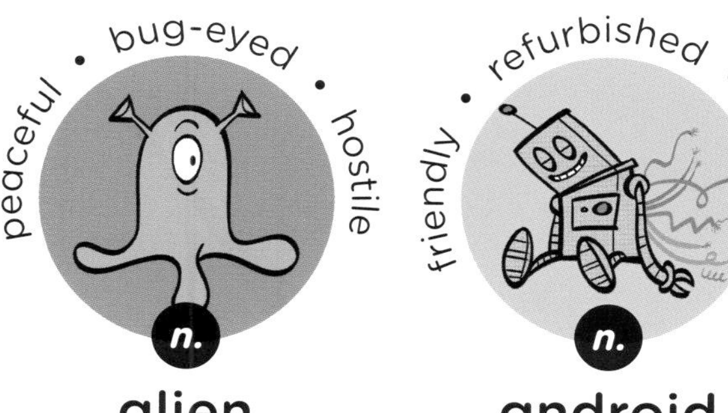

peaceful • bug-eyed • hostile

n.

alien

friendly • refurbished • glitching

n.

android

human • futuristic • expensive

n.

cryogenics

deep-freezing human bodies; like freezing yourself so you can wake up thousands of years later

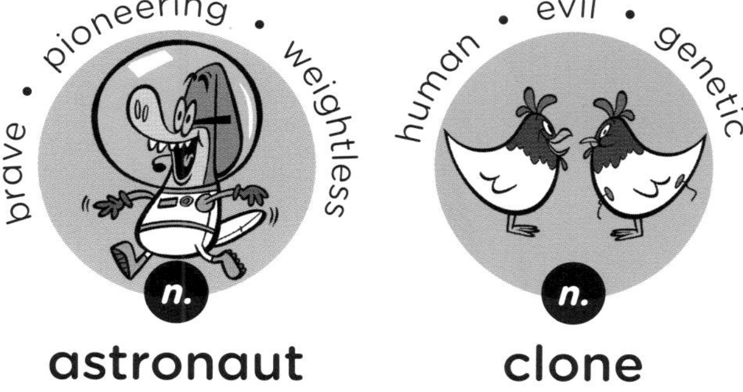

brave • pioneering • weightless

n.

astronaut

human • evil • genetic

n.

clone

lifelike • military • advanced

n.

cyborg

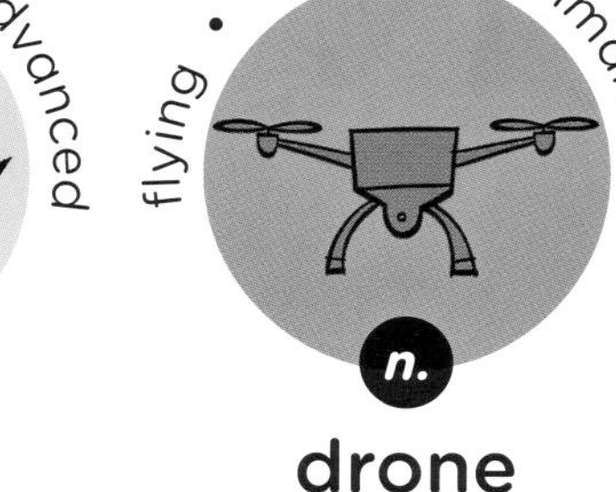

flying • armed • unmanned

n.

drone

skillful • anonymous • malicious

n.

hacker

young • billionaire • prolific

n.

inventor

rare • mistreated • telepathic

n.

mutant

evil • unfeeling • indestructible

n.

robot

famous • dangerous • erratic

n.

scientist

accidental • stranded • meddling

n.

time traveler

RunningMate 5000

determined

Emotion

TICKETS
SOLD OUT!
SOLD OU
SOLD OUT!

furious *adj.* angry or enraged; how you feel when tickets for your favorite band sell out

word pairs: reaction, pace, debate

grudge *n.* hatred or bitterness; when you stay angry with someone and won't forgive them

word pairs: hold, settle, harbor

livid *adj.* raging or furious; how you feel when you lose a video game

word pairs: face, glare, response

raging *adj.* furious or fuming; like an angry bull on a rampage

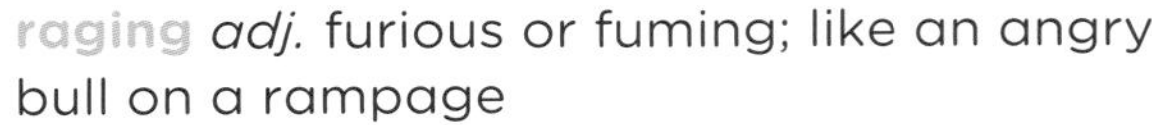

word pairs: bull, fire, debate

GAME OVER

irritated *adj.* annoyed or peeved; like when you hear an annoying song again and again

word pairs: skin, tone, glance

spiteful *adj.* hateful or mean; like purposefully spilling paint on someone's work to ruin it

word pairs: action, remark, gossip

angry words

word pair before:

hold a grudge

word pair after:

furious reaction
irritated skin
livid face
raging bull
spiteful action

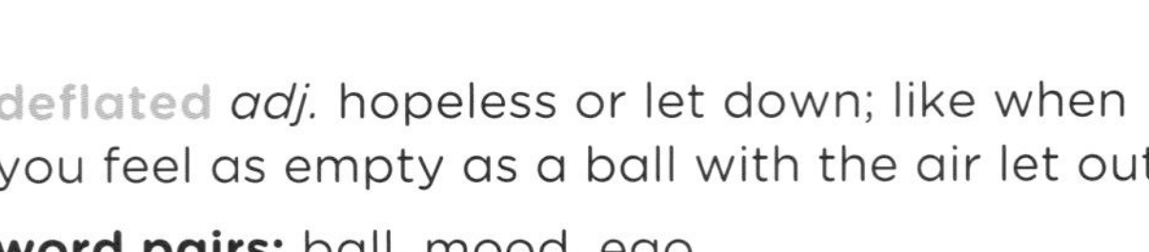

deflated *adj.* hopeless or let down; like when you feel as empty as a ball with the air let out

word pairs: ball, mood, ego

desperate *adj.* anxious or frantic; how you feel when you really need the bathroom

word pairs: need, attempt, situation

envious *adj.* jealous or resentful; when you want something that someone else has

word pairs: neighbor, rival, glance

humiliated *adj.* ashamed or embarrassed; how you feel if someone pulls a mean prank on you

word pairs: classmate, politician, candidate

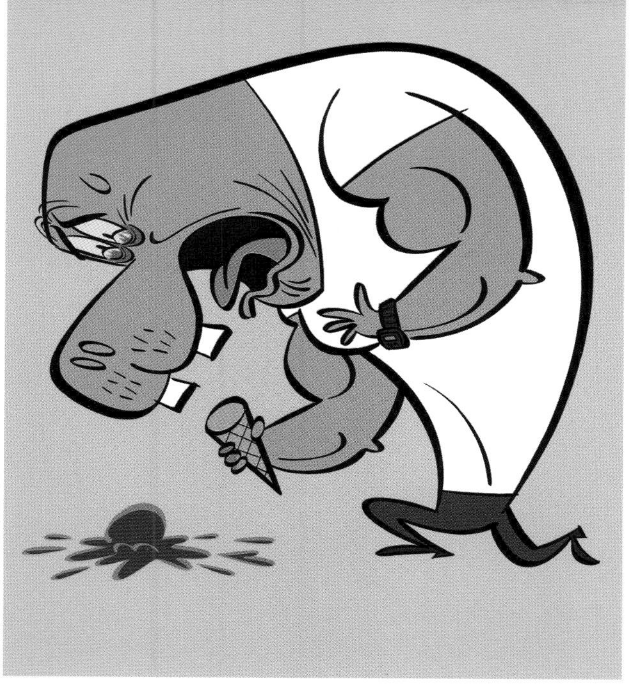

disheartened *adj.* sad, crushed, or disappointed; how you feel when you drop your ice cream

word pairs: expression, fans, voice

snubbed *adj.* ignored or rejected; how you feel if someone rudely turns you down

word pairs: admirer, player, expression

feeling bad words

word pair after:

deflated ball
desperate need
disheartened expression
envious neighbor
humiliated classmate
snubbed admirer

MATTRESS SALE!
SaLe!
50% OFF!
SOLD

contented *adj.* satisfied and comfortable; like feeling so calm and happy that you sleep well

word pairs: smile, heart, silence

ecstatic *adj.* blissful or thrilled; how you would feel if you won an award

word pairs: joy, crowd, celebration

gleeful *adj.* cheerful or merry; when you feel full of joy

word pairs: smile, laughter, grin

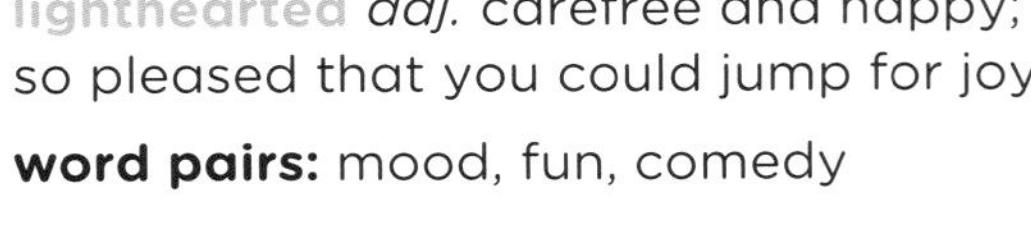

lighthearted *adj.* carefree and happy; so pleased that you could jump for joy

word pairs: mood, fun, comedy

exhilarated *adj.* excited or thrilled; like the feeling of riding a rollercoaster

word pairs: gasp, feeling, spirit

overjoyed *adj.* delighted and gleeful; like when you feel like partying

word pairs: reaction, parent, crowd

happy words

word pair after:

contented smile
ecstatic joy
exhilarated gasp
gleeful smile
lighthearted mood
overjoyed reaction

auspicious *adj.* hopeful or encouraging; like getting a sign that everything will go well

word pairs: sign, occasion, omen

encouraging *adj.* positive or motivating; like someone who cheers you on

word pairs: smile, news, response

optimistic *adj.* hopeful and positive; like being certain that the weather is going to get better

word pairs: attitude, view, outlook

SPF

promising *adj.* hopeful or encouraging; like a baby rocket scientist

word pairs: youngster, student, future

A
B
C

The Word
PEACE ACHIEVED!
PREZ

idealistic *adj.* very optimistic and unrealistic; like someone who dreams of a perfect world

word pairs: goal, vision, philosophy

sanguine *adj.* optimistic and cheery; like feeling happy even when things go wrong

word pairs: expectations, prediction, attitude

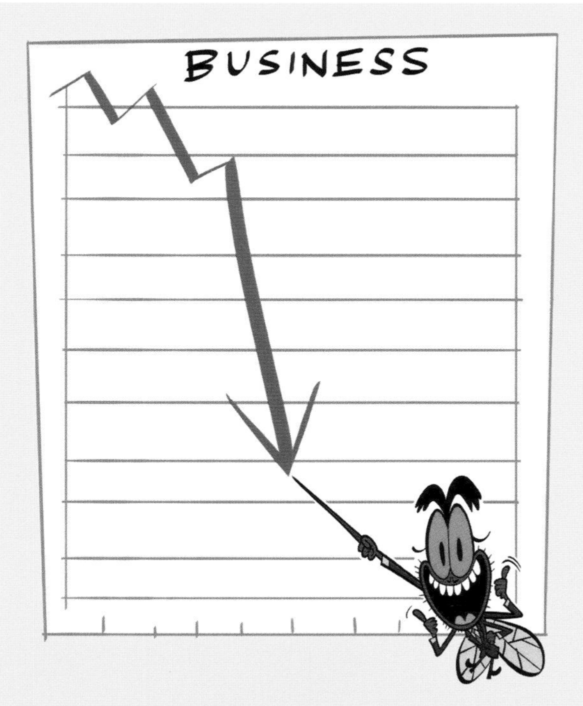
BUSINESS

hopeful words

word pair after:

auspicious sign
encouraging smile
idealistic goal
optimistic attitude
promising youngster
sanguine expectations

MILK

disgust *n.* a strong dislike or repulsion; like when you find a fly in your food

word pairs: deep, utter, profound

fixated *adj.* obsessed or focused; like a hungry tiger cub staring at her next meal

word pairs: mind, interest, desire

loathe *v.* to hate or dislike intensely; like how you feel about your least favorite food

word pairs: absolutely, intensely, universally

scorn *n.* dislike and contempt; what an environmentalist feels when they see littering

word pairs: bitter, public, utmost

love & hate words

infatuated *adj.* in love and obsessed; like falling for a dreamy singer

word pairs: fan, fool, admirer

yearning *n.* a strong desire or longing; like a prisoner who misses her friends

word pairs: deep, romantic, passionate

0010

word pair before:

deep **disgust**
absolutely **loathe**
bitter **scorn**
deep **yearning**

word pair after:

fixated mind
infatuated fan

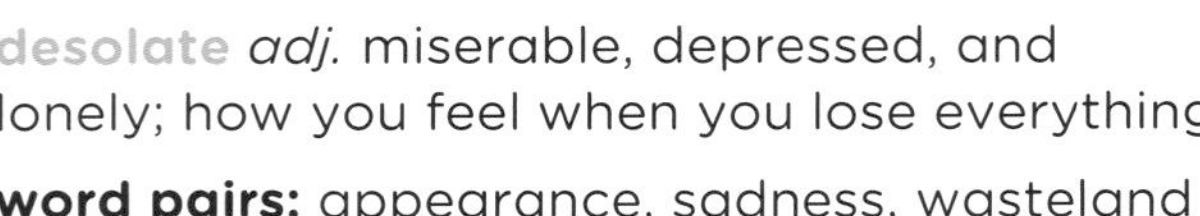

desolate *adj.* miserable, depressed, and lonely; how you feel when you lose everything

word pairs: appearance, sadness, wasteland

glum *adj.* sad or gloomy; when you feel like you're walking around under a black cloud

word pairs: mood, silence, expression

inconsolable *adj.* very unhappy or broken-hearted; like being impossible to cheer up

word pairs: despair, infant, sorrow

melancholy *adj.* depressed or gloomy; like someone who feels sad about everything

word pairs: thoughts, smile, song

ICE CREAM
FACIAL TISSUE

heartbroken *adj.* miserable or crushed; how you feel when you sob on the sofa eating ice cream

word pairs sobs, cry, fans

wistful *adj.* sad, longing, or nostalgic; like the sad feeling you get from some memories

word pairs sigh, smile, memory

OLD TOYS

sad words

word pair after:

desolate appearance
glum mood
heartbroken sobs
inconsolable despair
melancholy thoughts
wistful sigh

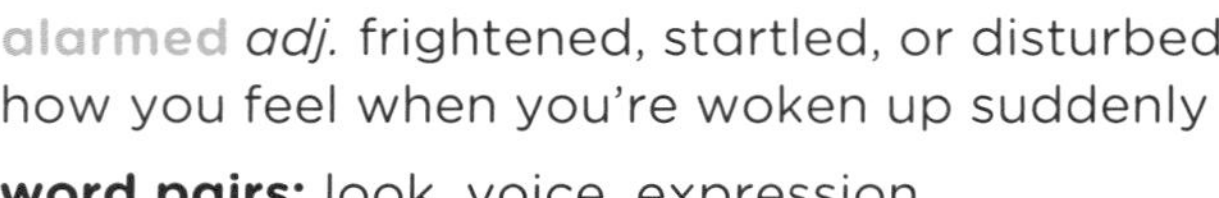

alarmed *adj.* frightened, startled, or disturbed; how you feel when you're woken up suddenly

word pairs: look, voice, expression

astonished *adj.* surprised or amazed; like when you've seen something you can't believe

word pairs: eyes, silence, spectator

speechless *adj.* dumbstruck or lost for words; how you feel when someone hangs up on you

word pairs: amazement, moment, rage

startled *adj.* surprised or frightened; like the feeling you get when someone jumps out at you

word pairs: expression, cry, deer

CALL
ENDED

JACKPOT!
2 18 35
39 51 59
JACKPOT!
WINNING NUMBERS
2 18 35
39 51 59

flabbergasted *adj.* shocked or amazed; like how you would feel if you won the lottery

word pairs: reaction, audience, onlooker

stunned *adj.* amazed or stupefied; like being so surprised you instantly freeze

word pairs: silence, surprise, disbelief

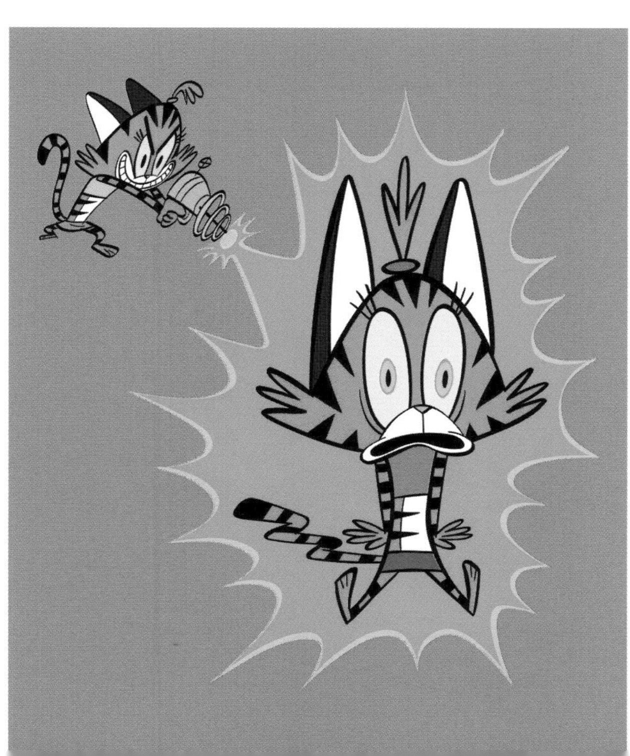

surprised words

word pair after:

alarmed look
astonished eyes
flabbergasted reaction
speechless amazement
startled expression
stunned silence

DESIRE DR.
DRIVE

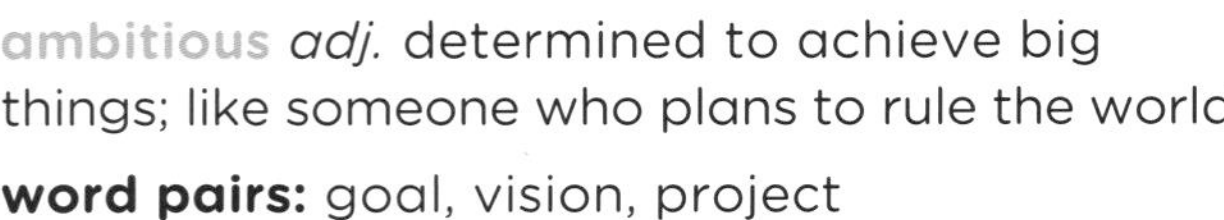

ambitious *adj.* determined to achieve big things; like someone who plans to rule the world

word pairs: goal, vision, project

committed *adj.* loyal and dedicated; like people who have promised to stay together

word pairs: couple, relationship, performance

determined *adj.* driven or completely set on; like working extra hard to get what you want

word pairs: effort, expression, opponent

persevere *v.* to keep going or carry on; like running all the way to the end of a marathon

word pairs: steadily, somehow, resolutely

RunningMate 5000

FINISH
76

dedicated *adj.* keen or devoted; when you care so much that you never give up

word pairs: employee, teacher, volunteer

tenacious *adj.* determined or strong-willed; like refusing to let go of something

word pairs: grasp, memory, attitude

trying hard words

word pair after:

ambitious goal
committed couple
dedicated employee
determined effort
persevere steadily
tenacious grasp

TEST

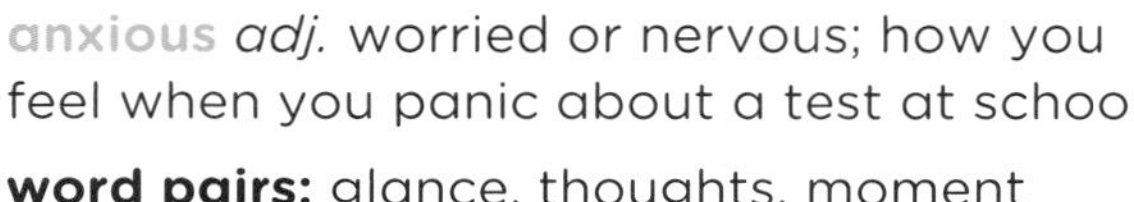

anxious *adj.* worried or nervous; how you feel when you panic about a test at school

word pairs: glance, thoughts, moment

apprehensive *adj.* nervous or afraid; like when you feel worried about a big decision

word pairs: feeling, face, glance

exasperated *adj.* annoyed or frustrated; when you feel like nothing is going your way

word pairs: state, sigh, grimace

flustered *adj.* nervous, muddled, and unsettled; how you act when you forget your homework

word pairs: student, manner, performance

Homework Excuses
50¢
each

distressed *adj.* worried and upset; you might get all sweaty and bite your nails

word pairs: look, voice, community

petrified *adj.* terrified or horrified; like being so frightened that you turn into stone

word pairs: horror, face, astonishment

worried words

word pair after:

anxious glance
apprehensive feeling
distressed look
exasperated state
flustered student
petrified horror

secluded

Robinson Crusoe

Setting

affluent *adj.* rich or wealthy; like a neighbor-hood where everyone lives in fancy houses

word pairs: area, neighborhood, lifestyle

bustling *adj.* crowded or lively; like a busy market full of shoppers

word pairs: market, port, metropolis

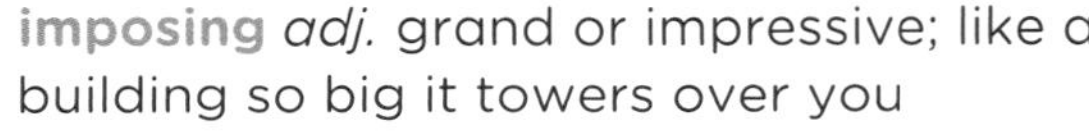

hectic *adj.* very busy or manic; how your day is when you have to do everything quickly

word pairs: schedule, day, lifestyle

imposing *adj.* grand or impressive; like a building so big it towers over you

word pairs: mansion, figure, presence

diverse *adj.* mixed or varied; like a group of people who are all different from each other

word pairs: community, mix, culture

polluted *adj.* dirty or foul; like smelly air that you try not to breathe in

word pairs: air, city, environment

city words

word pair after:

affluent area
bustling market
diverse community
hectic schedule
imposing mansion
polluted air

PIZZA!

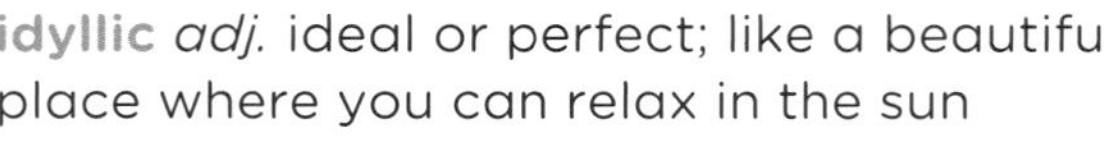

idyllic *adj.* ideal or perfect; like a beautiful place where you can relax in the sun

word pairs: countryside, town, childhood

lush *adj.* rich, flourishing, or overgrown; like a garden full of big, healthy plants

word pairs: greenery, garden, rainforest

scenic *adj.* beautiful and picturesque; like a postcard of the countryside

word pairs: route, walk, view

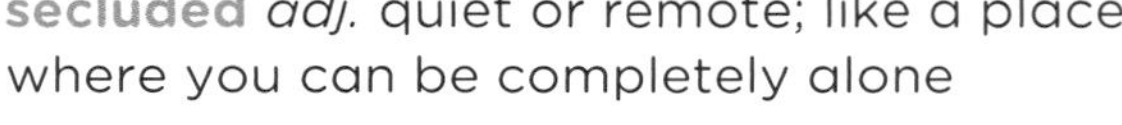

secluded *adj.* quiet or remote; like a place where you can be completely alone

word pairs: spot, beach, corner

rolling *adj.* rippling, wavy, or tumbling; like gentle hills that rise and fall like waves

word pairs: hills, waves, mist

verdant *adj.* green and leafy; like a lush valley where sheep graze on the grass

word pairs: valley, lawn, landscape

countryside words

word pair after:

idyllic countryside
lush greenery
rolling hills
scenic route
secluded spot
verdant valley

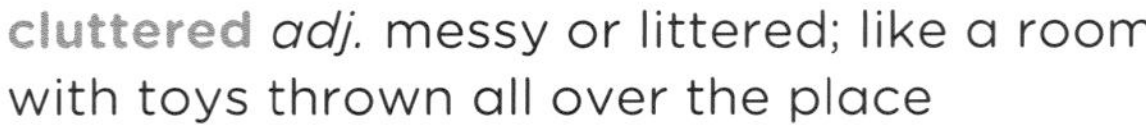

cluttered *adj.* messy or littered; like a room with toys thrown all over the place

word pairs: room, office, desk

dilapidated *adj.* run-down or shabby; like a house with broken windows and leaky ceilings

word pairs: house, school, mansion

palatial *adj.* vast or splendid; like a mansion where you live in the lap of luxury

word pairs: mansion, villa, surroundings

poky *adj.* tiny or cramped; like a cupboard under the stairs where there is no room to sit

word pairs: cupboard, room, apartment

immaculate *adj.* perfect or spotless; like a house that is so clean it shines and glitters

word pairs: house, lawn, appearance

sparse *adj.* scarce or few; like a big, empty room with hardly any furniture

word pairs: furniture, crowd, vegetation

LIVING ROOM

house words

word pair after:

cluttered room
dilapidated house
immaculate lawn
palatial mansion
poky cupboard
sparse furniture

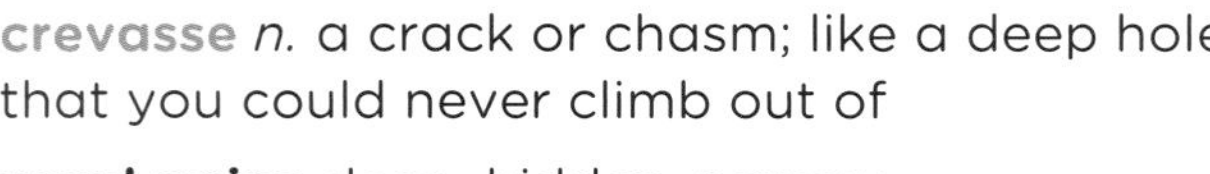

crevasse *n.* a crack or chasm; like a deep hole that you could never climb out of

word pairs: deep, hidden, narrow

precipitous *adj.* steep or dangerously high; like the edge of a very scary mountain

word pairs: cliff, slope, descent

steep *adj.* sharp and vertical; like the big, snowy drop beneath a cable car

word pairs: drop, path, stairs

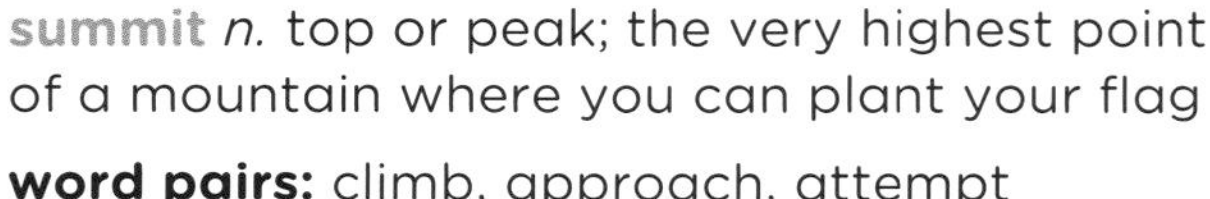

summit *n.* top or peak; the very highest point of a mountain where you can plant your flag

word pairs: climb, approach, attempt

W

rugged *adj.* rough, uneven, or craggy; like a stretch of coast full of big, jagged rocks

word pairs: coastline, terrain, beauty

towering *adj.* extremely tall; like a mountain looming over you

word pairs: peak, trees, rage

mountain words

word pair before:

deep **crevasse**
climb the **summit**

word pair after:

precipitous cliff
rugged coastline
steep drop
towering peak

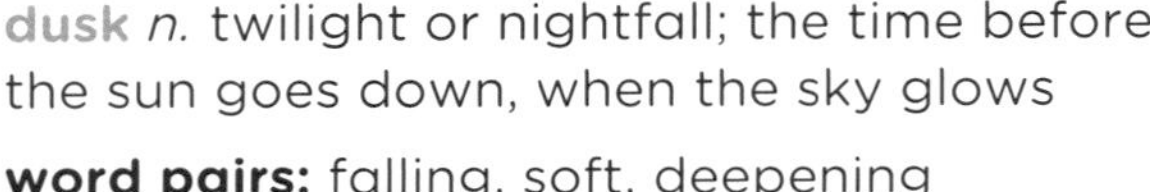
dusk *n.* twilight or nightfall; the time before the sun goes down, when the sky glows

word pairs: falling, soft, deepening

eerie *adj.* weird, ghostly, or creepy; like a spooky room full of skeletons and cobwebs

word pairs: silence, music, glow

nocturnal *adj.* nightly or active at night; like animals that come out to hunt in the dark

word pairs: creature, hunter, adventure

sleepless *adj.* wide awake and disturbed; like one of those nights when you can't sleep

word pairs: night, hour, soul

MILK

moonlit *adj.* lit up by the moon; like a bright night sky

word pairs: night, stroll, sea

twilight *n.* dusk or early evening; the soft light of evening that is too dim to read by

word pairs: dim, fading, perpetual

night words

word pair before:

deepening dusk
dim twilight

word pair after:

eerie silence
moonlit stroll
nocturnal creature
sleepless night

blaring *adj.* loud or booming; like speakers pumping out music so loud that they shake

word pairs: speaker, alarm, headline

deafening *adj.* very loud or noisy; like the sound of an airplane taking off

word pairs: noise, roar, silence

grating *adj.* harsh and annoying; like the sound of sharp nails scraping a blackboard

word pairs: sound, screech, personality

muffled *adj.* hushed or stifled; like the sound made when you speak into a pillow

word pairs: sound, thud, scream

ear-splitting *adj.* loud or piercing; like someone playing a flute right into your ear

word pairs: music, siren, screech

reverberating *adj.* echoing and vibrating; like crashing cymbals that shake your whole body

word pairs: crash, echo, explosion

noise words

word pair after:

blaring speaker
deafening roar
ear-splitting music
grating screech
muffled sound
reverberating crash

barren *adj.* empty or bare; like a lonely desert where nothing can grow

word pairs: desert, landscape, wasteland

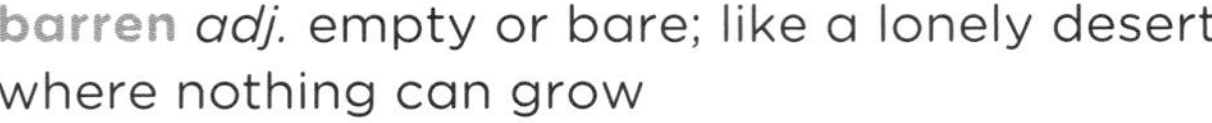

tangled *adj.* twisted or snarled; like a fly trapped in a spiderweb

word pairs: web, hair, undergrowth

impenetrable *adj.* dense and inaccessible; like a thick forest that you can't get through

word pairs: jungle, darkness, mystery

teeming *adj.* full or crowded; like a park that is overflowing with birds, insects, and animals

word pairs: wildlife, jungle, metropolis

overgrown *adj.* wild or tangled; like a jungle with plants growing on top of each other

word pairs: forest, garden, ruin

withered *adj.* wilted and drooping; like a dying tree that doesn't grow leaves anymore

word pairs: tree, flower, root

outdoor words

word pair after:

barren desert
impenetrable jungle
overgrown forest
tangled web
teeming wildlife
withered tree

Food Donations
thank You

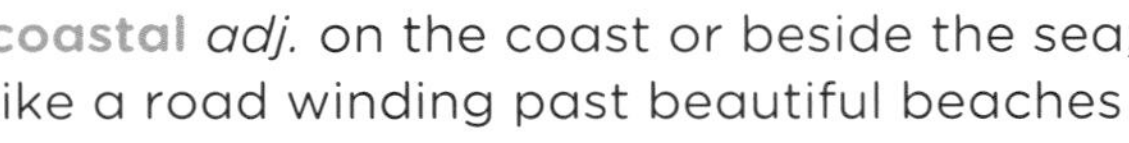

coastal *adj.* on the coast or beside the sea; like a road winding past beautiful beaches

word pairs: road, resort, scenery

deprived *adj.* poor or needy; like children who have no home, food, or clothes

word pairs: children, area, community

quaint *adj.* charming or picturesque; like a pretty, old-fashioned cottage

word pairs: cottage, street, custom

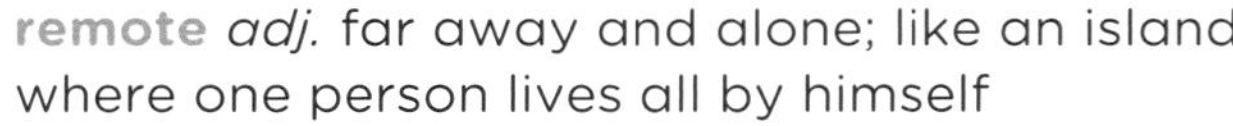

remote *adj.* far away and alone; like an island where one person lives all by himself

word pairs: island, village, chance

FOR
RENT

picturesque *adj.* attractive or scenic; like a village so pretty it could be on a postcard

word pairs: village, scene, beauty

rural *adj.* rustic or natural; like being in the countryside

word pairs: life, landscape, community

village words

word pair after:

coastal road
deprived children
picturesque village
quaint cottage
remote island
rural life

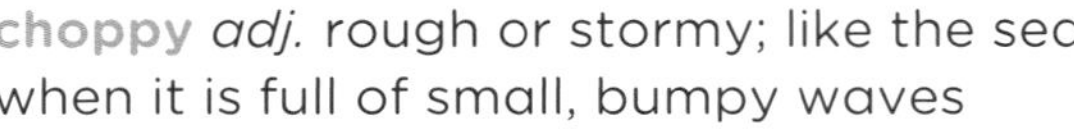

choppy *adj.* rough or stormy; like the sea when it is full of small, bumpy waves

word pairs: sea, waves, weather

frothy *adj.* foaming or bubbly; like a coffee covered in whipped cream

word pairs: cappuccino, water, foam

shimmering *adj.* gleaming or glistening; like a precious pearl when it catches the light

word pairs: beauty, water, surface

stagnant *adj.* stale or motionless; like a dirty pond where nothing is living or moving

word pairs: pond, swamp, sewage

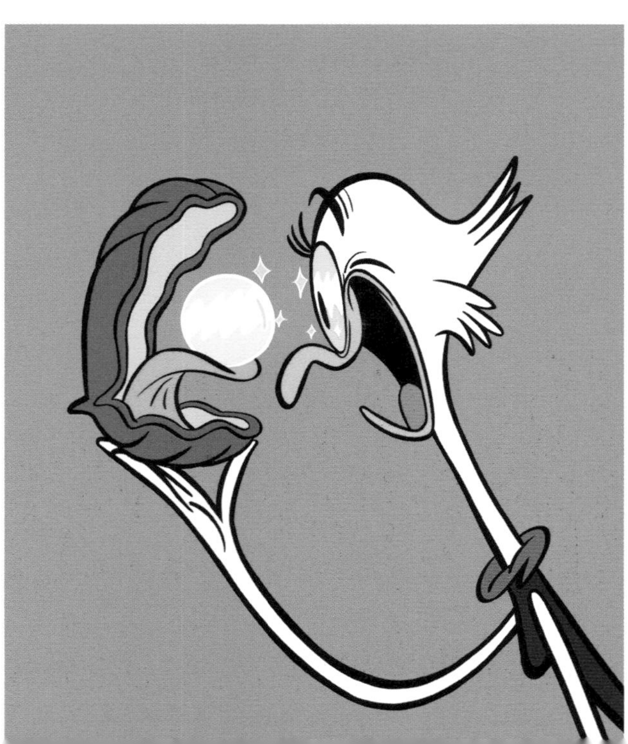

murky *adj.* dark, muddy, or cloudy; like water that's so dirty you can barely see through it

word pairs: water, sky, past

treacherous *adj.* dangerous or unsafe; like terrifying rapids that throw your boat around

word pairs: water, journey, enemy

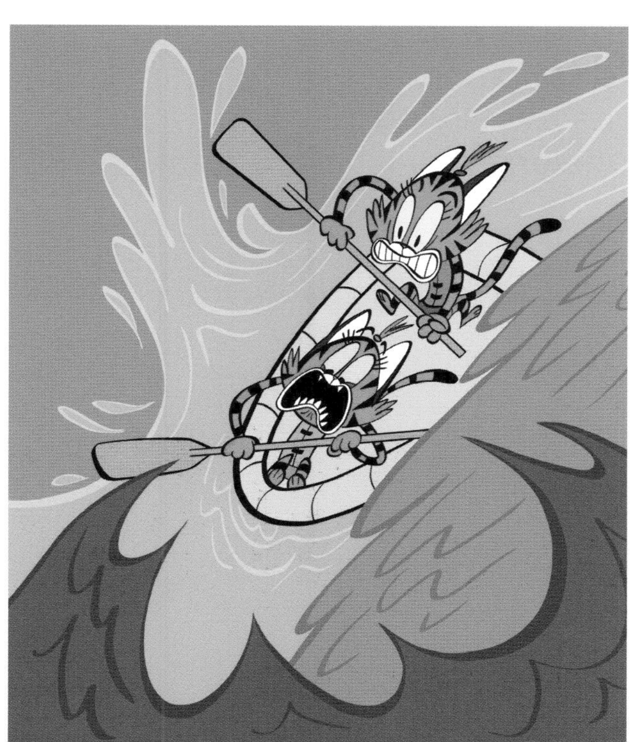

water words

word pair after:

choppy sea
frothy cappuccino
murky water
shimmering beauty
stagnant pond
treacherous journey

373 serene setting nouns

Take a tour of these wild nouns and word pairs, and set your story in its own living, breathing universe.

busy • congested • international
n.
airport
dark • narrow • winding
n.
alley
local • family-owned • artisan
n.
bakery
well-run • reputable • profitable
n.
bank
digital • interactive • garish
n.
billboard
local • organic • award-winning
n.
butcher shop
passing • honking • available
n.
cab
friendly • handy • late-night
n.
convenience store
wide • faded • unlit
n.
crosswalk
noisy • dense • bustling
n.
crowd
run-down • automated
n.
factory
colorful • spray-painted • rude
DOGZ SMEL
n.
graffiti
clean • overcrowded • austere
n.
hospital
five-star • trendy • charming
n.
hotel
flashing • blinking • buzzing
n.
neon sign
deep • dangerous • gaping
n.
pothole

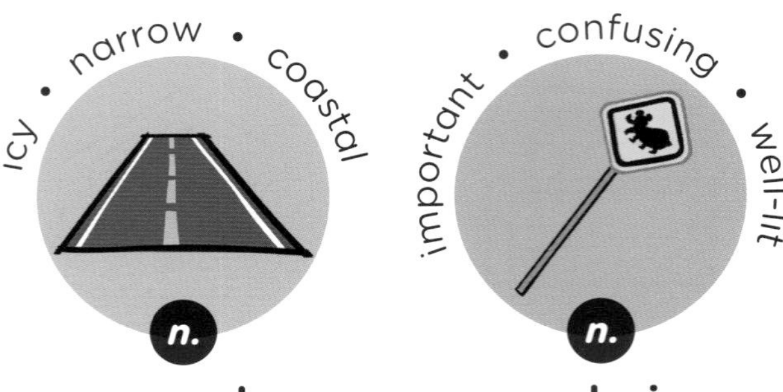

icy • narrow • coastal

n.

road

important • confusing • well-lit

n.

road sign

stinking • blocked • overflowing

n.

sewer

crowded • high-end • abandoned

n.

shopping mall

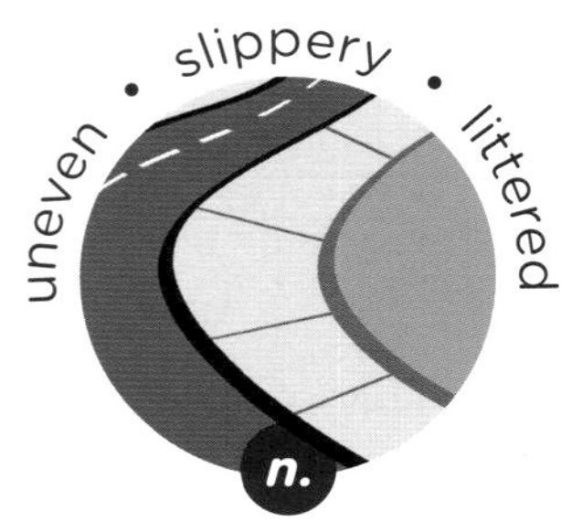

uneven • slippery • littered

n.

sidewalk

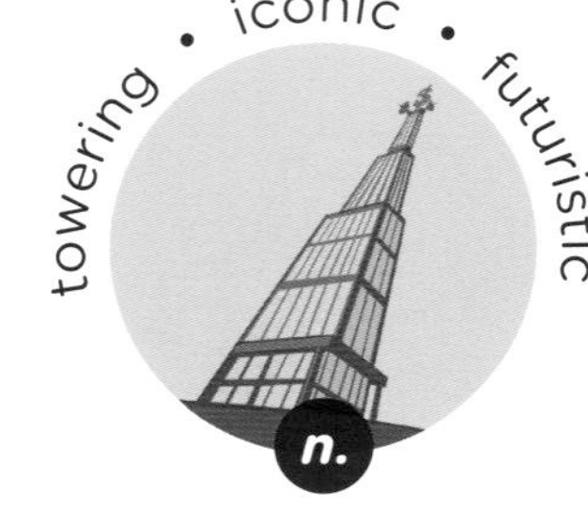

towering • iconic • futuristic

n.

skyscraper

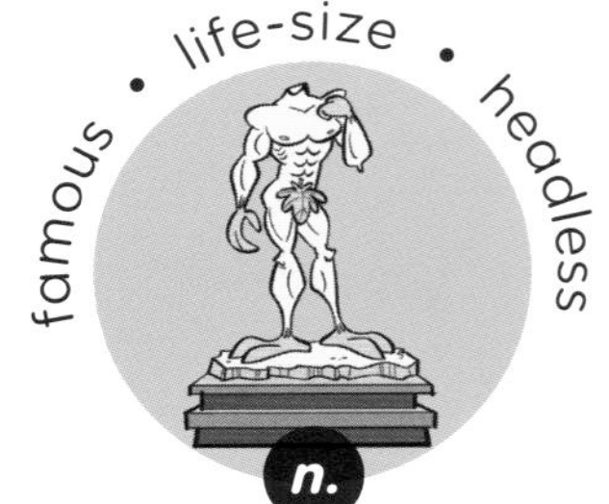

famous • life-size • headless

n.

statue

bright • flickering • crooked

n.

streetlamp

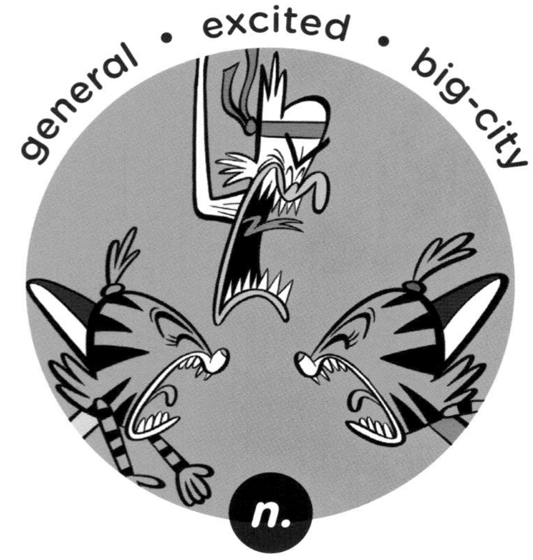

general • excited • big-city

n.

hubbub

a lot of noise caused by people talking over each other; like two basketball teams arguing about the referee

local • self-service • ransacked

n.

supermarket

eager • countless • stranded

n.

tourists

heavy • slow-moving • oncoming

n.

traffic

noisy • bustling • underground

n.

train station

CITIES > JUNKYARD

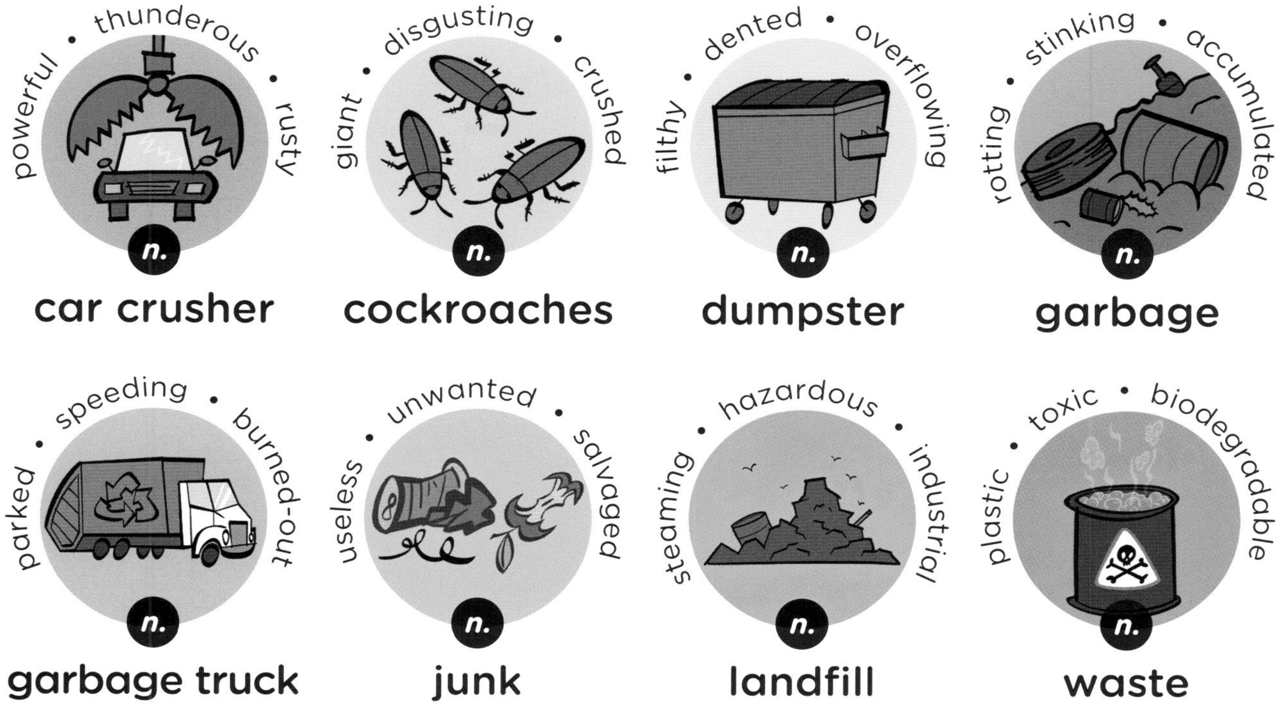
powerful • thunderous • rusty
n.
car crusher
giant • disgusting • crushed
n.
cockroaches
filthy • dented • overflowing
n.
dumpster
rotting • stinking • accumulated
n.
garbage
parked • speeding • burned-out
n.
garbage truck
useless • unwanted • salvaged
n.
junk
steaming • hazardous • industrial
n.
landfill
plastic • toxic • biodegradable
n.
waste

CITIES > PARK

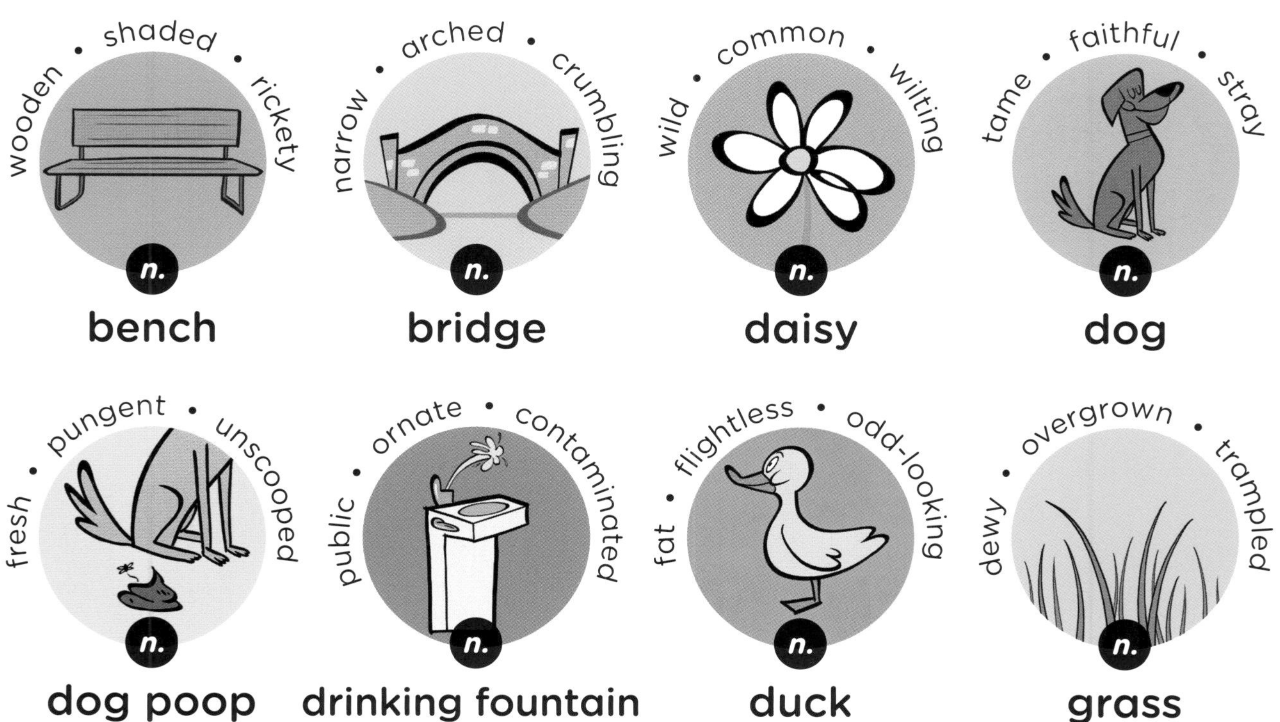
wooden • shaded • rickety
n.
bench
narrow • arched • crumbling
n.
bridge
wild • common • wilting
n.
daisy
tame • faithful • stray
n.
dog
fresh • pungent • unscooped
n.
dog poop
public • ornate • contaminated
n.
drinking fountain
fat • flightless • odd-looking
n.
duck
dewy • overgrown • trampled
n.
grass

CITIES > PARK

shallow • serene • polluted
n.
lake
scruffy • strutting • dim-witted
n.
pigeon
flowering • overgrown • potted
n.
plants
beloved • fenced-in • deserted
n.
playground
steep • slippery • spiraling
n.
slide
fluffy • nimble • inquisitive
n.
squirrel
rusty • squeaky • perilous
n.
swing set
fallen • hollow • lush
n.
trees

DRAMATIC > DANGER ZONE

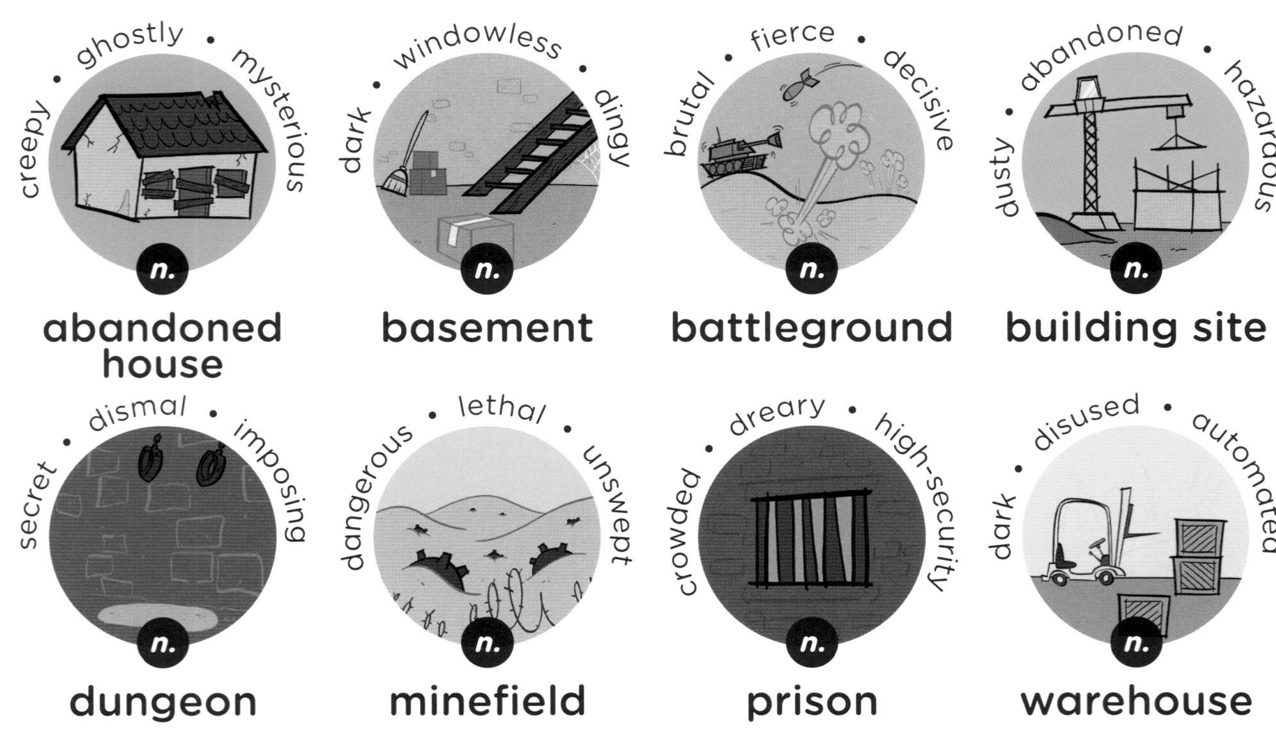
creepy • ghostly • mysterious
n.
abandoned house
dark • windowless • dingy
n.
basement
brutal • fierce • decisive
n.
battleground
dusty • abandoned • hazardous
n.
building site
secret • dismal • imposing
n.
dungeon
dangerous • lethal • unswept
n.
minefield
crowded • dreary • high-security
n.
prison
dark • disused • automated
n.
warehouse

DRAMATIC > SAFE HAVEN

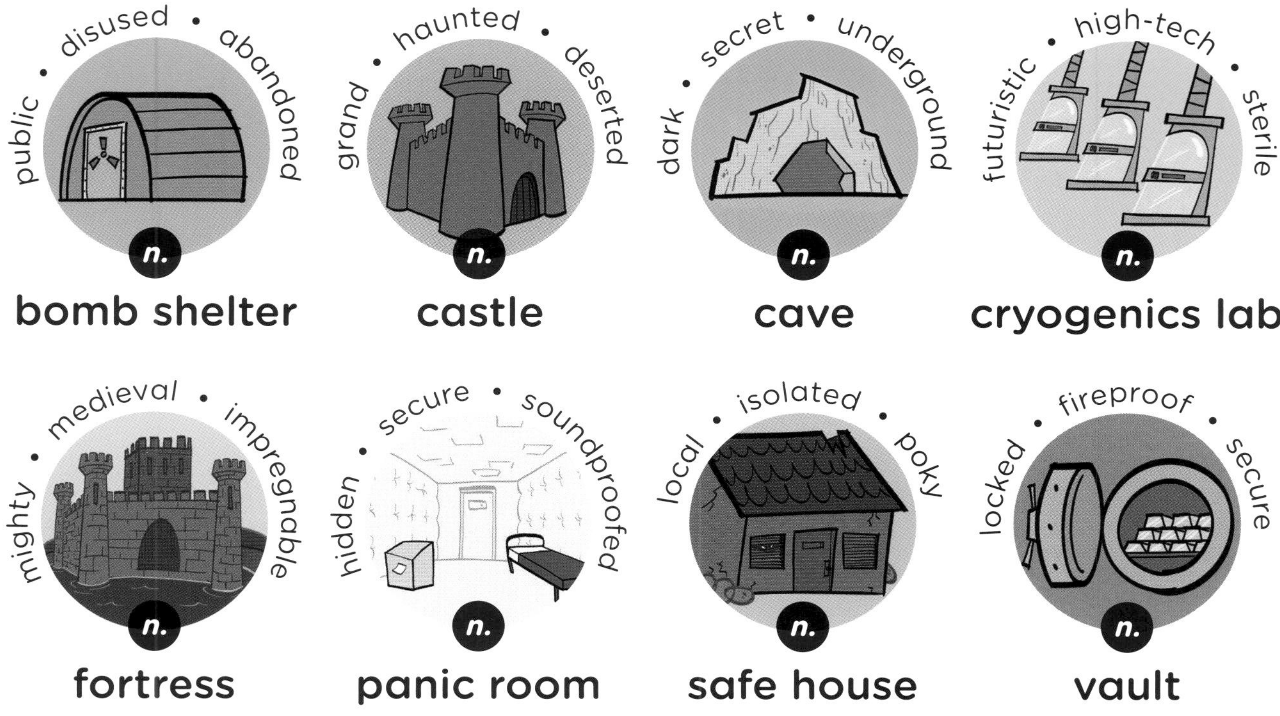

public • disused • abandoned
n.
bomb shelter
grand • haunted • deserted
n.
castle
dark • secret • underground
n.
cave
futuristic • high-tech • sterile
n.
cryogenics lab
mighty • medieval • impregnable
n.
fortress
hidden • secure • soundproofed
n.
panic room
local • isolated • poky
n.
safe house
locked • fireproof • secure
n.
vault

FARM > FARM ANIMALS

gentle • pregnant • grazing
n.
cow
old • adorable • stubborn
n.
goat
fluffy • scrawny • broody
n.
hen
tired • spirited • runaway
n.
horse
innocent • bleating • shorn
n.
lamb
greedy • grunting • squealing
n.
pig
proud • screeching • frenzied
n.
rooster
grazing • stray • jittery
n.
sheep

FARM > FARMYARD

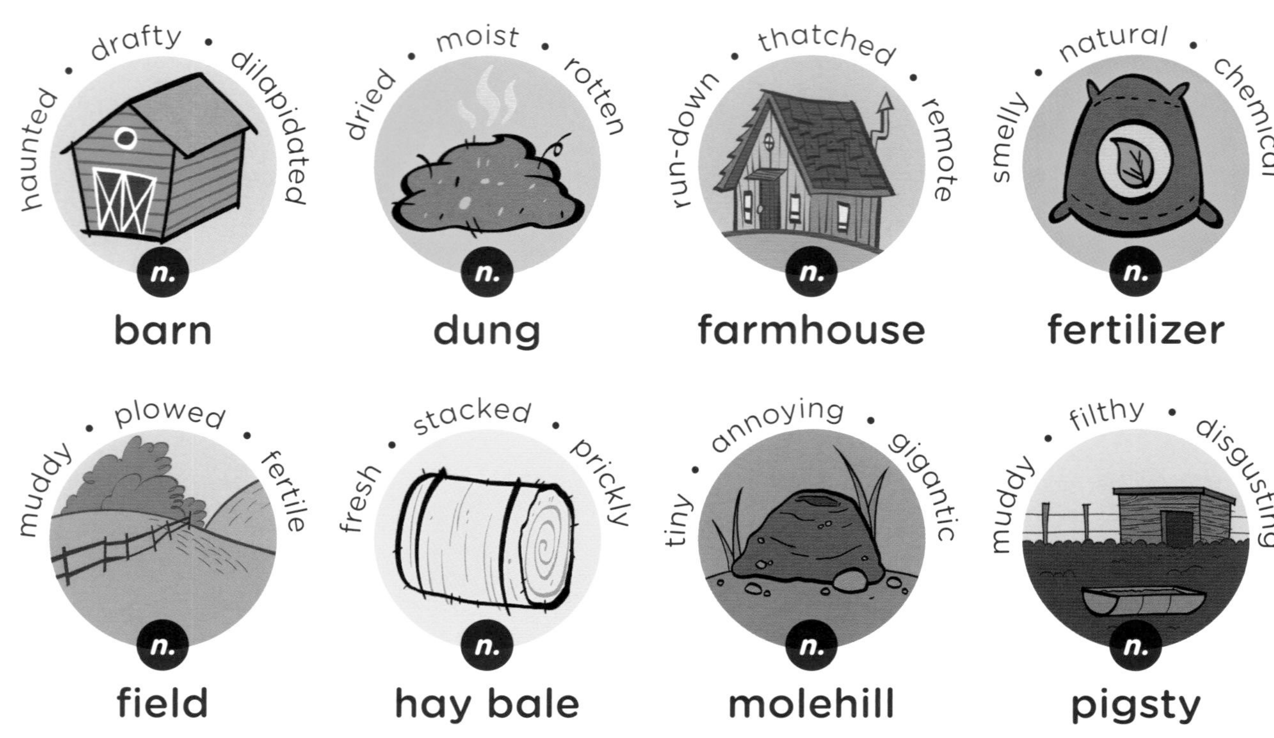
haunted • drafty • dilapidated
n.
barn
dried • moist • rotten
n.
dung
run-down • thatched • remote
n.
farmhouse
smelly • natural • chemical
n.
fertilizer
muddy • plowed • fertile
n.
field
fresh • stacked • prickly
n.
hay bale
tiny • annoying • gigantic
n.
molehill
muddy • filthy • disgusting
n.
pigsty

HOME > GARDEN

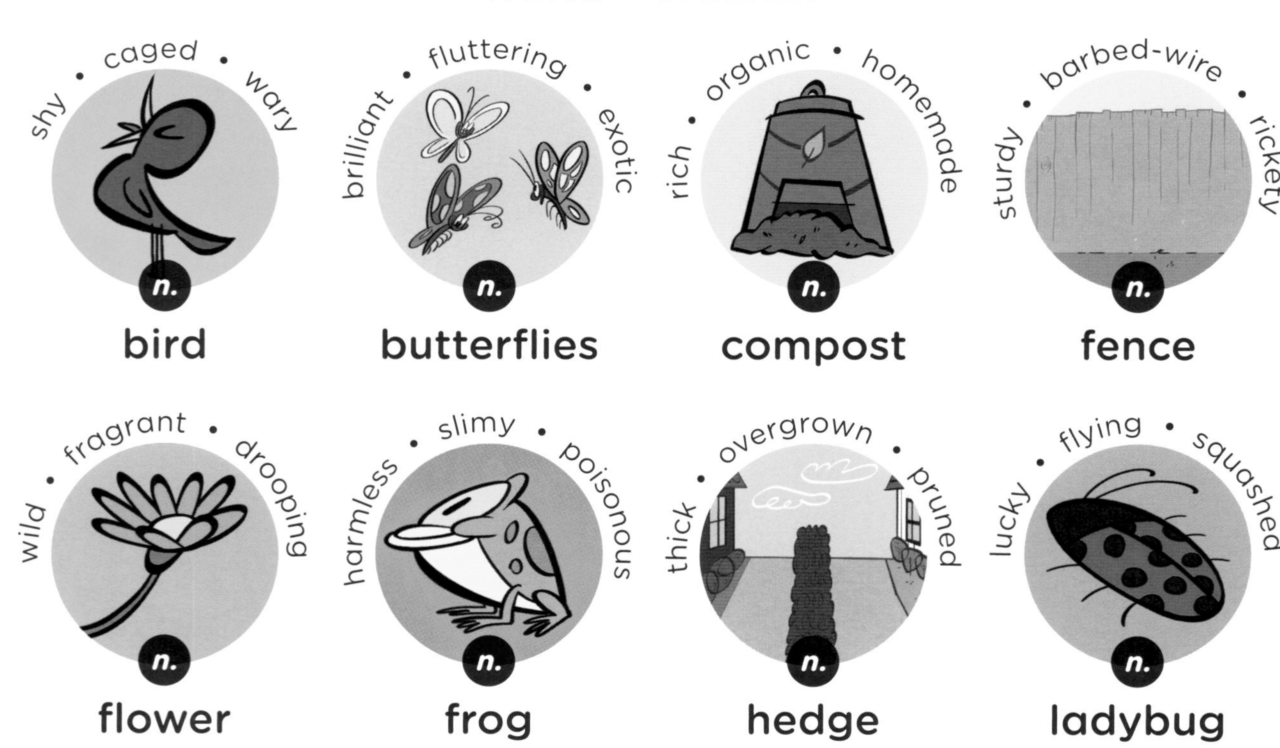
shy • caged • wary
n.
bird
brilliant • fluttering • exotic
n.
butterflies
rich • organic • homemade
n.
compost
sturdy • barbed-wire • rickety
n.
fence
wild • fragrant • drooping
n.
flower
harmless • slimy • poisonous
n.
frog
thick • overgrown • pruned
n.
hedge
lucky • flying • squashed
n.
ladybug

HOME > GARDEN

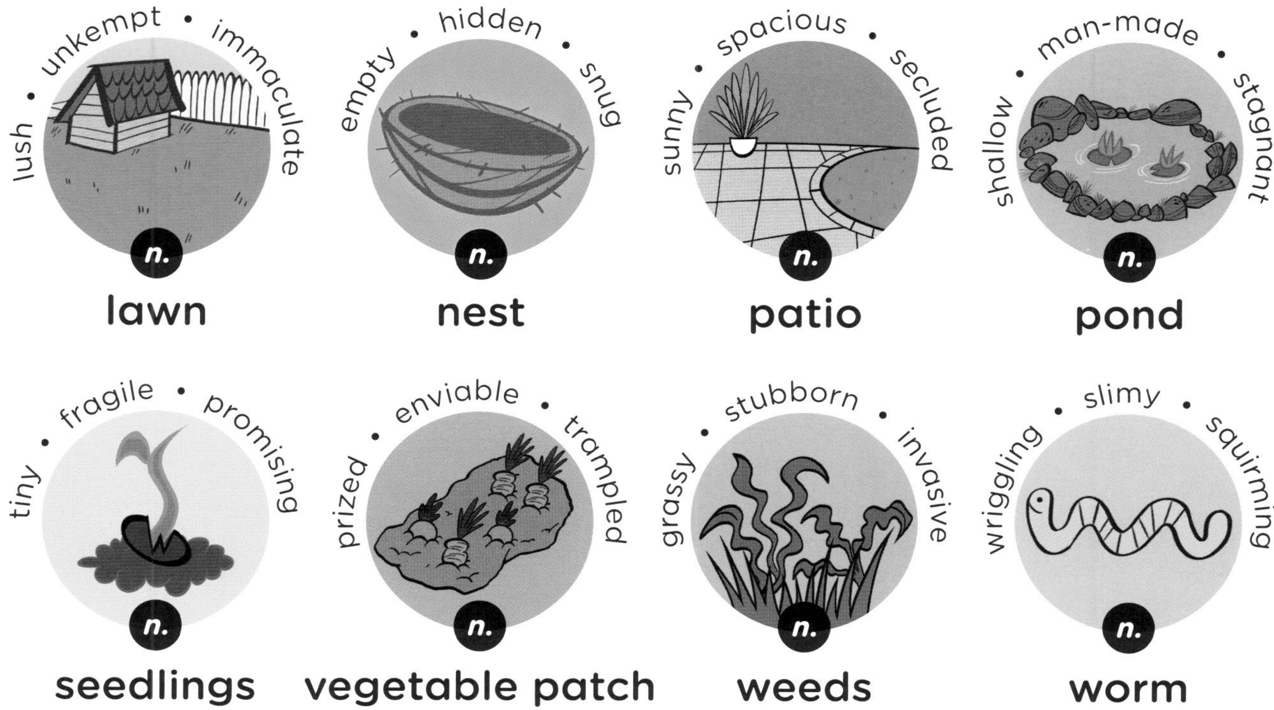
lush • unkempt • immaculate
n.
lawn
empty • hidden • snug
n.
nest
sunny • spacious • secluded
n.
patio
shallow • man-made • stagnant
n.
pond
tiny • fragile • promising
n.
seedlings
prized • enviable • trampled
n.
vegetable patch
grassy • stubborn • invasive
n.
weeds
wriggling • slimy • squirming
n.
worm

HOME > GEEK'S DEN

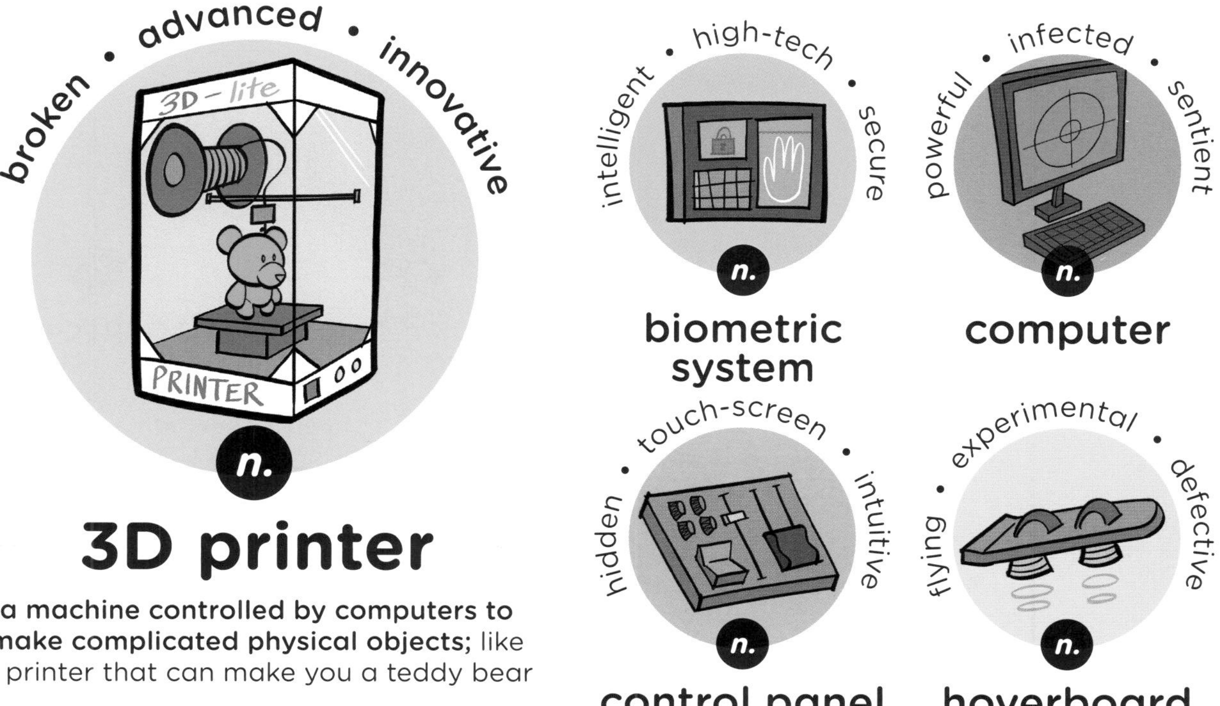
broken • advanced • innovative
3D - lite
PRINTER
n.
3D printer
intelligent • high-tech • secure
n.
biometric system
powerful • infected • sentient
n.
computer
hidden • touch-screen • intuitive
n.
control panel
flying • experimental • defective
n.
hoverboard

a machine controlled by computers to make complicated physical objects; like a printer that can make you a teddy bear

Action | Character | Emotion | Setting nouns | Taste & Smell | Weather

HOME > GEEK'S DEN

zooming • malfunctioning
n.
jetpack
stolen • compact • supercharged
n.
laptop
cracked • curved • interactive
n.
monitor
bulky • high-tech • infrared
n.
night vision goggles
booming • cutting-edge
n.
sound system
digital • flickering • flat-screen
n.
television
mobile • bulky • immersive
n.
VR headset
clever • magic • undetectable
n.
x-ray glasses

HOME > INTERIORS AND EXTERIORS

comfy • shabby • reclining
n.
armchair
dark • musty • poky
n.
attic
wooden • slippery • rickety
n.
banister
steamy • filthy • spotless
n.
bathroom
steaming • sunken • overflowing
n.
bathtub
warm • unmade • uncomfortable
n.
bed
untidy • immaculate • ransacked
n.
bedroom
built-in • crowded • groaning
n.
bookshelf

solid • crumbling • exposed
n.
bricks
locked • trophy • overhead
n.
cabinet
thick • stained • threadbare
n.
carpet
secret • damp • vast
n.
cellar
glittering • antique • ornate
n.
chandelier
smoky • blackened • crooked
n.
chimney
walk-in • mirrored • overstuffed
n.
closet
glass • stylish • antique
n.
coffee table
heavy • drawn • gaudy
n.
curtains
spacious • welcoming • elegant
n.
dining room
formal • elegant • communal
n.
dinner table
open • creaky • revolving
n.
door
dusty • roaring • wood-burning
n.
fireplace
empty • enormous • saltwater
n.
fishtank
wooden • carpeted • creaky
n.
floor
filthy • underground • cluttered
n.
garage

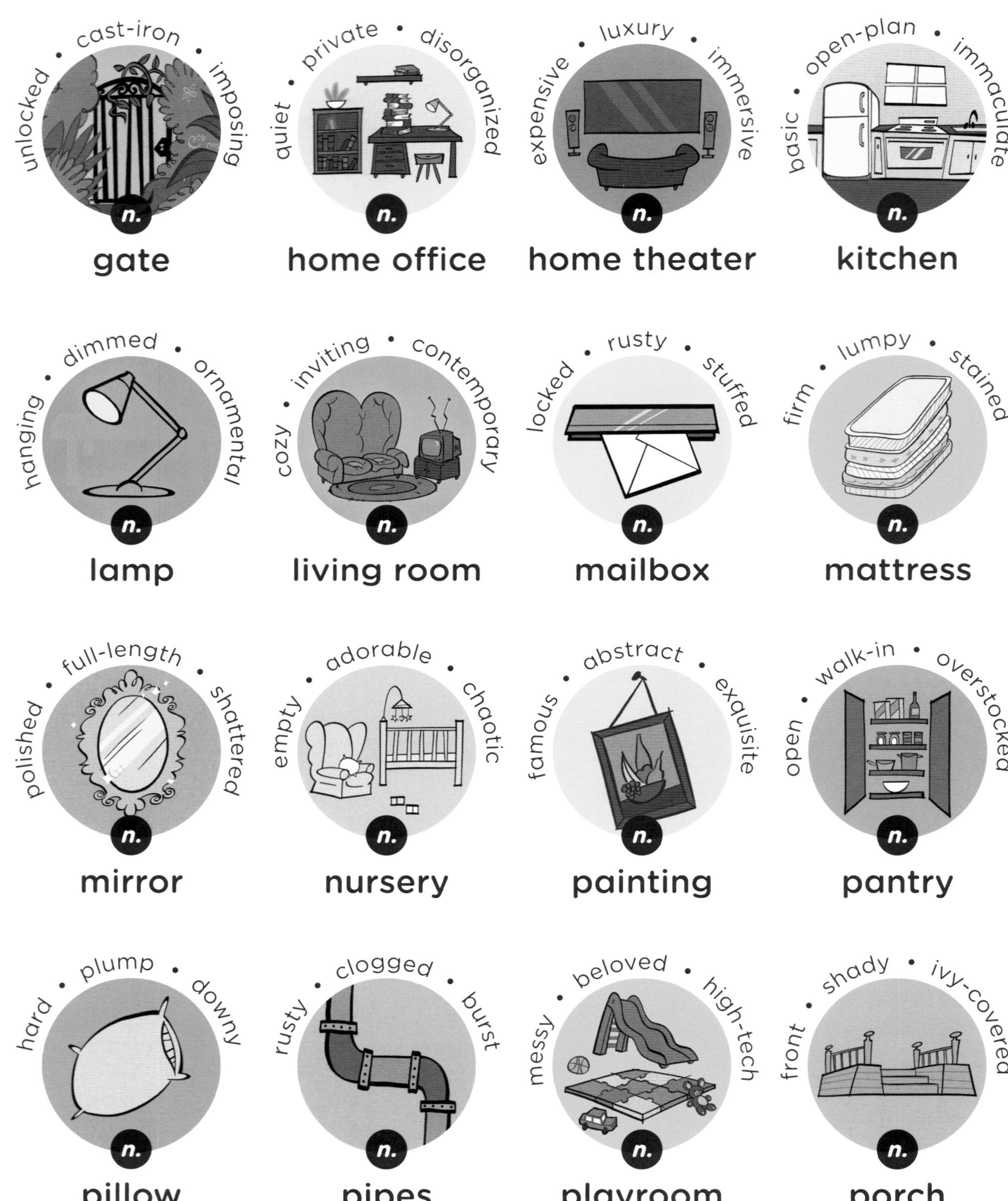
unlocked • cast-iron • imposing
n.
gate
quiet • private • disorganized
n.
home office
expensive • luxury • immersive
n.
home theater
basic • open-plan • immaculate
n.
kitchen
hanging • dimmed • ornamental
n.
lamp
cozy • inviting • contemporary
n.
living room
locked • rusty • stuffed
n.
mailbox
firm • lumpy • stained
n.
mattress
polished • full-length • shattered
n.
mirror
empty • adorable • chaotic
n.
nursery
famous • abstract • exquisite
n.
painting
open • walk-in • overstocked
n.
pantry
hard • plump • downy
n.
pillow
rusty • clogged • burst
n.
pipes
messy • beloved • high-tech
n.
playroom
front • shady • ivy-covered
n.
porch

leaky • tiled • thatched
n.
roof
thick • bearskin • shaggy
n.
rug
ice-cold • steamy • invigorating
n.
shower
plush • sagging • threadbare
n.
sofa
modern • built-in • roof-mounted
n.
solar panels
bright • airy • leafy
n.
solarium
secret • spiraling • creaky
n.
staircase
three-legged • sturdy • wobbly
n.
stool

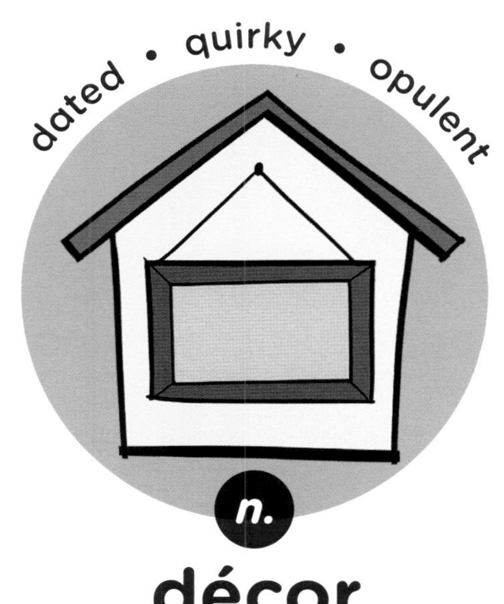
dated • quirky • opulent
n.

décor

the things in a room that make it comfortable and look nice; like furniture, pictures, wallpaper, and ornaments

square • hand-painted • cracked
n.
tiles
stinking • outdoor • unflushed
n.
toilet
patterned • floral • peeling
n.
wallpaper
broken • grimy • shuttered
n.
windows

new • humble • temporary
n.
abode
empty • high-rise • cramped
n.
apartment
charming • detached • squat
n.
bungalow
dark • lakeside • remote
n.
cabin
romantic • alpine • luxurious
n.
chalet
seaside • quaint • whitewashed
n.
cottage
large • communal • unpatrolled
n.
dormitory
grand • vacant • dilapidated
n.
house
floating • moored • ramshackle
n.
houseboat
mud • beachside • primitive
n.
hut
wooden • safari • exclusive
n.
lodge
red-brick • grand • restored
n.
manor
elegant • aristocratic • opulent
n.
mansion
royal • vast • enchanted
n.
palace
stylish • luxurious • sprawling
n.
penthouse
private • princely • spacious
n.
residence

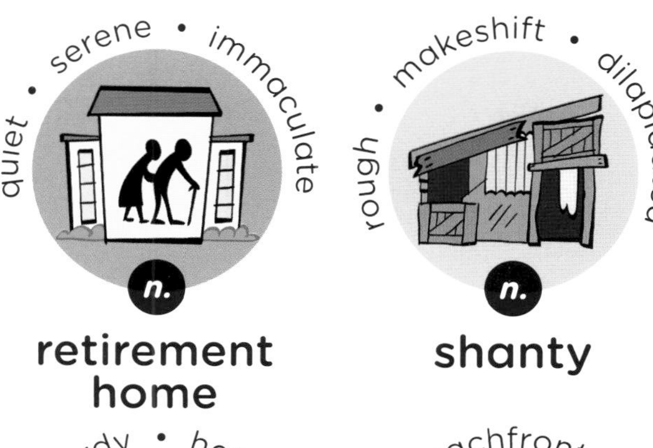
quiet • serene • immaculate
n.
rough • makeshift • dilapidated
n.

retirement home

shanty

tiny • sturdy • half-finished
n.
modern • beachfront • detached
n.

tree house

villa

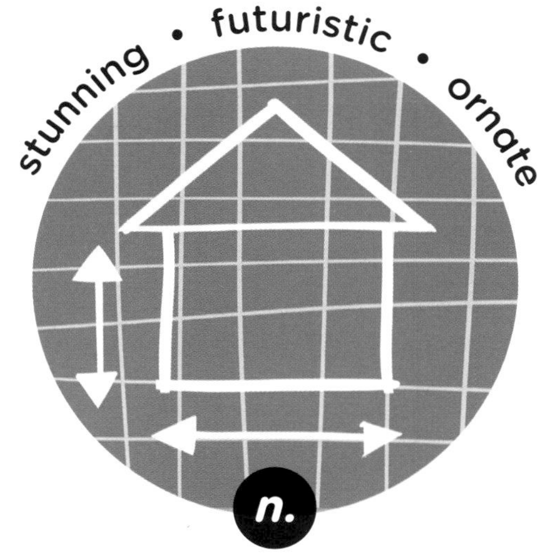
stunning • futuristic • ornate
n.

architecture

the designing and making of buildings;
like carefully planning and constructing your dream home

LANDSCAPES > COUNTRYSIDE

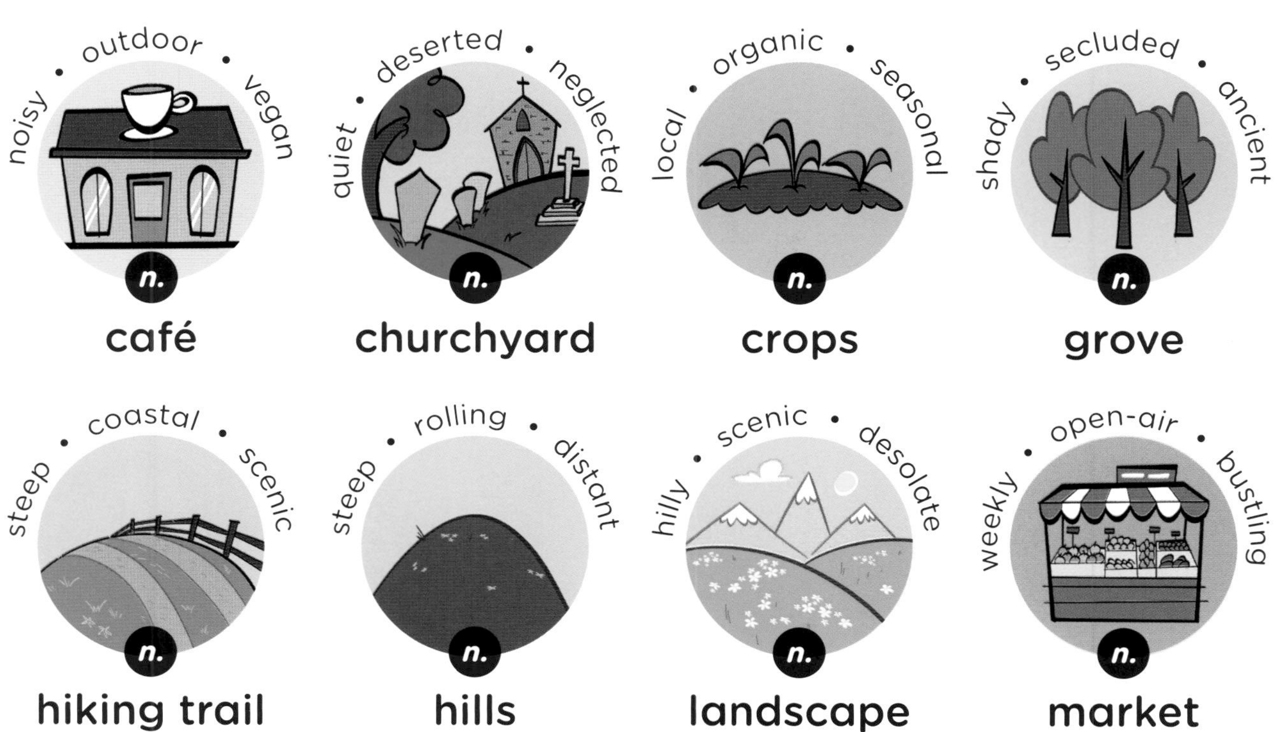
noisy • outdoor • vegan
n.
café
quiet • deserted • neglected
n.
churchyard
local • organic • seasonal
n.
crops
shady • secluded • ancient
n.
grove
steep • coastal • scenic
n.
hiking trail
steep • rolling • distant
n.
hills
hilly • scenic • desolate
n.
landscape
weekly • open-air • bustling
n.
market

LANDSCAPES > COUNTRYSIDE

grassy • snowy • moonlit
n.
meadow
beautiful • overgrown • fragrant
n.
orchard
green • lush • abundant
n.
pasture
muddy • narrow • dead-end
n.
path
wooden • heavy • horse-drawn
n.
plow
quiet • cobbled • bustling
n.
street
old • grand • raucous
n.
town hall
rusty • powerful • heavy-duty
n.
tractor

LANDSCAPES > DESERT

giant • wild • prickly
n.
cactus
thirsty • overloaded • tethered
n.
camel
endless • barren • arid
n.
desert
fine • volcanic • atmospheric
n.
dust
rare • harmless • venomous
n.
lizard
cute • curious • sharp-eyed
n.
meerkat
peaceful • distant • fertile
n.
oasis
deadly • venomous • monstrous
n.
scorpion

distant • cruel • shimmering

n.

mirage

an optical illlusion caused by bending light rays; like when you're lost in the desert and think you can see water in the distance

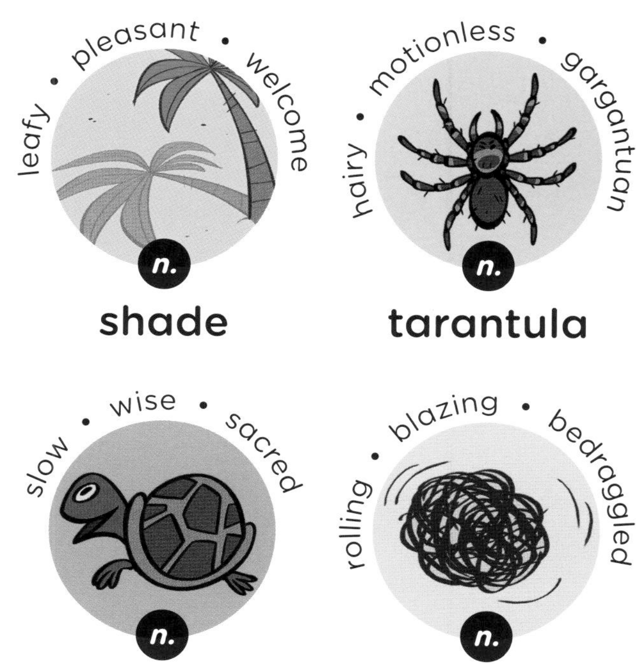

leafy • pleasant • welcome

n.

shade

hairy • motionless • gargantuan

n.

tarantula

slow • wise • sacred

n.

tortoise

rolling • blazing • bedraggled

n.

tumbleweed

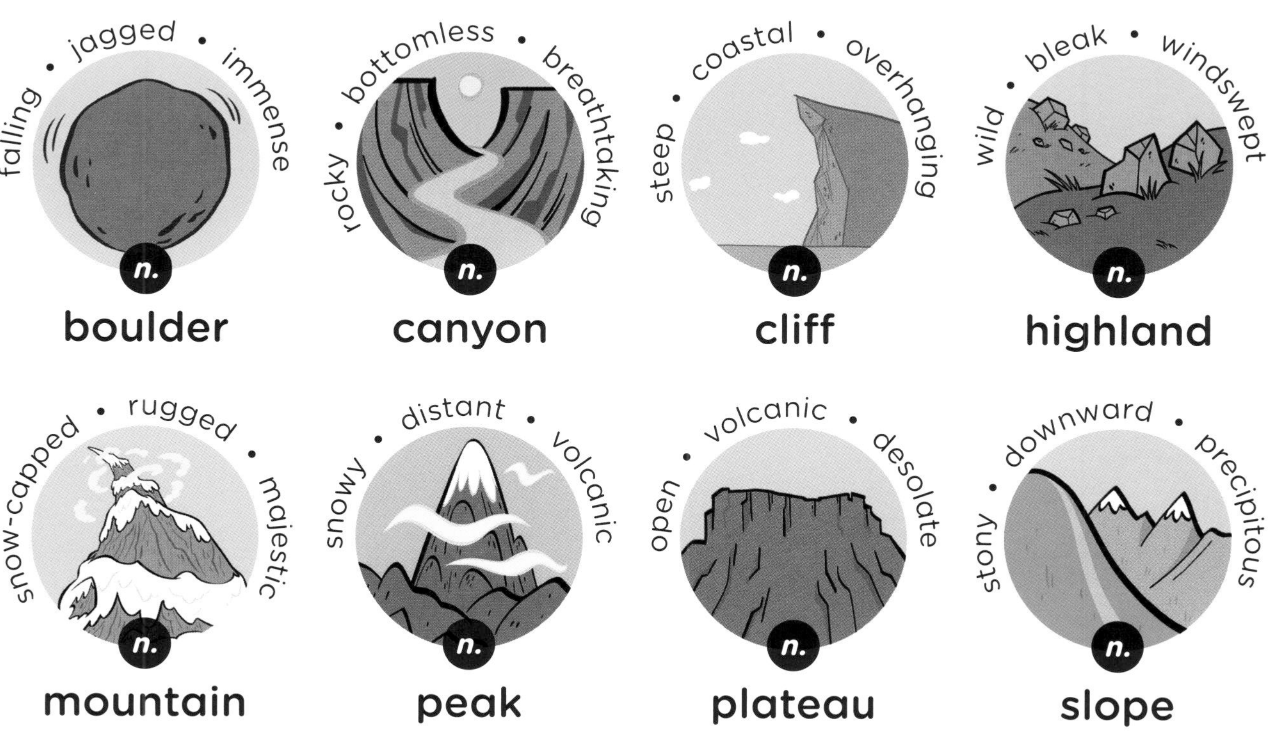

falling • jagged • immense

n.

boulder

rocky • bottomless • breathtaking

n.

canyon

steep • coastal • overhanging

n.

cliff

wild • bleak • windswept

n.

highland

snow-capped • rugged • majestic

n.

mountain

snowy • distant • volcanic

n.

peak

open • volcanic • desolate

n.

plateau

stony • downward • precipitous

n.

slope

playful • majestic • elusive
n.
arctic fox
floating • enormous • submerged
n.
iceberg
melting • immense • advancing
n.
glacier
a huge mass of moving ice;
like a slow-moving, frozen river
polar • thawing • colossal
n.
icecap
cozy • hidden • abandoned
n.
igloo
howling • shaggy • gaunt
n.
husky
horned • gigantic • mysterious
n.
narwhal
friendly • waddling • comical
n.
penguin
mighty • playful • endangered
n.
polar bear
swimming • curious • lovable
n.
puffin
stray • harnessed • timid
n.
reindeer
wooden • loaded • overturned
n.
sled
fat • enormous • beached
n.
walrus

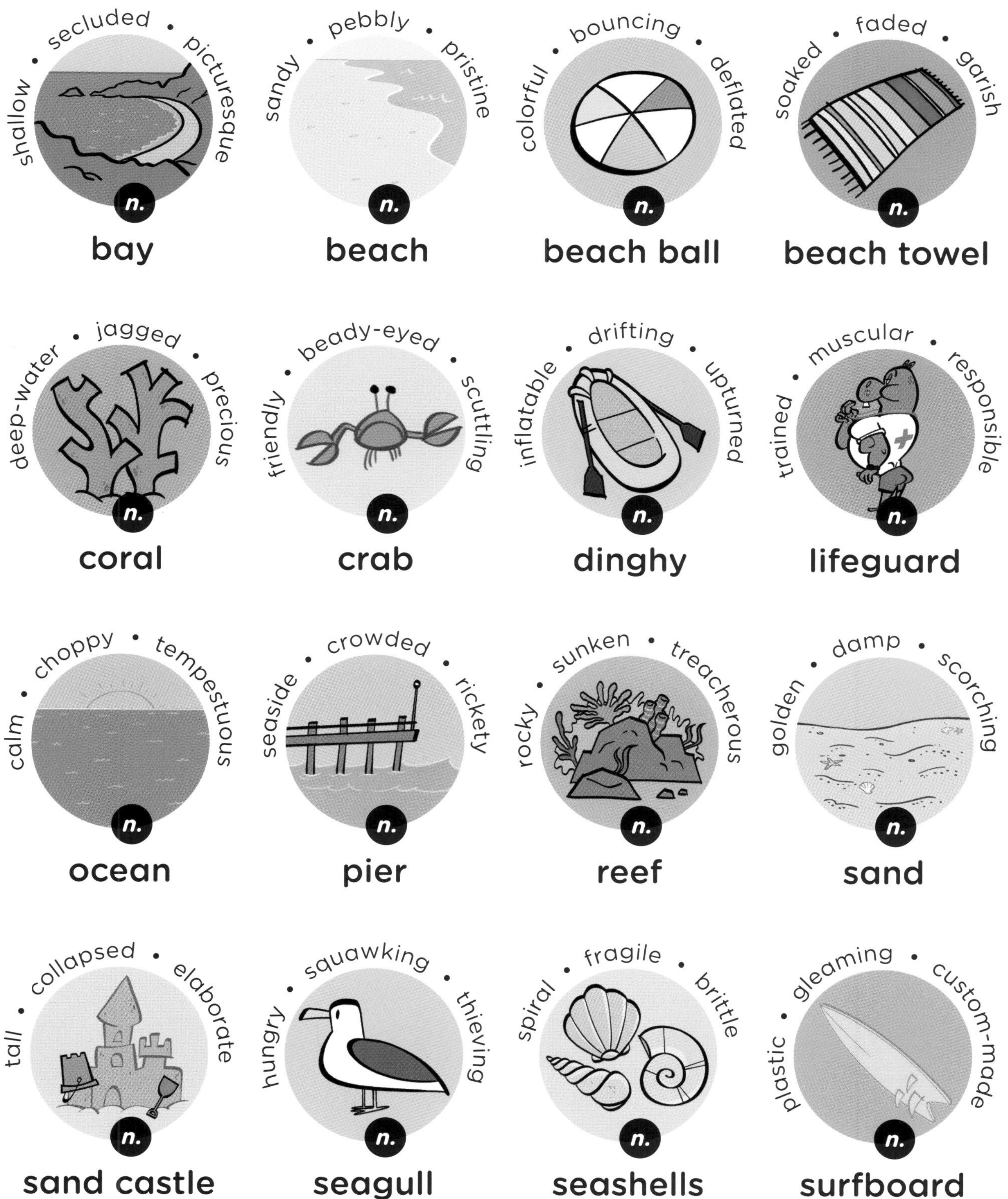
shallow • secluded • picturesque
n.
bay
sandy • pebbly • pristine
n.
beach
colorful • bouncing • deflated
n.
beach ball
soaked • faded • garish
n.
beach towel
deep-water • jagged • precious
n.
coral
friendly • beady-eyed • scuttling
n.
crab
inflatable • drifting • upturned
n.
dinghy
trained • muscular • responsible
n.
lifeguard
calm • choppy • tempestuous
n.
ocean
seaside • crowded • rickety
n.
pier
rocky • sunken • treacherous
n.
reef
golden • damp • scorching
n.
sand
tall • collapsed • elaborate
n.
sand castle
hungry • squawking • thieving
n.
seagull
spiral • fragile • brittle
n.
seashells
plastic • gleaming • custom-made
n.
surfboard

LANDSCAPES > TROPICAL

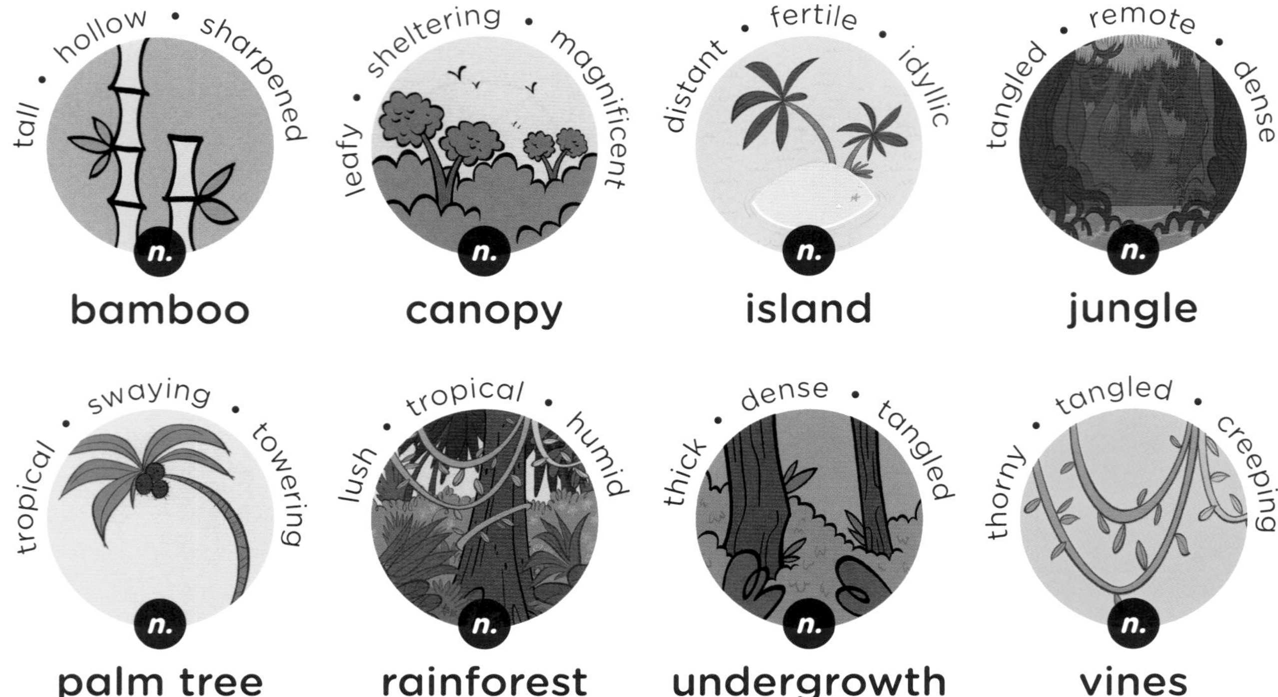
tall • hollow • sharpened
n.
bamboo
leafy • sheltering • magnificent
n.
canopy
distant • fertile • idyllic
n.
island
tangled • remote • dense
n.
jungle
tropical • swaying • towering
n.
palm tree
lush • tropical • humid
n.
rainforest
thick • dense • tangled
n.
undergrowth
thorny • tangled • creeping
n.
vines

LANDSCAPES > UNDER THE SEA

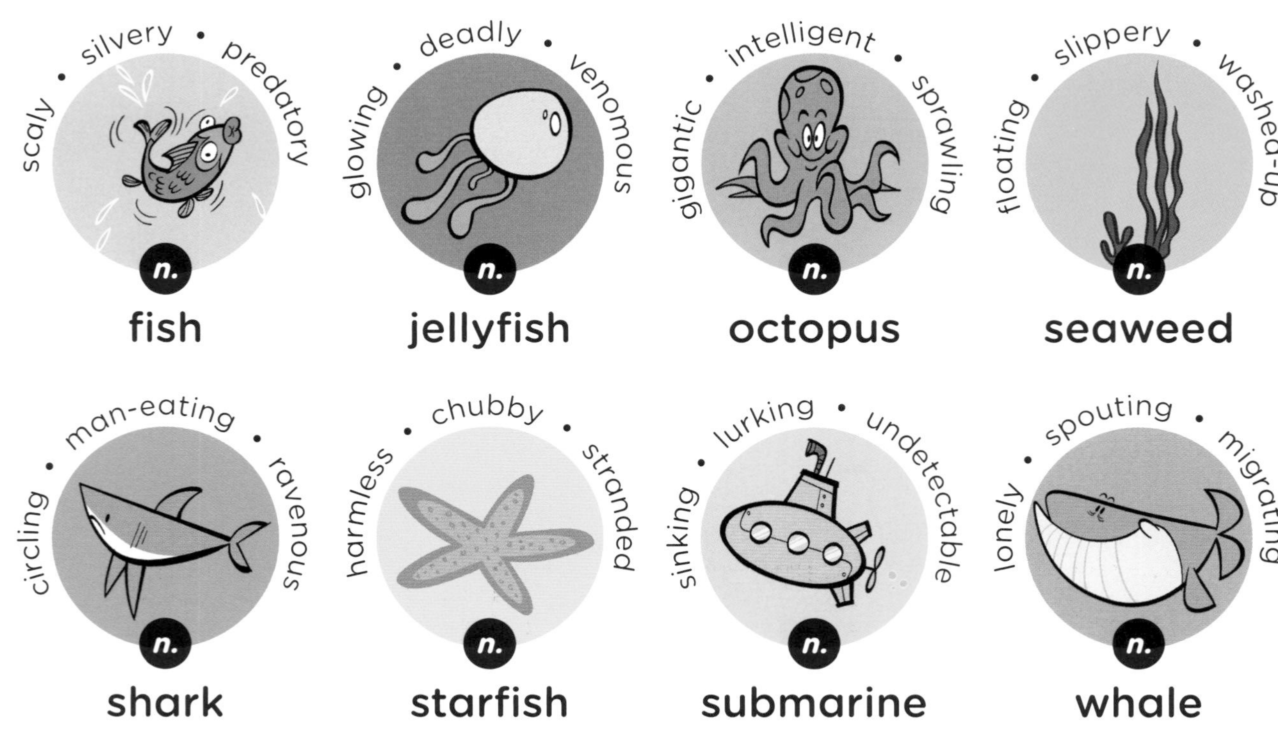
scaly • silvery • predatory
n.
fish
glowing • deadly • venomous
n.
jellyfish
gigantic • intelligent • sprawling
n.
octopus
floating • slippery • washed-up
n.
seaweed
circling • man-eating • ravenous
n.
shark
harmless • chubby • stranded
n.
starfish
sinking • lurking • undetectable
n.
submarine
lonely • spouting • migrating
n.
whale

muddy • slippery • marshy 
n.
bank

clear • babbling • sparkling 
n.
brook

winding • polluted • sluggish 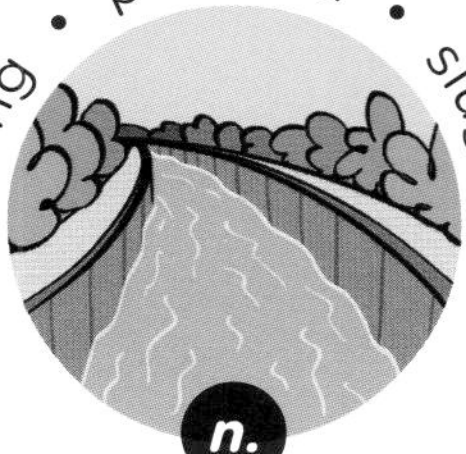
n.
canal

narrow • swollen • meandering 
n.
creek

rich • marshy • flooded 
n.
delta

shallow • sleepy • tranquil 
n.
lagoon

deadly • raging • unstoppable 
n.
riptide

winding • mighty • turbulent 
n.
river

wild • frothy • challenging

n.
rapids

a very fast-moving and rough part of a river; like a terrifying stretch of white water that throws you from your canoe

hot • natural • sulfurous
n.
spring

shallow • sparkling • meandering
n.
stream

powerful • foaming • cascading
n.
waterfall

crashing • lapping • choppy
n.
waves

LANDSCAPES > WETLAND

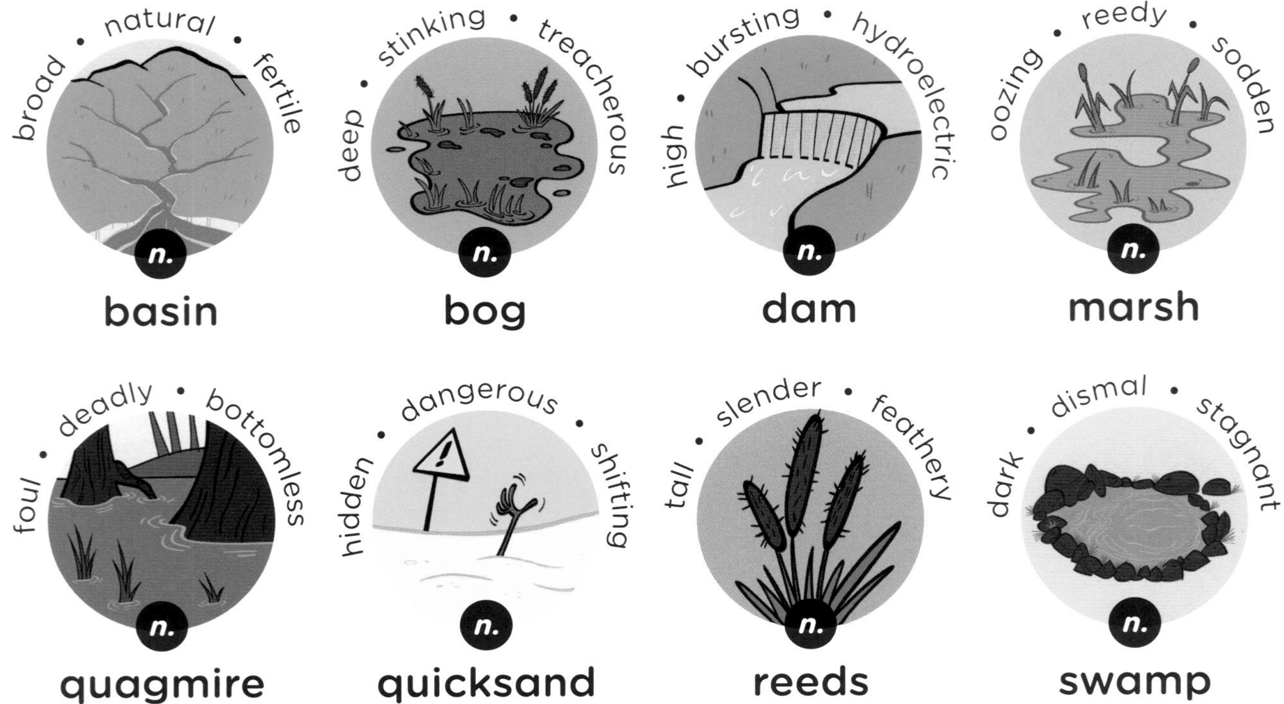
broad • natural • fertile
n.
basin
deep • stinking • treacherous
n.
bog
high • bursting • hydroelectric
n.
dam
oozing • reedy • sodden
n.
marsh
foul • deadly • bottomless
n.
quagmire
hidden • dangerous • shifting
n.
quicksand
tall • slender • feathery
n.
reeds
dark • dismal • stagnant
n.
swamp

LANDSCAPES > WOODLAND

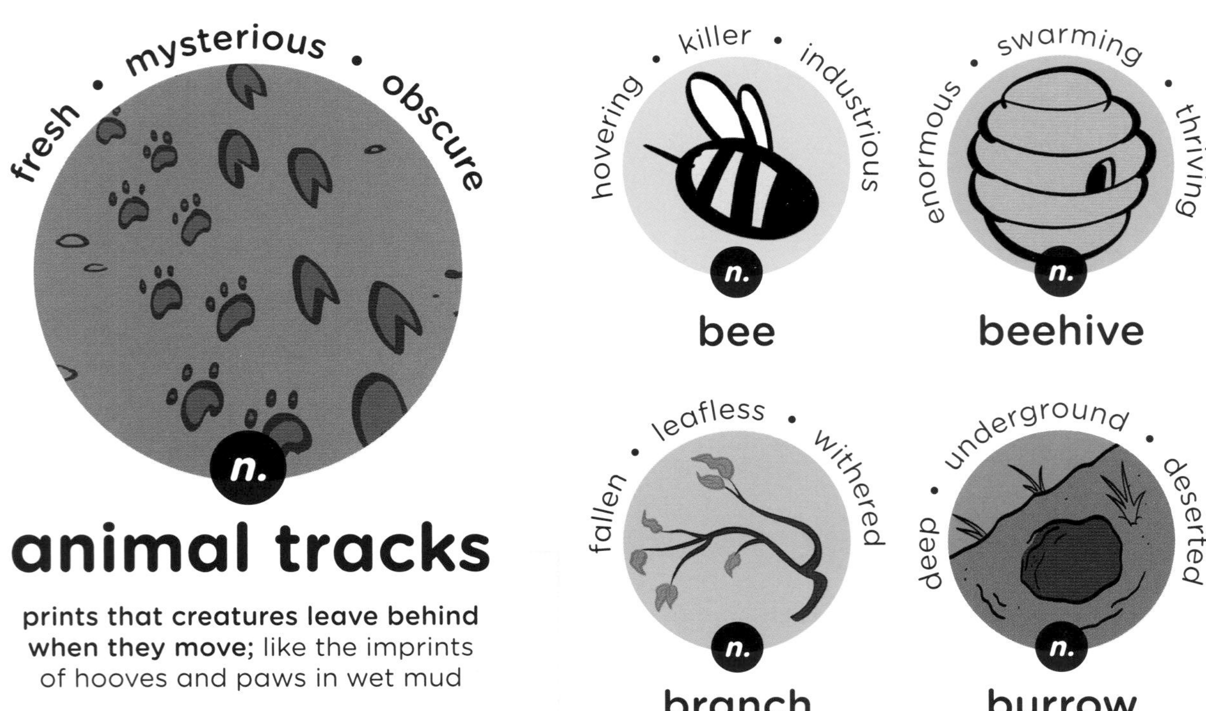
fresh • mysterious • obscure
n.
hovering • killer • industrious
n.
bee
enormous • swarming • thriving
n.
beehive
fallen • leafless • withered
n.
branch
deep • underground • deserted
n.
burrow

animal tracks

prints that creatures leave behind when they move; like the imprints of hooves and paws in wet mud

LANDSCAPES > WOODLAND

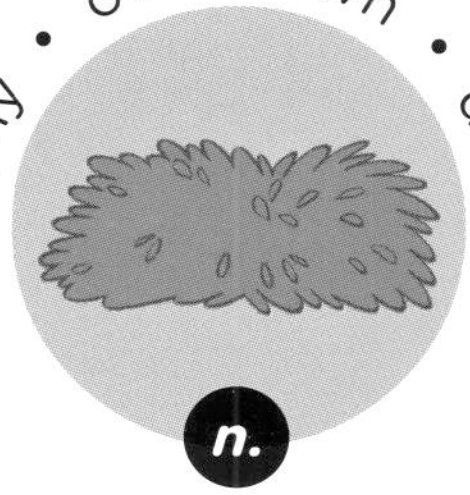

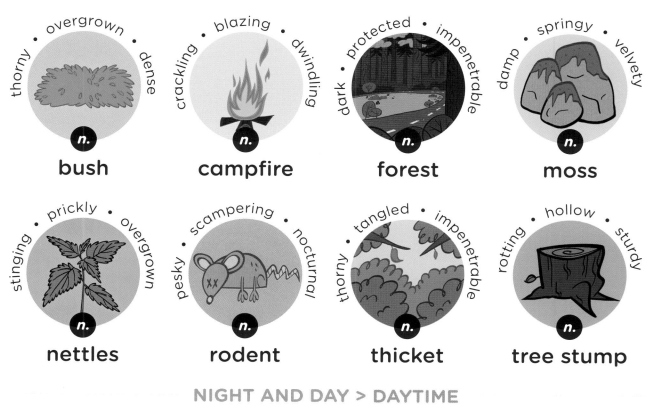

bush *n.* — thorny • overgrown • dense

campfire *n.* — crackling • blazing • dwindling

forest *n.* — dark • protected • impenetrable

moss *n.* — damp • springy • velvety

nettles *n.* — stinging • prickly • overgrown

rodent *n.* — pesky • scampering • nocturnal

thicket *n.* — thorny • tangled • impenetrable

tree stump *n.* — rotting • hollow • sturdy

NIGHT AND DAY > DAYTIME

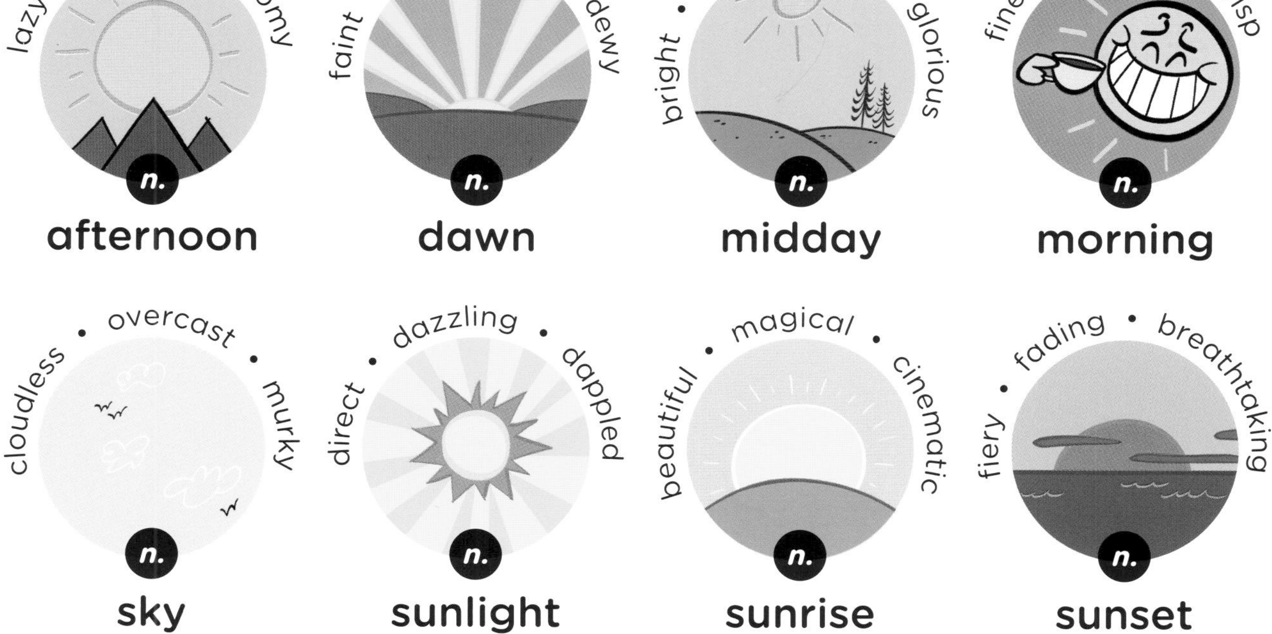

afternoon *n.* — lazy • balmy • gloomy

dawn *n.* — faint • glimmering • dewy

midday *n.* — bright • approaching • glorious

morning *n.* — fine • radiant • crisp

sky *n.* — cloudless • overcast • murky

sunlight *n.* — direct • dazzling • dappled

sunrise *n.* — beautiful • magical • cinematic

sunset *n.* — fiery • fading • breathtaking

NIGHT AND DAY > NIGHTTIME

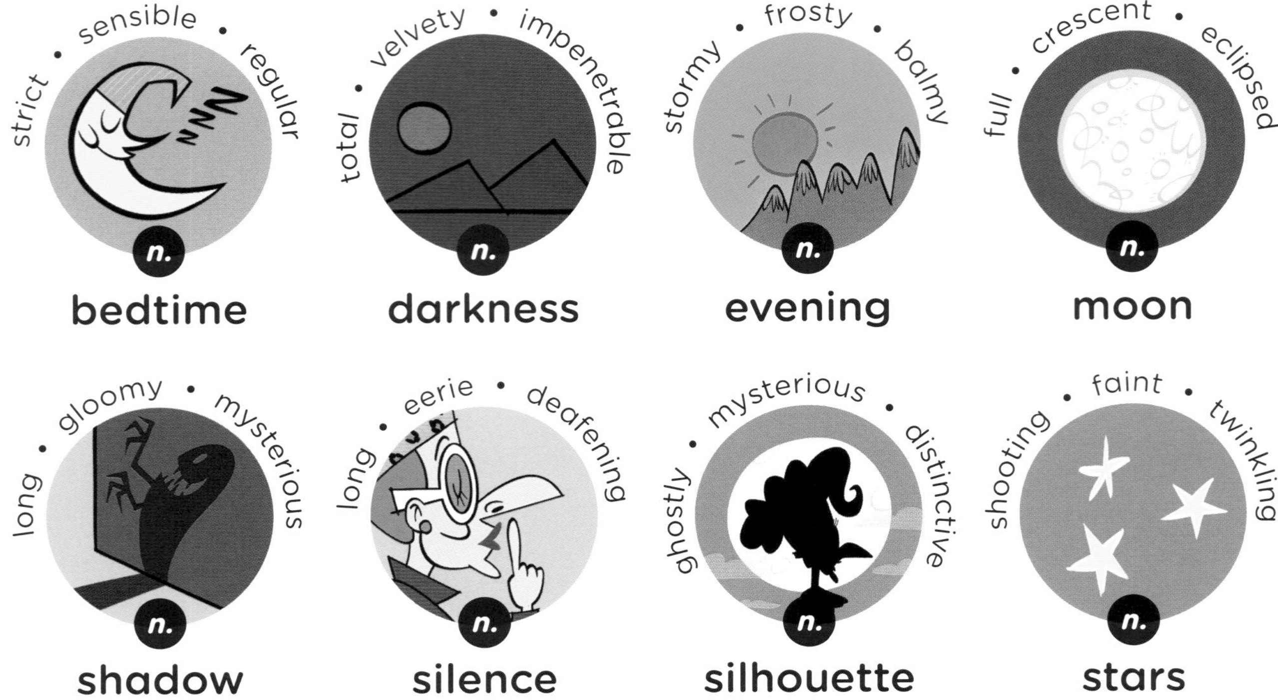
strict • sensible • regular
n.
bedtime
total • velvety • impenetrable
n.
darkness
stormy • frosty • balmy
n.
evening
full • crescent • eclipsed
n.
moon
long • gloomy • mysterious
n.
shadow
long • eerie • deafening
n.
silence
ghostly • mysterious • distinctive
n.
silhouette
shooting • faint • twinkling
n.
stars

SPACE

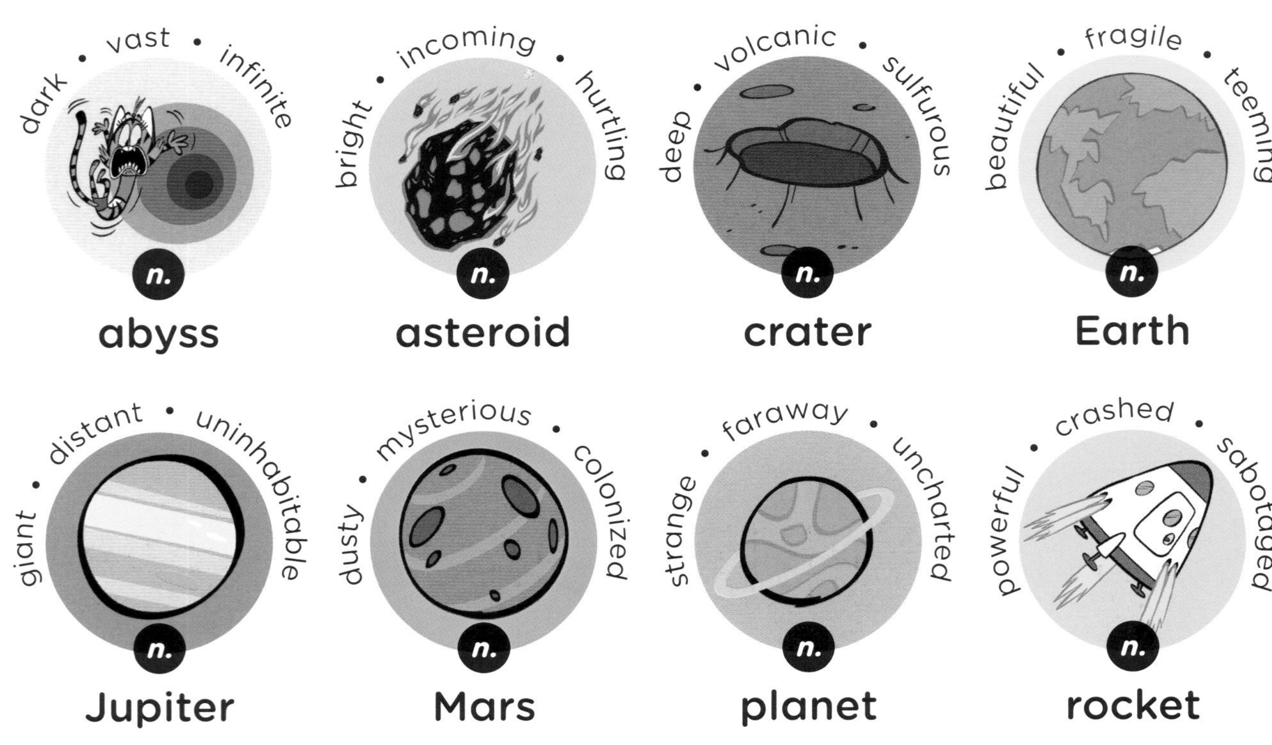
dark • vast • infinite
n.
abyss
bright • incoming • hurtling
n.
asteroid
deep • volcanic • sulfurous
n.
crater
beautiful • fragile • teeming
n.
Earth
giant • distant • uninhabitable
n.
Jupiter
dusty • mysterious • colonized
n.
Mars
strange • faraway • uncharted
n.
planet
powerful • crashed • sabotaged
n.
rocket

SPACE

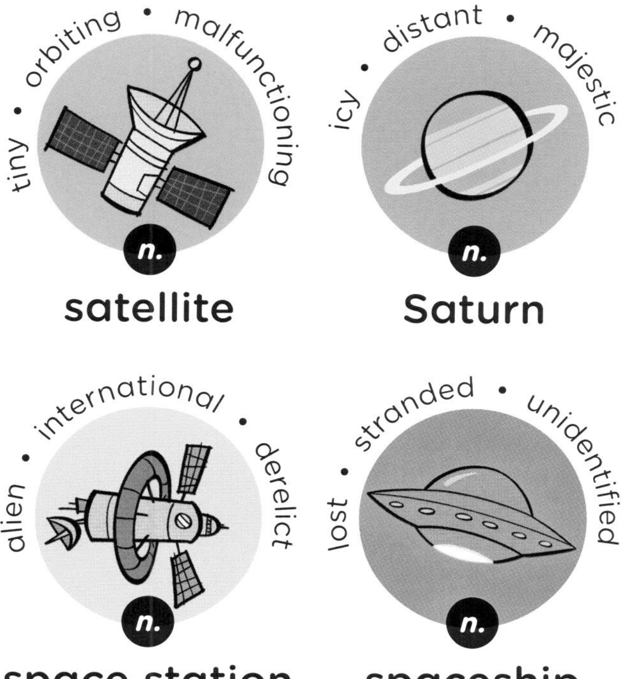

tiny • orbiting • malfunctioning
n.
satellite
icy • distant • majestic
n.
Saturn
alien • international • derelict
n.
space station
lost • stranded • unidentified
n.
spaceship

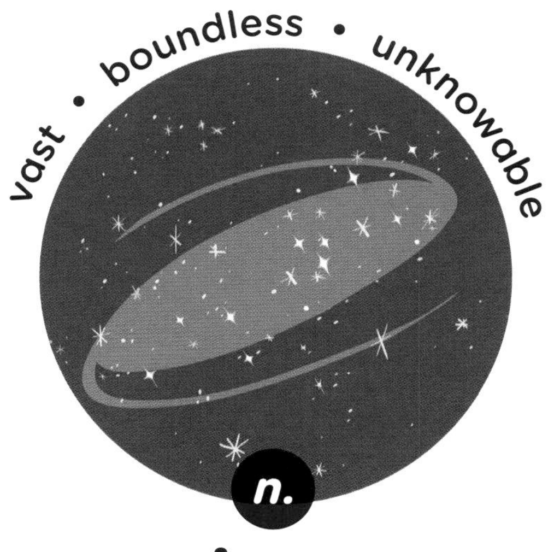

vast • boundless • unknowable
n.

universe

all of space, time, and everything else; all the planets, galaxies, and things you can and can't see

WILDLIFE > ANIMALS

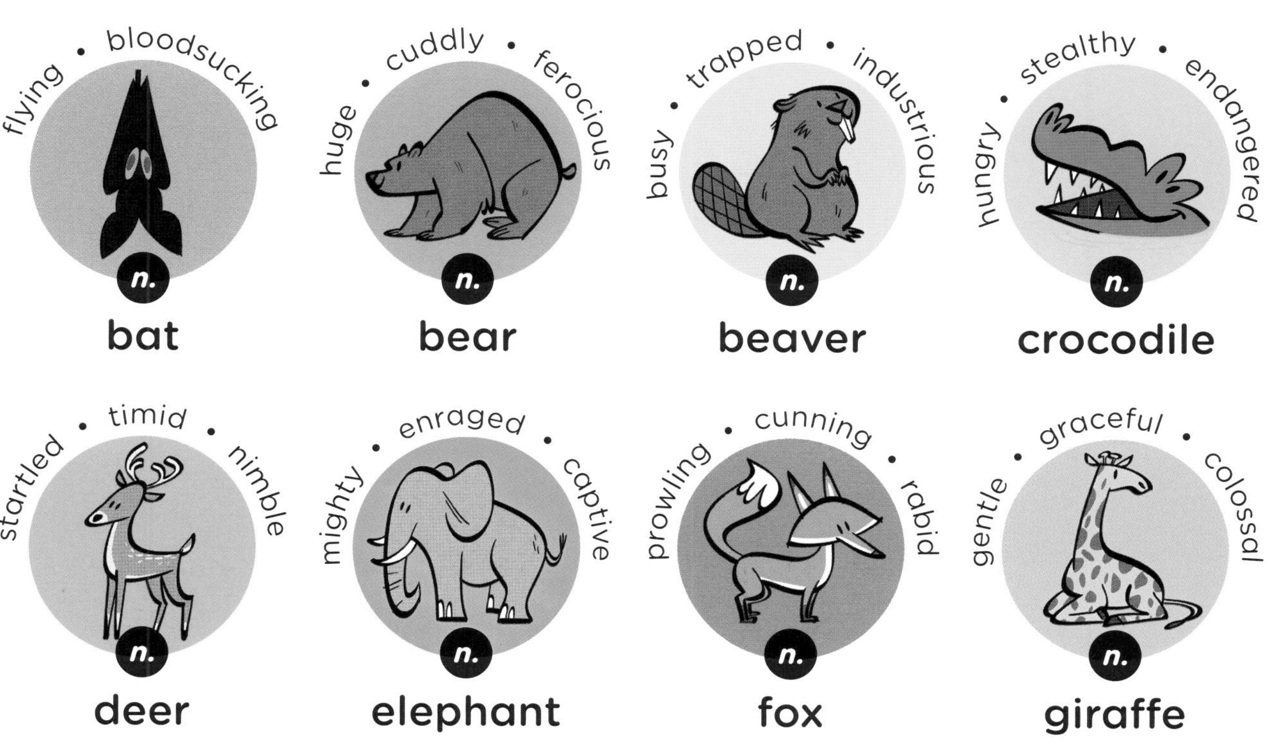

flying • bloodsucking
n.
bat
huge • cuddly • ferocious
n.
bear
busy • trapped • industrious
n.
beaver
hungry • stealthy • endangered
n.
crocodile
startled • timid • nimble
n.
deer
mighty • enraged • captive
n.
elephant
prowling • cunning • rabid
n.
fox
gentle • graceful • colossal
n.
giraffe

WILDLIFE > ANIMALS

hopping • frightened • tame
n.
hare
roaring • caged • magnificent
n.
lion
rescued • orphaned • solitary
n.
orangutan
cute • sleek • playful
n.
otter
rare • raging • endangered
n.
rhinoceros
hissing • slithering • venomous
n.
snake
striped • man-eating • tranquilized
n.
tiger
hungry • howling • lone
n.
wolf

WILDLIFE > BIRDS

young • unseen • intruding
n.
cuckoo
soaring • watchful • majestic
n.
eagle
pink • beautiful • fabulous
n.
flamingo
hungry • fierce • marauding
n.
hawk
slender • elegant • solitary
n.
heron
little • speckled • hovering
n.
hummingbird
clever • thieving • mischievous
n.
magpie
huge • strutting • rapid
n.
ostrich

WILDLIFE > BIRDS

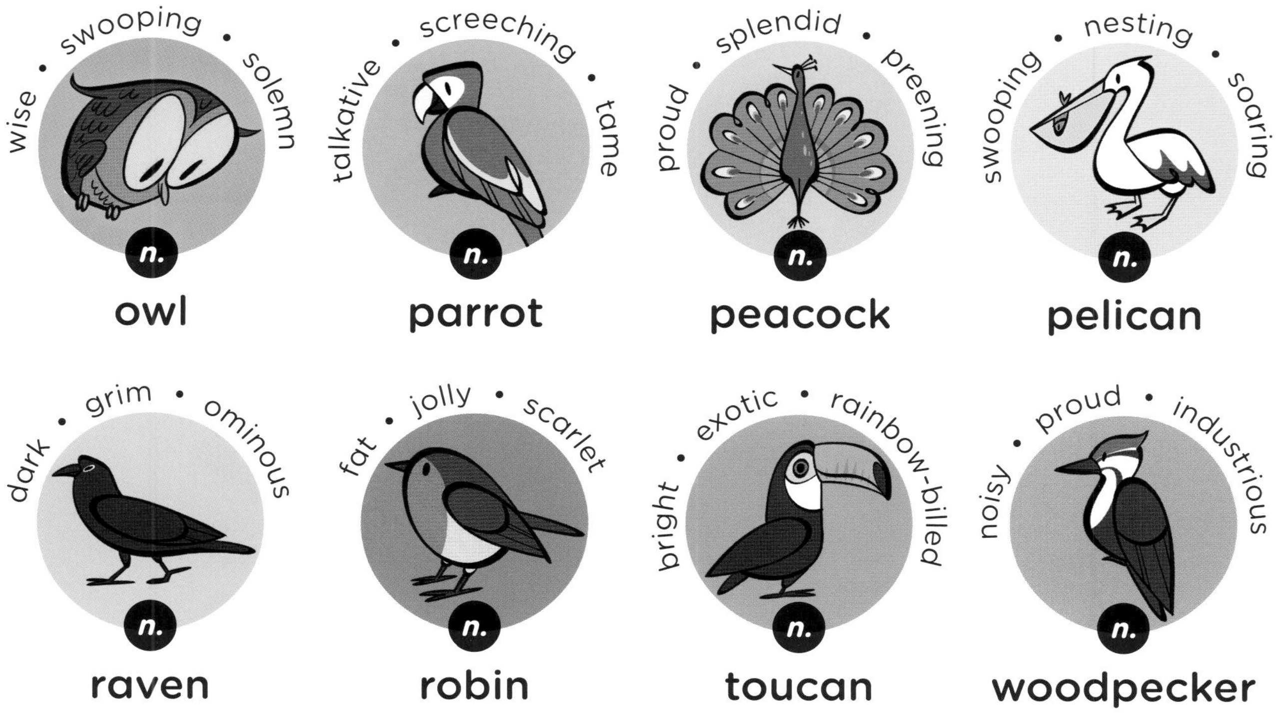
wise • swooping • solemn
n.
owl
talkative • screeching • tame
n.
parrot
proud • splendid • preening
n.
peacock
swooping • nesting • soaring
n.
pelican
dark • grim • ominous
n.
raven
fat • jolly • scarlet
n.
robin
bright • exotic • rainbow-billed
n.
toucan
noisy • proud • industrious
n.
woodpecker

WILDLIFE > GROUPS OF ANIMALS

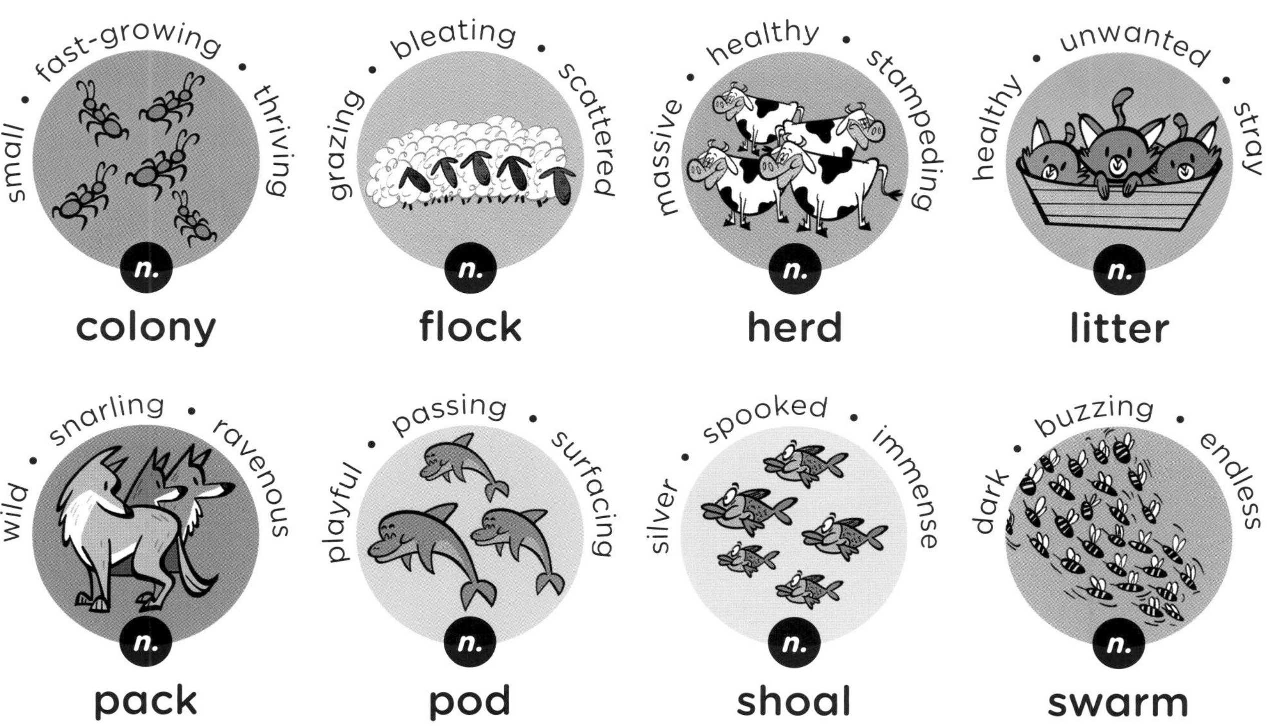
small • fast-growing • thriving
n.
colony
grazing • bleating • scattered
n.
flock
massive • healthy • stampeding
n.
herd
healthy • unwanted • stray
n.
litter
wild • snarling • ravenous
n.
pack
playful • passing • surfacing
n.
pod
silver • spooked • immense
n.
shoal
dark • buzzing • endless
n.
swarm

savor

Taste & Smell

CHOCOLATE
MILK

irresistible *adj.* appealing and inviting; like something you can't help reaching for

word pairs: temptation, craving, urge

moist *adj.* damp or not dry; like a fluffy chocolate cake that oozes chocolate syrup

word pairs: cake, soil, towel

scrumptious *adj.* tasty or delicious; like a fancy selection of cakes

word pairs: cakes, dessert, feast

succulent *adj.* juicy and fresh; like perfectly ripe peaches that are full of delicious juice

word pairs: peaches, lobster, steak

mouthwatering *adj.* looking or smelling delicious; like something that makes you drool

word pairs: treat, smell, recipe

tantalizing *adj.* tempting and tormenting; like delicious doughnuts that you can't reach

word pairs: food, possibility, glimpse

delicious words

word pair after:

irresistible temptation
moist cake
mouthwatering treat
scrumptious cakes
succulent peaches
tantalizing food

inedible *adj.* not fit for eating; like a pizza covered in nuts and bolts

word pairs: meal, mushroom, leaves

nauseating *adj.* sickening or disgusting; like a rotten sandwich

word pairs: stench, fear, opinions

repulsive *adj.* disgusting or gross; like an ugly gargoyle that makes you feel sick

word pairs: creature, odor, manners

stale *adj.* old, hard, and crusty; like bread that has gone hard because you left it out

word pairs: bread, air, sweat

disgusting words

rancid *adj.* foul or rotten; like milk that has been left out for days and gone sour

word pairs: milk, meat, smell

unpalatable *adj.* unappealing or off-putting; like a can of gross, brown dog food

word pairs: food, mush, truth

Dog
FOOD

word pair after:

inedible meal
nauseating stench
rancid milk
repulsive creature
stale bread
unpalatable food

Weather

demolish *v.* to destroy or eat up; when you gobble something up until there's nothing left

word pairs: lunch, cake, house

devour *v.* to eat hungrily or gobble up; when you swallow your dinner quickly and hungrily

word pairs: meal, steak, book

guzzle *v.* to gobble or devour; like gulping down a huge carton of milk all at once

word pairs: drink, gas, gallons

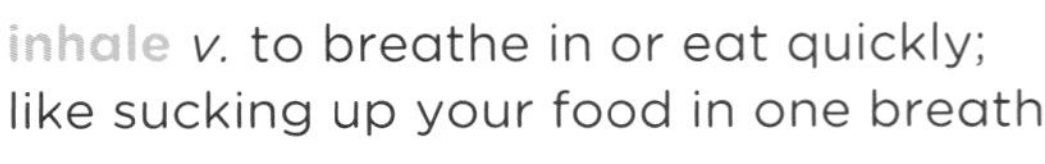

inhale *v.* to breathe in or eat quickly; like sucking up your food in one breath

word pairs: food, gas, fumes

MILK
2%

DONUTS
DONUTS

gorge *v.* to stuff yourself or overeat; when you eat a giant mountain of food and feel sick

word pairs: shamelessly, greedily, completely

savor *v.* to enjoy or appreciate; when you eat very slowly so you can enjoy every bite

word pairs: taste, mouthful, moment

eating words

word pair after:

demolish your lunch
devour a meal
gorge shamelessly
guzzle a drink
inhale food
savor the taste

bland *adj.* plain or flavorless; like food that is tasteless and boring

word pairs: food, smile, statement

peppery *adj.* spicy or fiery; like food that makes your face turn red and your eyes run

word pairs: taste, sauce, aftertaste

sugary *adj.* very sticky and sweet; how your bath would taste if it were full of doughnuts

word pairs: doughnuts, cereal, drink

tangy *adj.* flavorful and sharp; like the sour taste of a grapefruit

word pairs: fruit, jam, sauce

Grit

savory *adj.* salty or spicy; like pizza sauce or a peppery steak

word pairs: steak, stew, snack

tart *adj.* sharp and sour; like the taste of freshly squeezed lemonade

word pairs: flavor, apple, reply

flavor words

word pair after:

bland food
peppery taste
savory steak
sugary doughnuts
tangy fruit
tart flavor

COFFEE!
COFFEE!

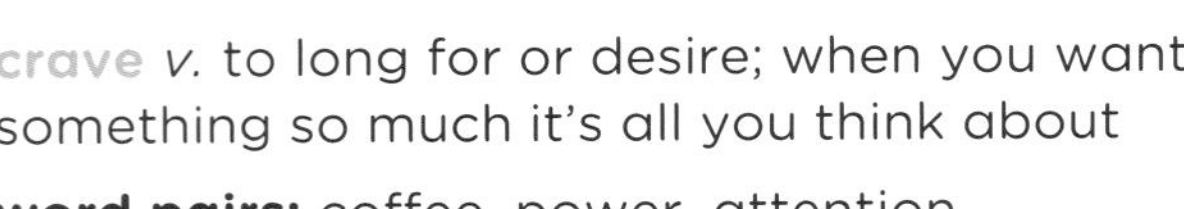
crave *v.* to long for or desire; when you want something so much it's all you think about

word pairs: coffee, power, attention

famished *adj.* very hungry or ravenous; how you feel when you're wild with hunger

word pairs: beast, lion, traveler

parched *adj.* dry or thirsty; how your throat feels if you run out of water in the desert

word pairs: throat, lips, desert

ravenous *adj.* hungry or starving; like you could eat an entire dinner in one bite

word pairs: dog, appetite, shark

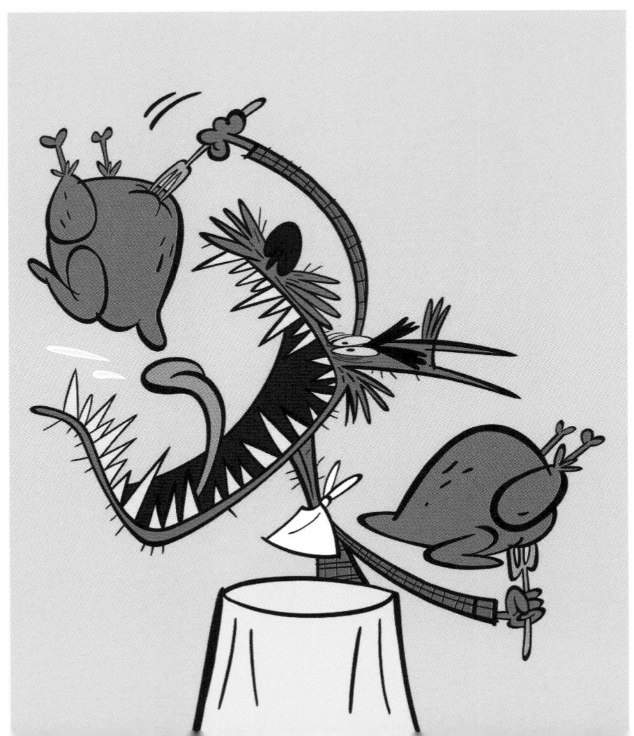

insatiable *adj.* greedy or impossible to satisfy; so hungry you never fill up

word pairs: appetite, greed, curiosity

voracious *adj.* greedy or very hungry; like having a never-ending hunger for hamburgers

word pairs: appetite, predator, reader

hungry or thirsty words

word pair after:

crave coffee
famished beast
insatiable appetite
parched throat
ravenous dog
voracious appetite

hearty *adj.* filling and wholesome; like a healthy bowl of stew on a winter's day

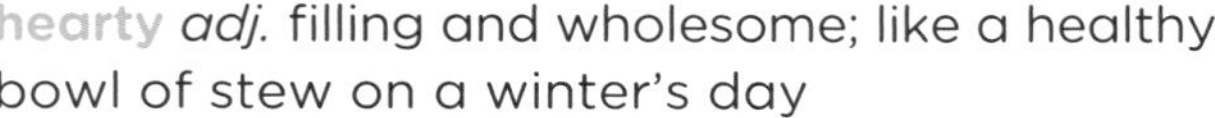

word pairs: stew, breakfast, welcome

humble *adj.* modest, plain, and simple; like a bowl of simple soup for dinner

word pairs: meal, offering, abode

meager *adj.* small, limited, or not enough; like a meal made up of a single bean

word pairs: portion, meal, wage

sumptuous *adj.* lavish and luxurious; like a banquet made up of the finest food and drink

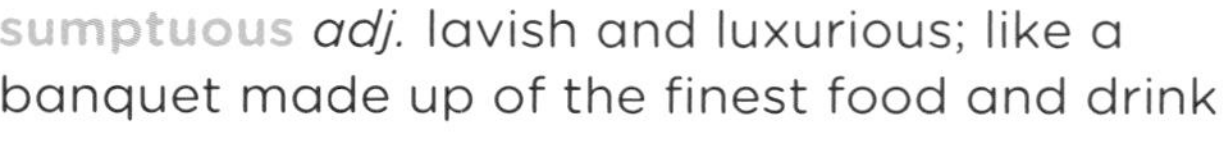

word pairs: dinner, breakfast, feast

lavish *adj.* sumptuous and luxurious; like a huge banquet for just one person

word pairs: banquet, gift, lifestyle

wholesome *adj.* healthy or good for you; like a bag of fresh fruit and vegetables

word pairs: meal, diet, fun

meal words

word pair after:

hearty stew
humble meal
lavish banquet
meager portion
sumptuous dinner
wholesome meal

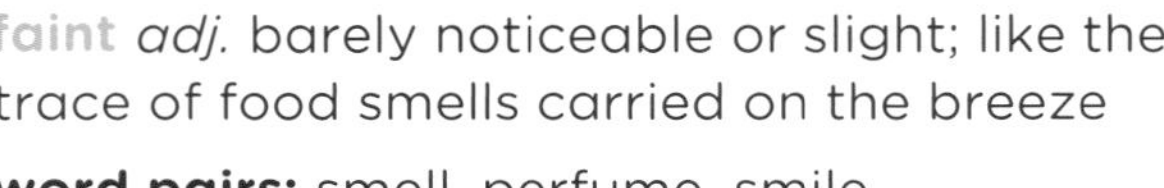

faint *adj.* barely noticeable or slight; like the trace of food smells carried on the breeze

word pairs: smell, perfume, smile

fragrance *n.* a sweet smell or perfume; like the odor of delicious herbs or exotic flowers

word pairs: floral, sweet, subtle

odor *n.* a smell or stink; like the fumes from someone's armpits

word pairs: unpleasant, strong, offensive

overpowering *adj.* overwhelming or unbearable; like a smell that knocks you over

word pairs: smell, force, urge

smell words

musty *adj.* stuffy and stale; like the smell of a stinky sweater that has never been washed

word pairs: clothes, smell, attic

pungent *adj.* very strong and smelly; like the stench of sweaty sneakers after a day of sports

word pairs: smell, sauce, feet

word pair before:

floral fragrance
unpleasant odor

word pair after:

faint perfume
musty clothes
overpowering smell
pungent feet

putrid *adj.* rotten and decayed; like an old, moldy sandwich

word pairs: food, smell, meat

stench *n.* an odor or stink; like the smell of someone who hasn't showered for days

word pairs: unbearable, foul, overpowering

reek *v.* to stink or smell; like the worst breath

word pairs: breath, sewer, swamp

toxic *adj.* poisonous or harmful; like dangerous radioactive waste

word pairs: waste, chemicals, gas

scent *n.* a smell or aroma; like the particular smell that someone leaves behind

word pairs: strong, lingering, unmistakable

whiff *n.* a sniff or trace; like the smell of your favorite pie wafting through the air

word pairs: delicious, faint, distinct

smell words

word pair before:

his breath reeked
strong scent
unbearable stench
delicious whiff

word pair after:

putrid food
toxic waste

WORD-O's

167 decadent taste & smell nouns

Hungry for more? Devour these red-hot nouns and their sizzling word pairs.

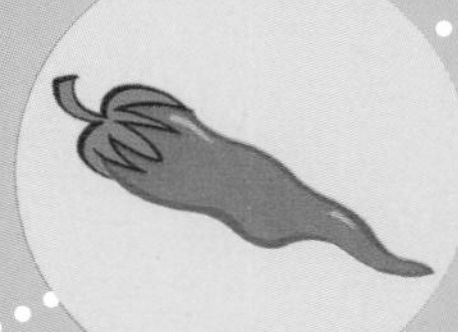

BAKING

handheld • buzzing • electric
n.
blender
gooey • dense • decadent
n.
brownie
moist • frosted • scrumptious
n.
cake
towering • tiered • toppling
n.
cake stand
melted • rich • bittersweet
n.
chocolate
warm • freshly baked • fortune
n.
cookie
whipped • clotted • curdled
n.
cream
frosted • gluten-free • decorated
n.
cupcakes
glazed • deep-fried • stale
n.
doughnut
piped • whipped • slathered
n.
frosting
spiced • decorated • fragrant
n.
gingerbread
rich • melted • homemade
n.
ice cream
sugary • crushed • tempting
n.
macaron
blueberry • half-eaten • mini
n.
muffin
floured • heavy • wooden
n.
rolling pin
broken • accurate • precise
n.
scale

BAKING

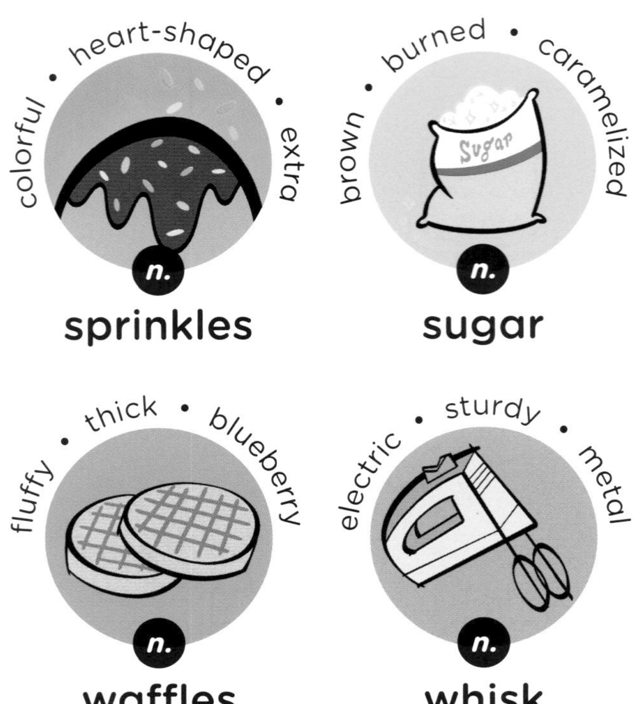

sprinkles (n.) — colorful • heart-shaped • extra

sugar (n.) — brown • burned • caramelized

waffles (n.) — fluffy • thick • blueberry

whisk (n.) — electric • sturdy • metal

sweet tooth (n.) — huge • raging • incurable

a taste for sugary food;
like a person who is always ready for dessert

BREAKFAST

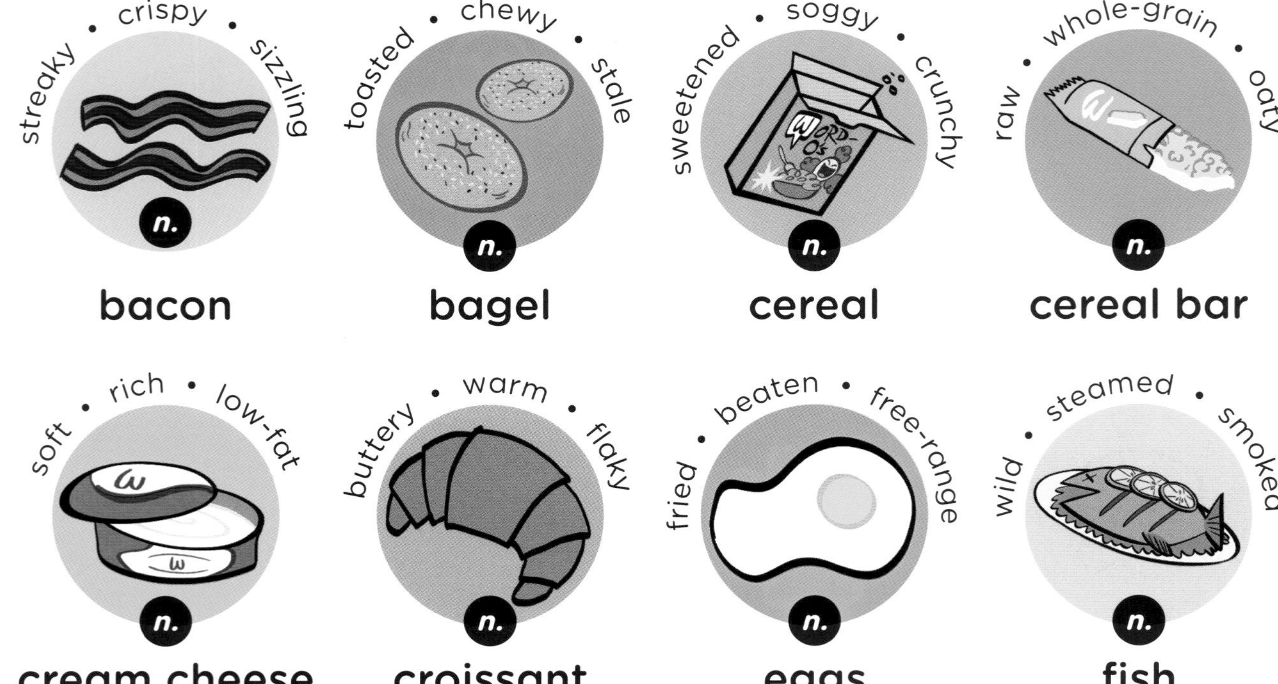

bacon (n.) — streaky • crispy • sizzling

bagel (n.) — toasted • chewy • stale

cereal (n.) — sweetened • soggy • crunchy

cereal bar (n.) — raw • whole-grain • oaty

cream cheese (n.) — soft • rich • low-fat

croissant (n.) — buttery • warm • flaky

eggs (n.) — fried • beaten • free-range

fish (n.) — wild • steamed • smoked

BREAKFAST

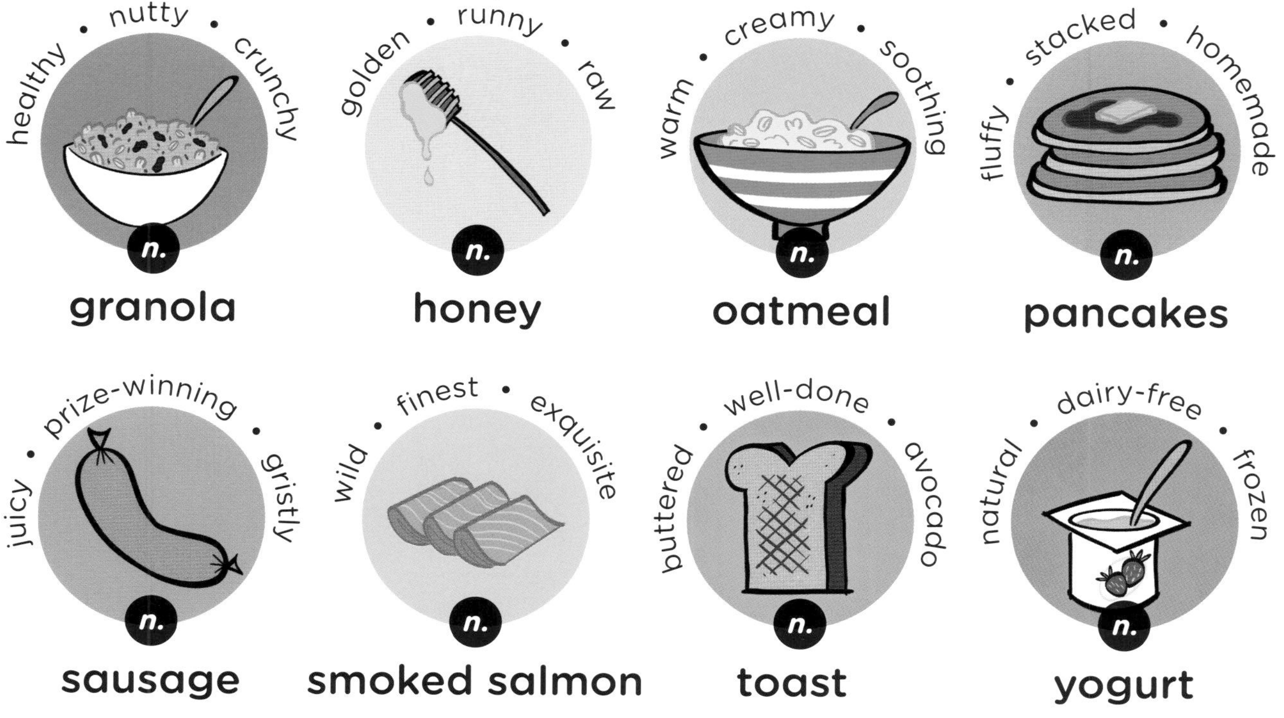
healthy • nutty • crunchy
n.
granola
golden • runny • raw
n.
honey
warm • creamy • soothing
n.
oatmeal
fluffy • stacked • homemade
n.
pancakes
juicy • prize-winning • gristly
n.
sausage
wild • finest • exquisite
n.
smoked salmon
buttered • well-done • avocado
n.
toast
natural • dairy-free • frozen
n.
yogurt

COOKING

wooden • disposable • slippery
n.
chopsticks
wooden • floured • porous
n.
cutting board
imported • fancy • spewing
n.
espresso machine
huge • two-pronged • loaded
n.
fork
sizzling • hot • electric
n.
grill
blunt • steak • serrated
n.
knife
dirty • high-powered • humming
n.
microwave
empty • blazing • wood-fired
n.
oven

COOKING

non-stick • cast-iron • roasting
n.
pan
dull • sharp • industrial
n.
peeler
fine • dirty • heavy
n.
silverware
red-hot • bamboo • rotating
n.
skewer
rubber • plastic • missing
n.
spatula
heaped • serving • edible
n.
spoon
pop-up • faulty • electric
n.
toaster
heavy • dented • flaming
n.
wok

DRINKS

iced • frothy • skinny
n.
cappuccino
strong • steaming • undrinkable
n.
coffee
fruity • powerful • sugar-loaded
n.
energy drink
rich • steaming • decadent
n.
hot chocolate
sweet • refreshing • legendary
n.
iced tea
fruit • freshly squeezed • spilled
n.
juice
mint • spiced • chilled
n.
lassi
ice-cold • homemade • tart
n.
lemonade

DRINKS

spilled • lukewarm • scalding
MILK
n.
milk
thick • frothy • spoon-bending
n.
milkshake
fruity • fancy • tasty
n.
mocktail
frozen • thick • sugary
n.
slushy
healthy • tropical • disgusting
n.
smoothie
sugary • addictive • delicious
n.
soda
herbal • loose-leaf • weak
n.
tea
ice-cold • sparkling • boiling
n.
water

FRUITS AND VEGETABLES

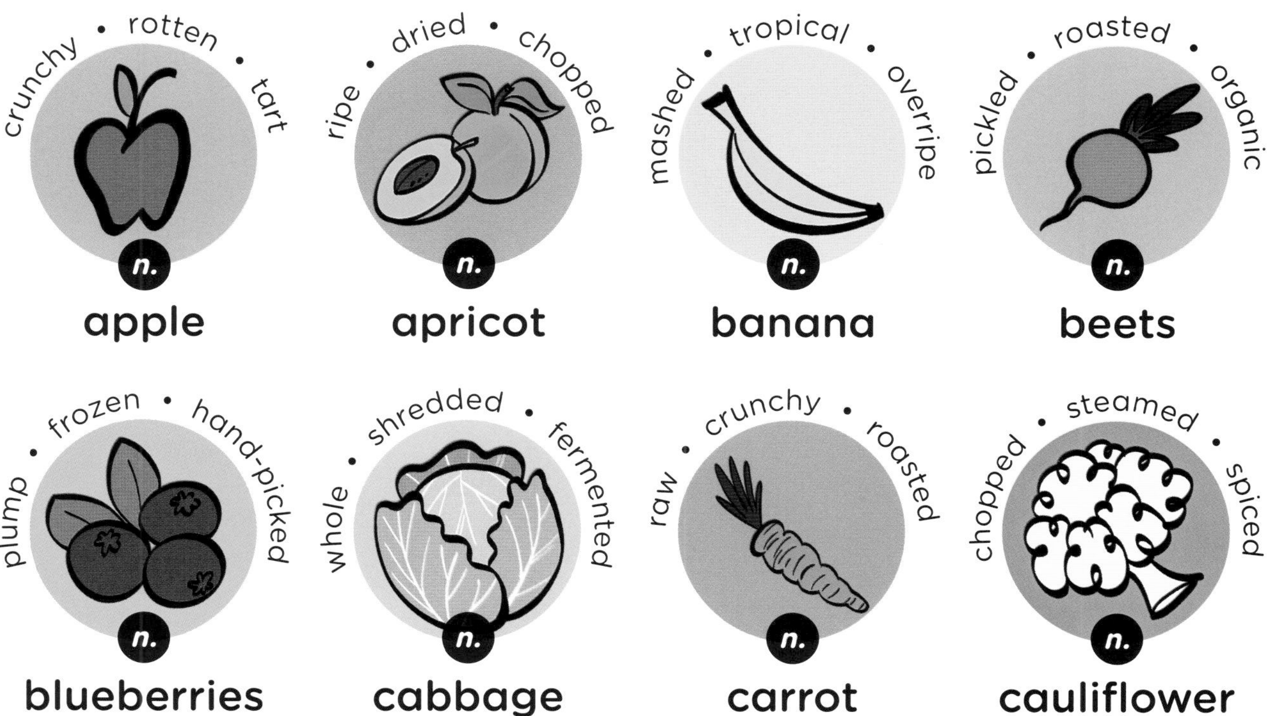
crunchy • rotten • tart
n.
apple
ripe • dried • chopped
n.
apricot
mashed • tropical • overripe
n.
banana
pickled • roasted • organic
n.
beets
plump • frozen • hand-picked
n.
blueberries
whole • shredded • fermented
n.
cabbage
raw • crunchy • roasted
n.
carrot
chopped • steamed • spiced
n.
cauliflower

FRUITS AND VEGETABLES

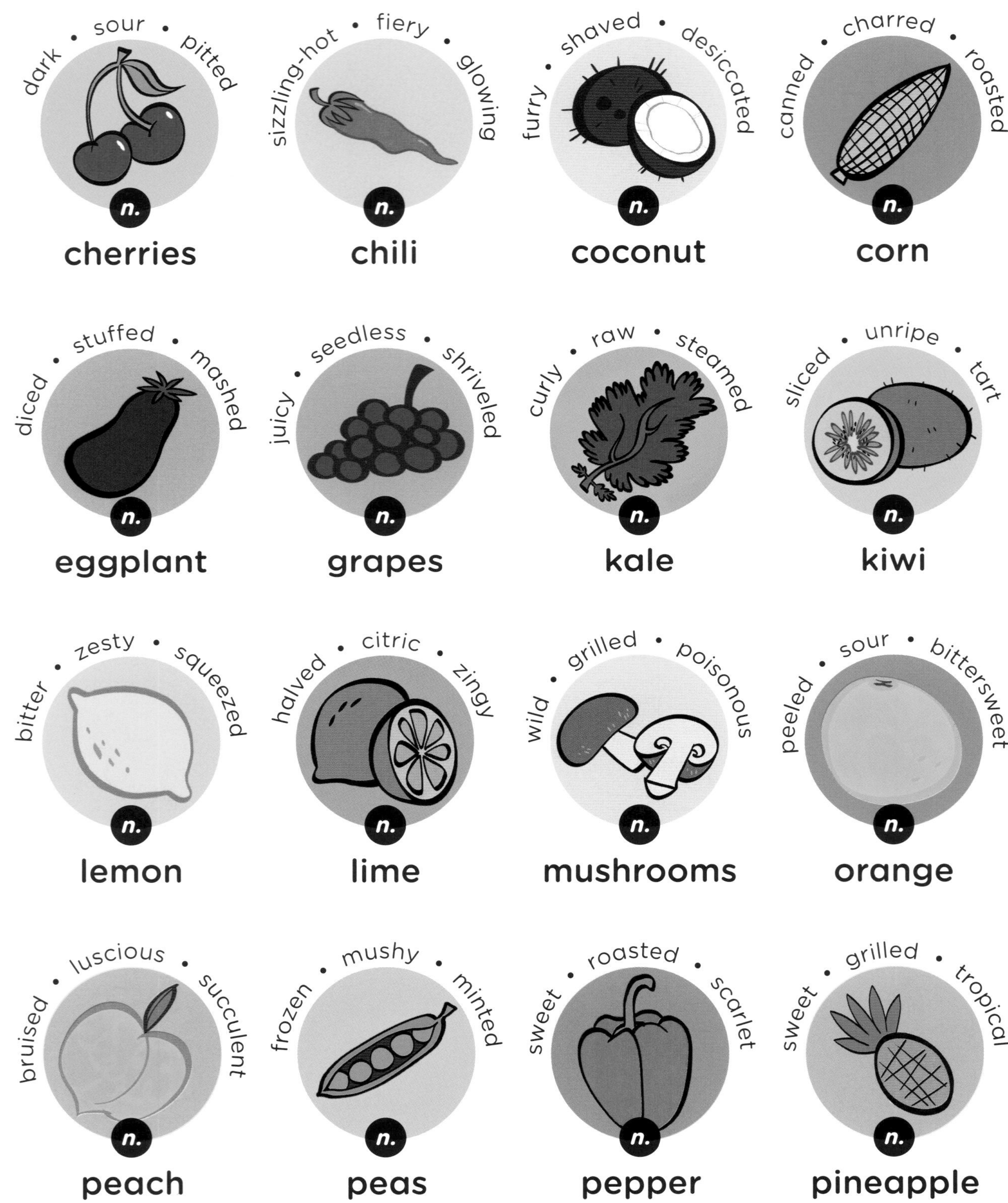
dark • sour • pitted
n.
cherries
sizzling-hot • fiery • glowing
n.
chili
furry • shaved • desiccated
n.
coconut
canned • charred • roasted
n.
corn
diced • stuffed • mashed
n.
eggplant
juicy • seedless • shriveled
n.
grapes
curly • raw • steamed
n.
kale
sliced • unripe • tart
n.
kiwi
bitter • zesty • squeezed
n.
lemon
halved • citric • zingy
n.
lime
wild • grilled • poisonous
n.
mushrooms
peeled • sour • bittersweet
n.
orange
bruised • luscious • succulent
n.
peach
frozen • mushy • minted
n.
peas
sweet • roasted • scarlet
n.
pepper
sweet • grilled • tropical
n.
pineapple

FRUITS AND VEGETABLES

fat • stewed • delicious
n.

plum

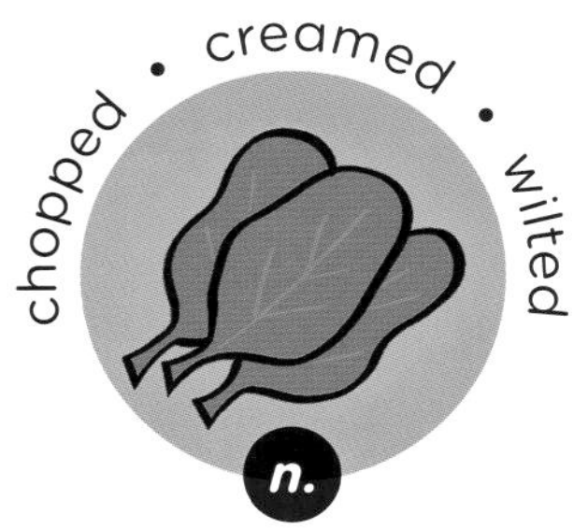
chopped • creamed • wilted
n.

spinach

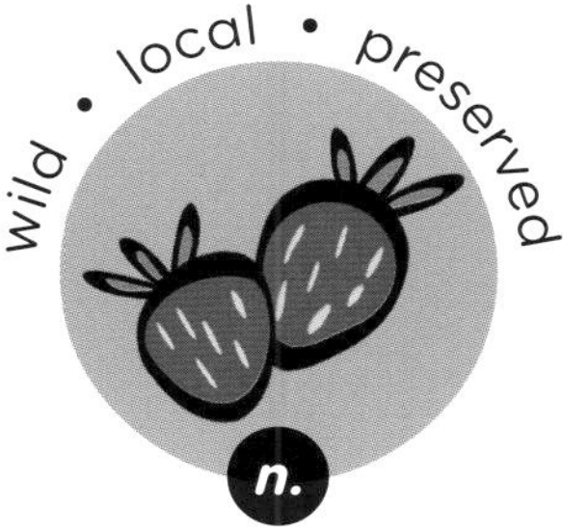
wild • local • preserved
n.

strawberries

watermelon

ice-cold • seedless • exploding

n.

healthy • strict • ethical
n.

vegan

a person who doesn't eat anything from animals; someone who never eats meat, cheese, or eggs

INGREDIENTS

melted • burned • salted
n.

butter

grated • pungent • nutty
n.

cheese

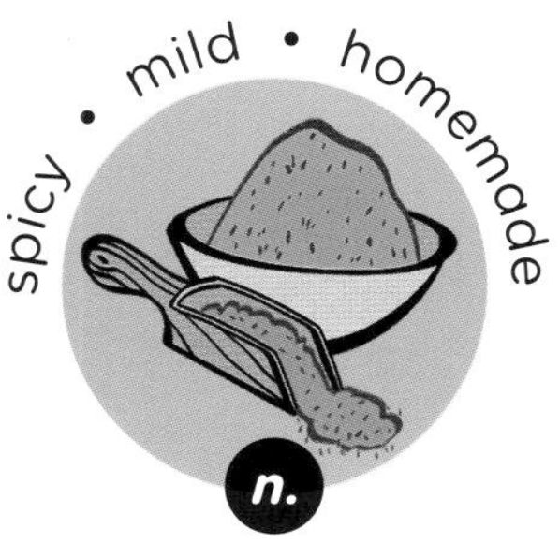
spicy • mild • homemade
n.

curry powder

sifted • heaped • gluten-free
n.

flour

crushed • raw • roasted
n.

garlic

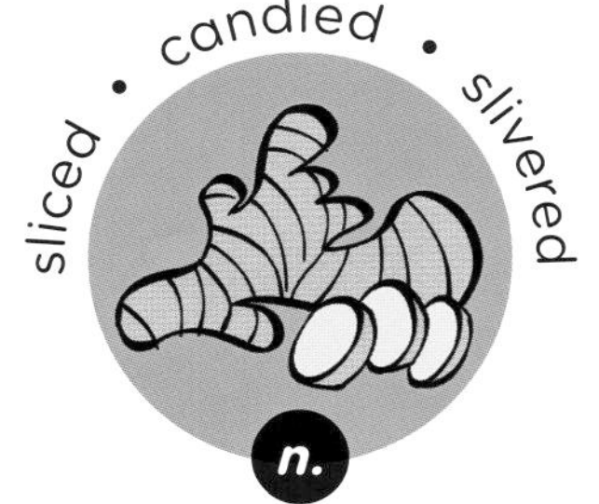
sliced • candied • slivered
n.

ginger

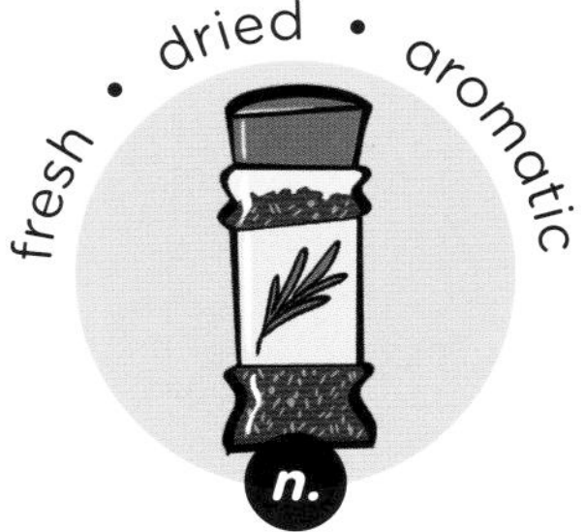
fresh • dried • aromatic
n.

herbs

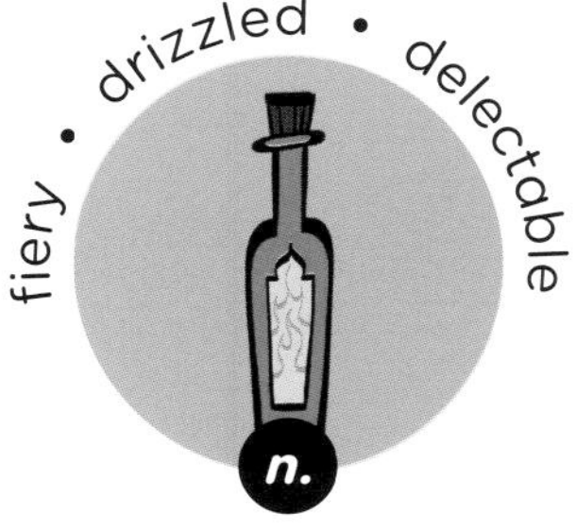
fiery • drizzled • delectable
n.

hot sauce

INGREDIENTS

hot • healthy • organic
n.
olive oil
raw • caramelized • fried
n.
onion
black • cracked • whole
n.
peppercorns
pure • delicate • expensive
n.
saffron
table • excess • sea
n.
salt
dark • aged • low-sodium
n.
soy sauce
vegetable • chicken • salty
n.
stock
strong • balsamic • sufficient
n.
vinegar

MEAT AND FISH

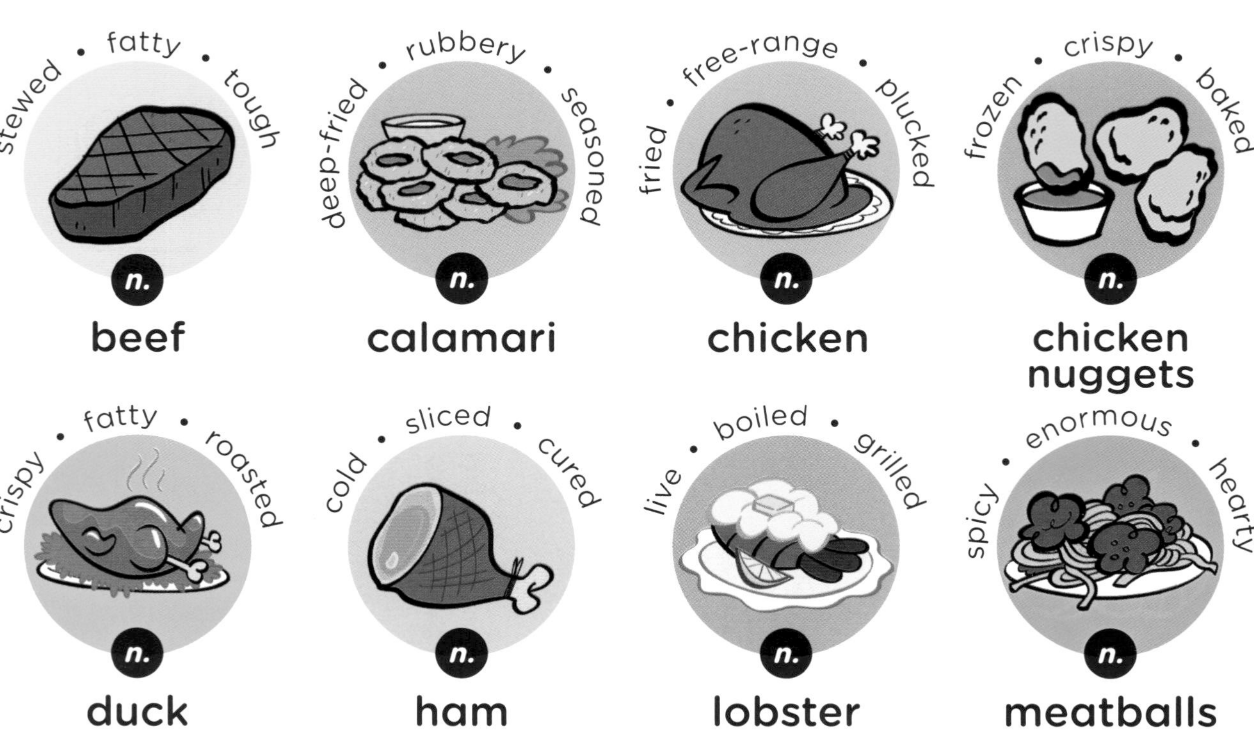
stewed • fatty • tough
n.
beef
deep-fried • rubbery • seasoned
n.
calamari
fried • free-range • plucked
n.
chicken
frozen • crispy • baked
n.
chicken nuggets
crispy • fatty • roasted
n.
duck
cold • sliced • cured
n.
ham
live • boiled • grilled
n.
lobster
spicy • enormous • hearty
n.
meatballs

MEAT AND FISH

plump • local • exquisite
n.
oysters
jumbo • frozen • imported
n.
prawns
wild • farmed • poached
n.
salmon
plump • seared • marinated
n.
scallops
rare • sizzling • marbled
n.
steak
raw • expensive • exotic
n.
sushi
canned • seared • sustainable
n.
tuna
stuffed • oversized • leftover
n.
turkey

RESTAURANTS > EATING OUT

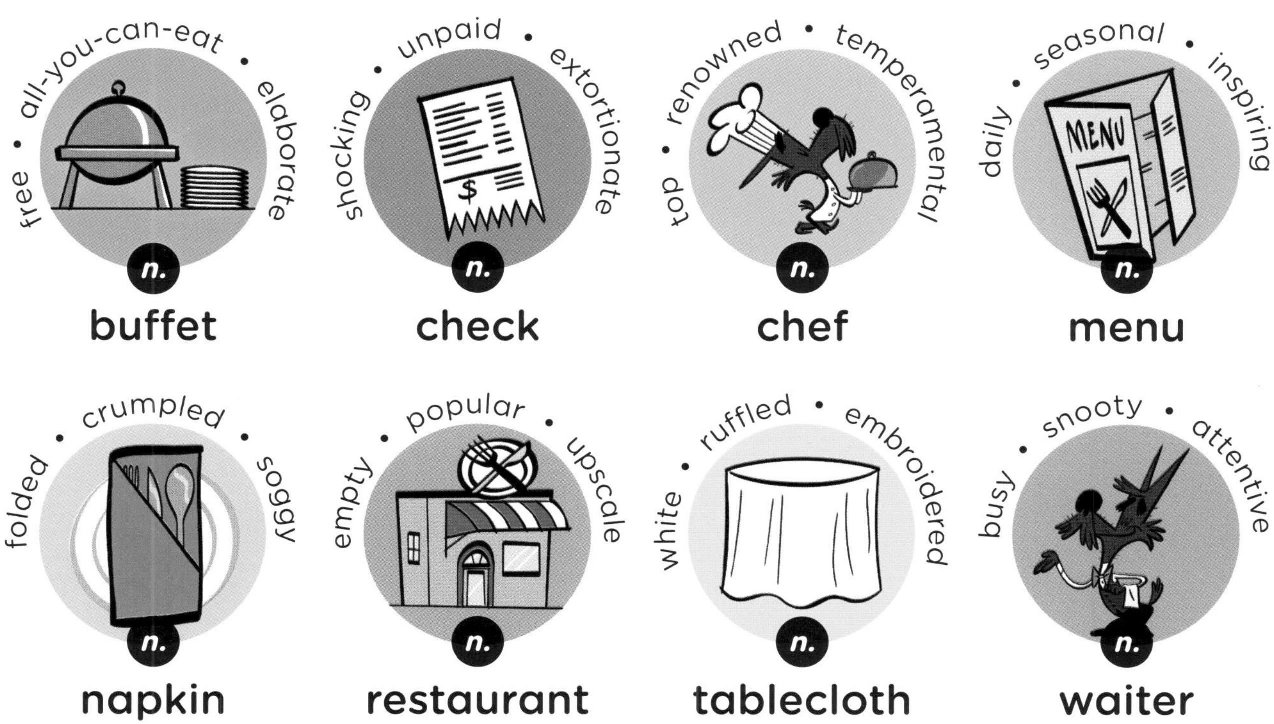
free • all-you-can-eat • elaborate
n.
buffet
shocking • unpaid • extortionate
$
n.
check
top • renowned • temperamental
n.
chef
daily • seasonal • inspiring
MENU
n.
menu
folded • crumpled • soggy
n.
napkin
empty • popular • upscale
n.
restaurant
white • ruffled • embroidered
n.
tablecloth
busy • snooty • attentive
n.
waiter

RESTAURANTS > FAST FOOD

steamed • deep-fried • glutinous
n.
dumplings
salty • greasy • soggy
n.
fries
juicy • towering • succulent
n.
hamburger
grilled • half-eaten • foot-long
n.
hotdog
spicy • authentic • magnificent
n.
kebab
fried • instant • spicy
n.
noodles
frozen • wood-fired • leftover
n.
pizza
soft • spicy • crunchy
n.
taco

STAPLES

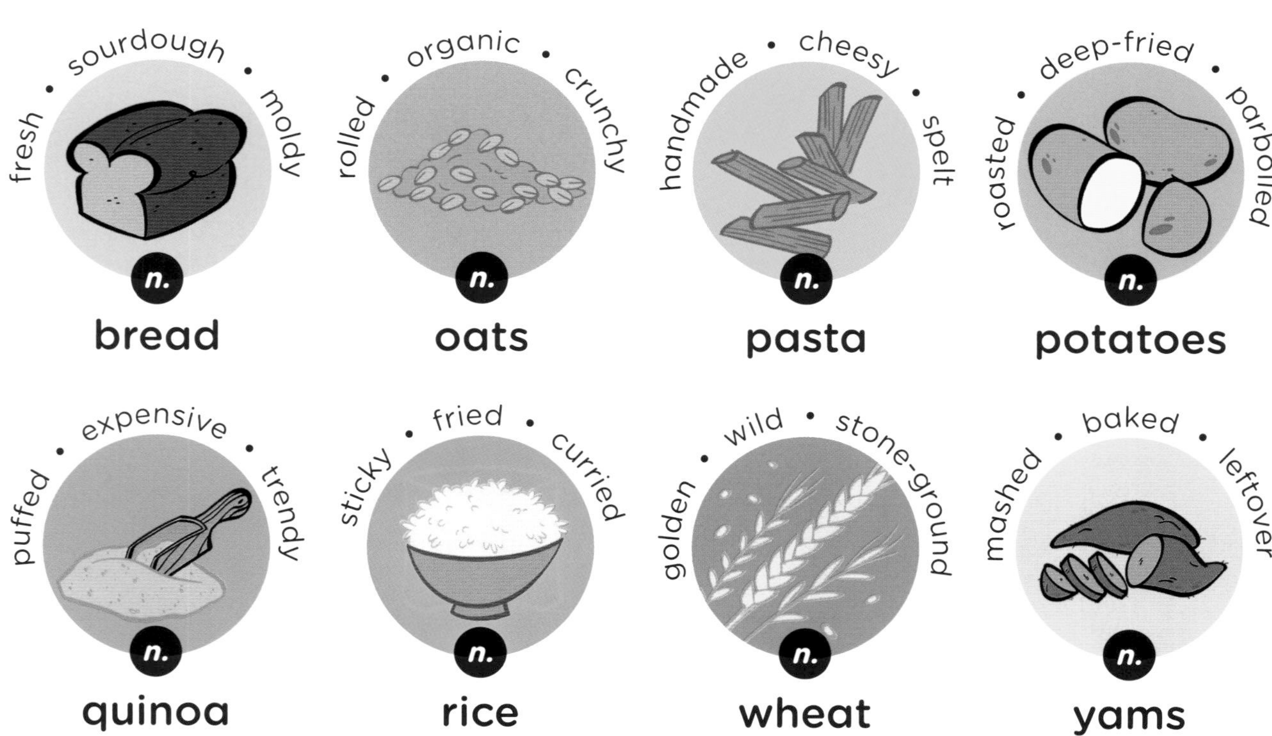
fresh • sourdough • moldy
n.
bread
rolled • organic • crunchy
n.
oats
handmade • cheesy • spelt
n.
pasta
roasted • deep-fried • parboiled
n.
potatoes
puffed • expensive • trendy
n.
quinoa
sticky • fried • curried
n.
rice
golden • wild • stone-ground
n.
wheat
mashed • baked • leftover
n.
yams

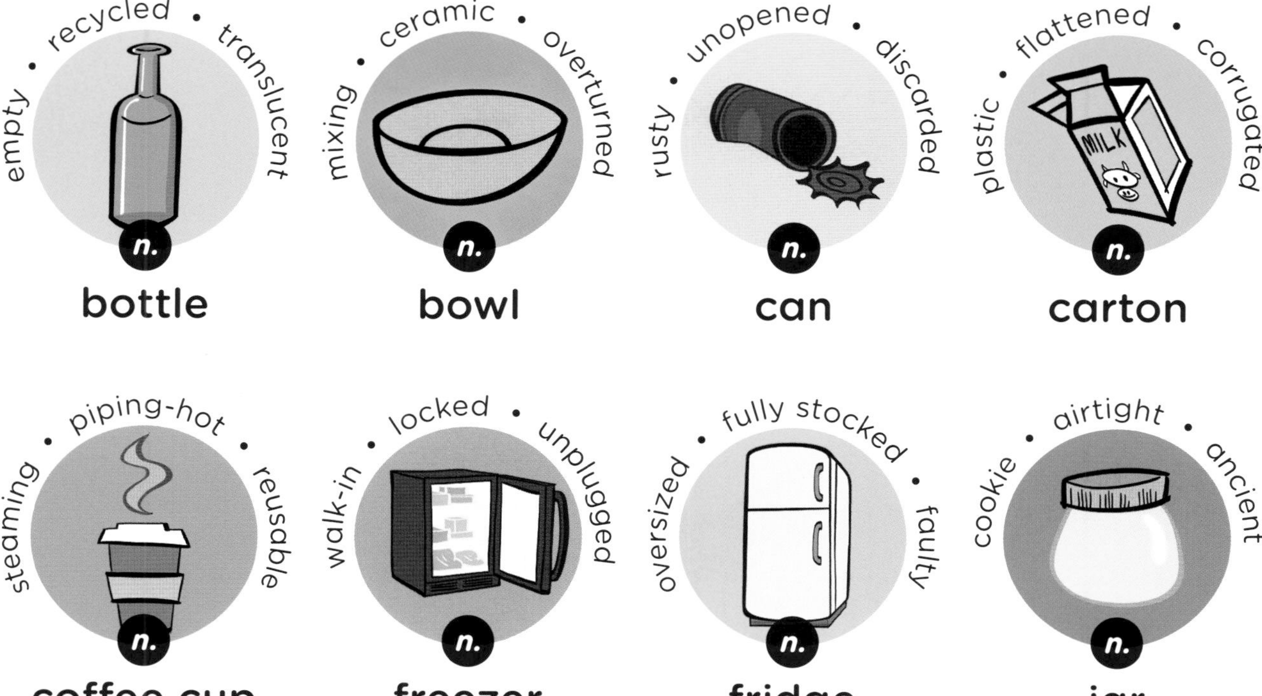

empty • recycled • translucent
n.
bottle
mixing • ceramic • overturned
n.
bowl
rusty • unopened • discarded
n.
can
plastic • flattened • corrugated
MILK
n.
carton
steaming • piping-hot • reusable
n.
coffee cup
walk-in • locked • unplugged
n.
freezer
oversized • fully stocked • faulty
n.
fridge
cookie • airtight • ancient
n.
jar

rotting • composting • avoidable
n.

food waste

scraps or uneaten leftovers;
like fishbones and apple cores
that are thrown away after a meal

dirty • chipped • steaming
n.
mug
cracked • paper • heaped
n.
plate
steaming • scalding • talking
n.
teapot
sealed • big-bellied • replenished
n.
thermos

flurry

Weather

billowing *adj.* swelling or expanding; like a cloud that has grown so big you can bounce on it

word pairs: clouds, sails, waves

dense *adj.* thick, solid, or heavy; like a cloud so thick you need a knife to cut through it

word pairs: clouds, forest, fog

overcast *adj.* cloudy or gray; how the sky looks when dark clouds block out all the sunshine

word pairs: weather, morning, conditions

swirling *adj.* spiraling or twirling; like clouds spinning around after a plane whizzes past

word pairs: mist, smoke, snowflakes

TALL TALES

hazy *adj.* cloudy or misty; like a fog that makes it hard to see clearly

word pairs: sky, sunshine, memories

wispy *adj.* thin or fine; like clouds that are feathery and light

word pairs: clouds, beard, voice

cloudy words

word pair after:

billowing clouds
dense fog
hazy sky
overcast morning
swirling mist
wispy clouds

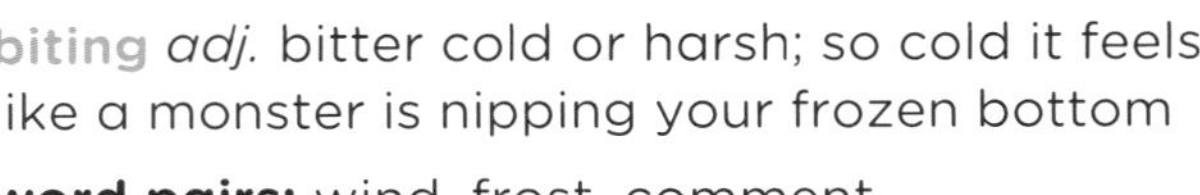

biting *adj.* bitter cold or harsh; so cold it feels like a monster is nipping your frozen bottom

word pairs: wind, frost, comment

brisk *adj.* sharp or crisp; like the cold air on your face when you go for a winter walk

word pairs: air, walk, trade

frosty *adj.* freezing or icy; the kind of cold that feels like you have a layer of ice over you

word pairs: air, breath, silence

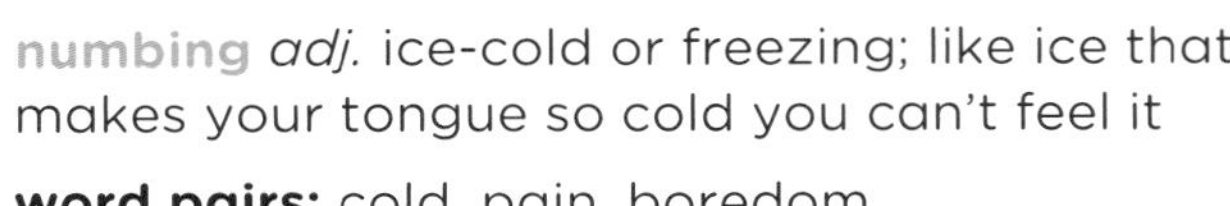

numbing *adj.* ice-cold or freezing; like ice that makes your tongue so cold you can't feel it

word pairs: cold, pain, boredom

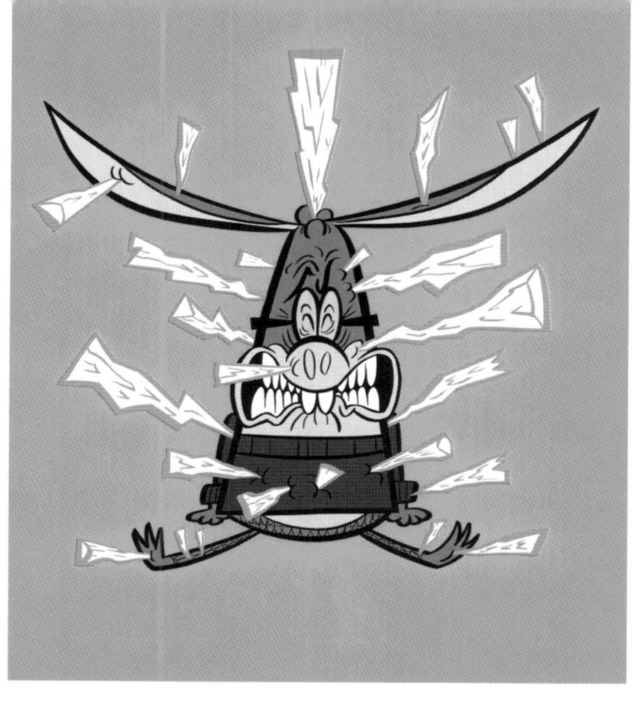

cold words

excruciating *adj.* extremely painful; how it would feel to be pricked all over by sharp icicles

word pairs: agony, detail, experience

penetrating *adj.* piercing or sharp; like freezing air that goes straight to your bones

word pairs: cold, gaze, odor

word pair after:

biting wind
brisk air
excruciating agony
frosty breath
numbing pain
penetrating cold

HOT!
FRESH!
I.O.U.
DOUGHNUTS!

bleak *adj.* gloomy or depressing; like a miserable day when your doughnuts are gone

word pairs: day, future, reality

dreary *adj.* boring or miserable; like a dull job doing the same thing over and over again

word pairs: work, winter, afternoon

SMILE
HANG IN THERE

downpour *n.* a heavy rainstorm; a big burst of rain that soaks you to the skin

word pairs: heavy, torrential, thundery

ominous *adj.* scary, threatening, or menacing; like a huge, dark tornado spinning toward you

word pairs: clouds, sign, shadow

drab *adj.* dull or gray; like a dark, gloomy day

word pairs: day, uniform, existence

splattered *adj.* splashed or sprinkled; like heavy raindrops that ruin your painting

word pairs: water, paint, mud

dark and rainy words

word pair before:

heavy downpour

word pair after:

bleak reality
drab day
dreary work
ominous clouds
splattered water

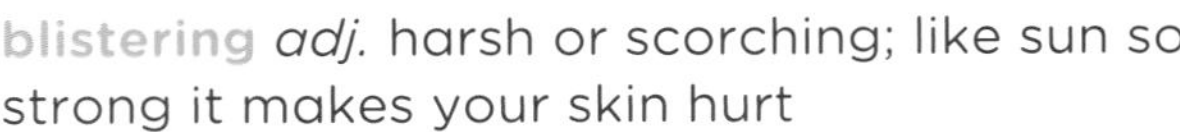

blistering *adj.* harsh or scorching; like sun so strong it makes your skin hurt

word pairs: sunburn, speed, critique

oppressive *adj.* heavy, harsh, or overpowering; like heat so strong you feel like it is crushing you

word pairs: heat, laws, silence

clammy *adj.* soggy or moist; like your skin when you are sweaty or feverish

word pairs: sweat, weather, handshake

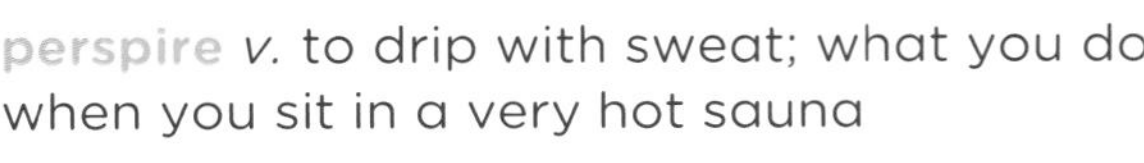

perspire *v.* to drip with sweat; what you do when you sit in a very hot sauna

word pairs: heavily, profusely, visibly

gleaming *adj.* shining or bright; like teeth that have been scrubbed clean by the dentist

word pairs: smile, light, sword

radiant *adj.* bright, brilliant, or glowing; like a very large and powerful light bulb

word pairs: glow, skin, beauty

hot words

word pair after:

blistering sunburn
clammy sweat
gleaming smile
oppressive heat
perspire heavily
radiant glow

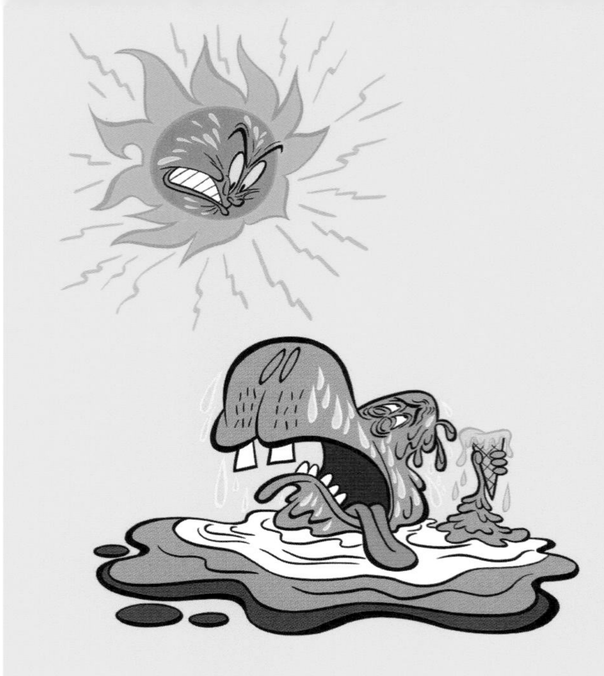

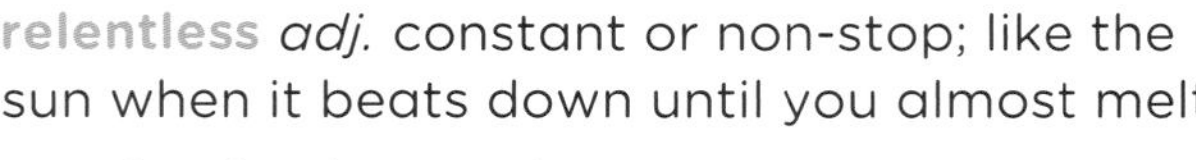

relentless *adj.* constant or non-stop; like the sun when it beats down until you almost melt

word pairs: heat, rain, pressure

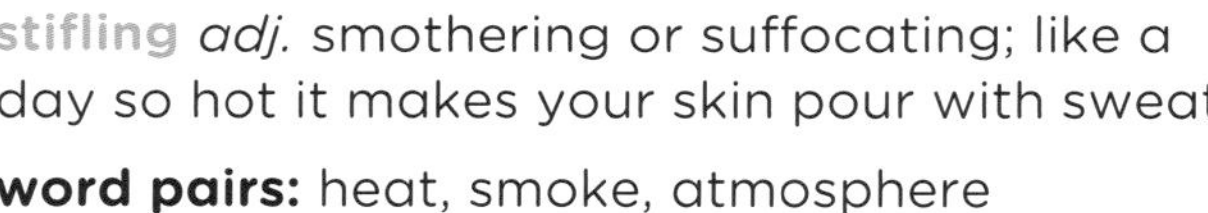

stifling *adj.* smothering or suffocating; like a day so hot it makes your skin pour with sweat

word pairs: heat, smoke, atmosphere

scorching *adj.* red-hot or blazing; the kind of heat that will roast a marshmallow

word pairs: rays, summer, desert

suffocating *adj.* stuffy or smothering; like clothes so tight around your neck you can't breathe

word pairs: feeling, heat, fumes

searing *adj.* burning or scorching; like a day so hot that you can cook food on the pavement

word pairs: heat, pain, honesty

sweltering *adj.* very hot or baking; like weather that makes you desperate for some shade

word pairs: heat, day, heatwave

hot words

word pair after:

relentless heat
scorching rays
searing pain
stifling atmosphere
suffocating feeling
sweltering heatwave

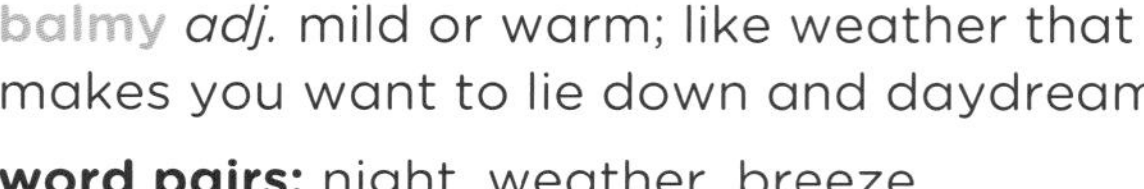

balmy *adj.* mild or warm; like weather that makes you want to lie down and daydream

word pairs: night, weather, breeze

dewy *adj.* moist or damp; like grass that is covered in droplets of water in the morning

word pairs: grass, cobweb, complexion

serene *adj.* peaceful or calm; like how you feel when you've done some relaxing yoga

word pairs: moment, beauty, weather

temperate *adj.* mild or pleasant; like a place where the weather is never too hot or too cold

word pairs: weather, climate, person

rustling *adj.* crackling or swishing; the sound of fall leaves being shaken from a tree

word pairs: leaves, papers, fabric

tranquil *adj.* peaceful or blissfully quiet; how you feel when you take a nap in the shade

word pairs: surroundings, garden, atmosphere

pleasant words

word pair after:

balmy night
dewy grass
rustling leaves
serene moment
temperate weather
tranquil surroundings

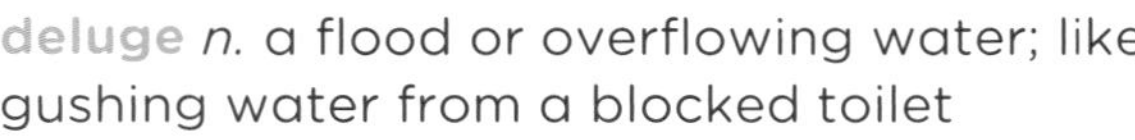

deluge *n.* a flood or overflowing water; like gushing water from a blocked toilet

word pairs: sudden, torrential, catastrophic

lashing *adj.* thrashing or beating; like heavy rain smacking you in the face

word pairs: rain, wind, tail

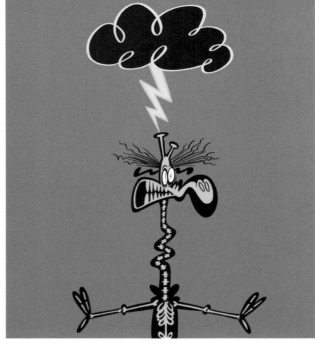

electrifying *adj.* thrilling or stunning; like an exciting storm full of lightning and thunder

word pairs: storm, story, performance

tempestuous *adj.* stormy, wild, or violent; when the wind and the sea are out of control

word pairs: weather, sea, relationship

incessant *adj.* endless or non-stop; like a loud phone conversation that goes on and on

word pairs: chatter, downpour, repetition

torrential *adj.* falling heavily or forcefully; like the rain in a violent storm

word pairs: rain, downpour, thunderstorm

stormy words

word pair before:

sudden **deluge**

word pair after:

electrifying storm
incessant chatter
lashing rain
tempestuous weather
torrential downpour

blustery *adj.* windy or gusty; like gusts of wind that turn your umbrella inside out

word pairs: conditions, wind, afternoon

flurry *n.* a short, swirling gust; like a burst of whirling snow that flies around your head

word pairs: brief, initial, constant

howl *v.* to cry or wail; like wind so strong that it makes a sound

word pairs: loudly, fiercely, miserably

whirlwind *n.* like a hurricane or tornado; like wind that spins and sweeps everything up

word pairs: violent, sudden, destructive

gust *n.* a blast of air or strong breeze; like a puff of wind so strong it blows things away

word pairs sudden, strong, violent

windswept *adj.* windblown and untidy; how you look when you are blown around by the wind

word pairs beach, hair, island

windy words

word pair before:

brief flurry
sudden gust
violent whirlwind

word pair after:

blustery conditions
howl loudly
windswept beach

97 whistling weather nouns

Deafening thunder or perfect blue skies? Discover the nouns and word pairs that will transform your story from a gentle breeze into an unstoppable whirlwind.

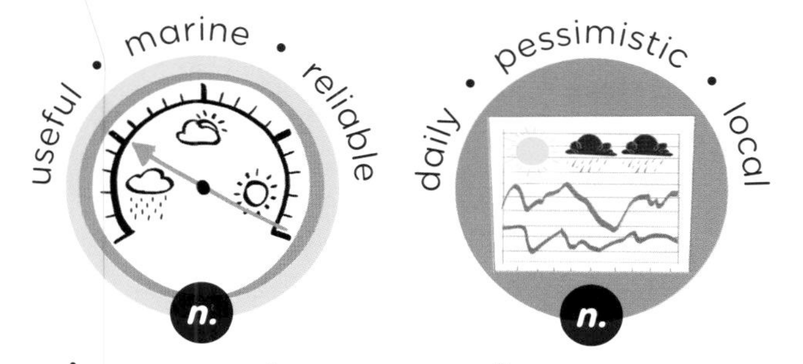

useful • marine • reliable

n.

barometer

daily • pessimistic • local

n.

forecast

extreme • man-made • accelerated

n.

global warming

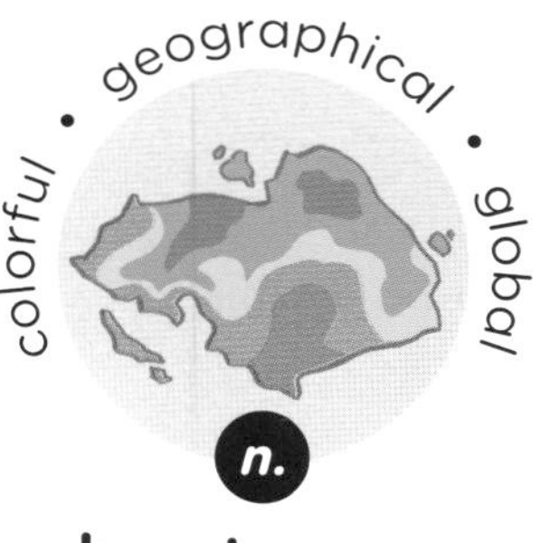

colorful • geographical • global

n.

heat map

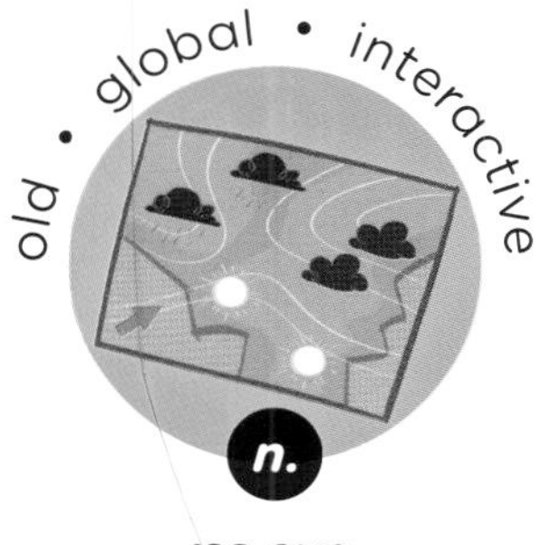

old • global • interactive

n.

map

respected • renowned • incompetent

n.

meteorologist

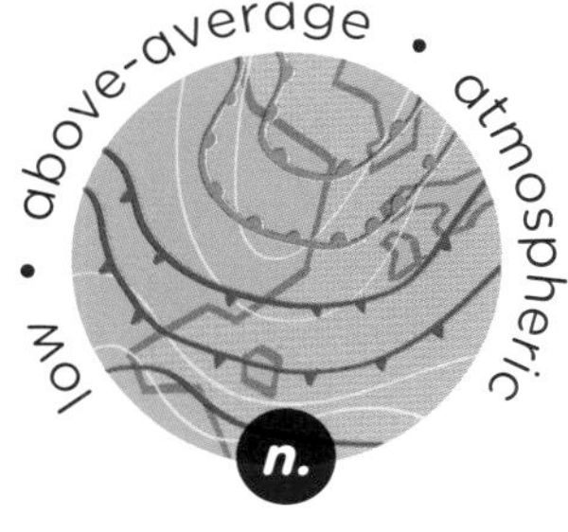

low • above-average • atmospheric

n.

pressure

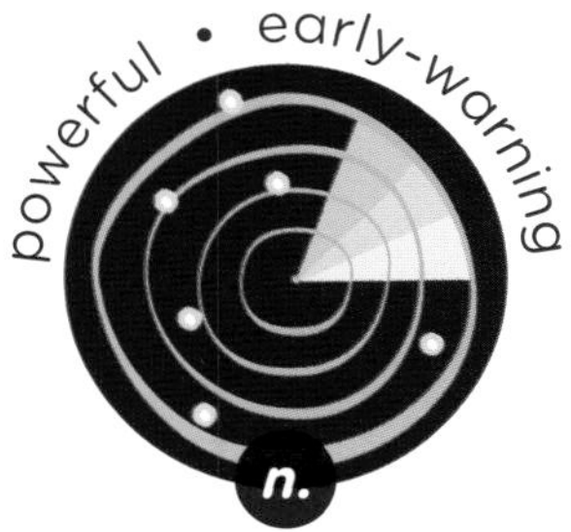

powerful • early-warning

n.

radar

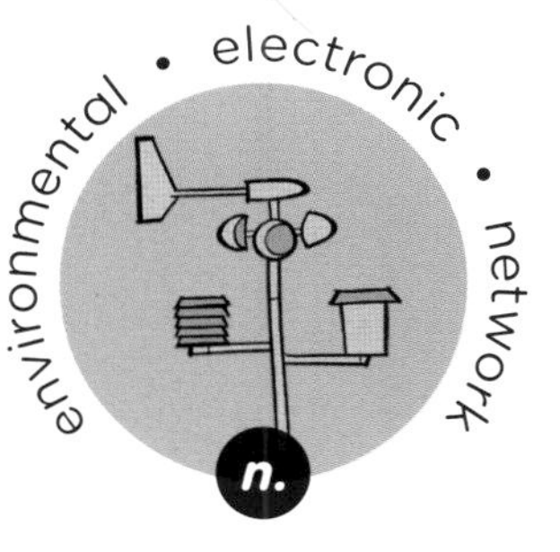

environmental • electronic • network

n.

sensor

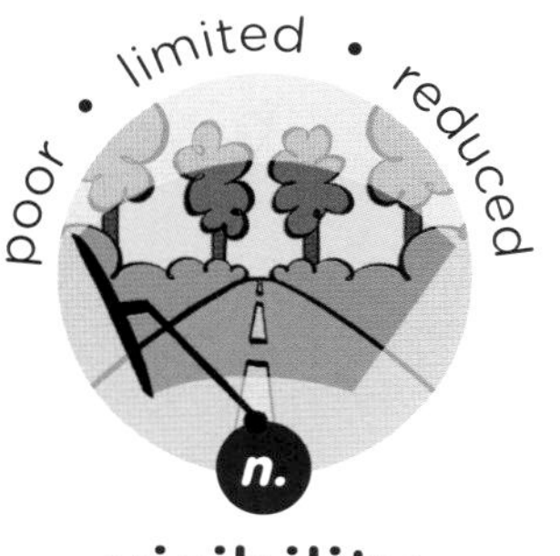

poor • limited • reduced

n.

visibility

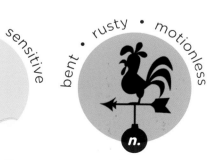

floating • lost • sensitive

n.

weather balloon

bent • rusty • motionless

n.

weathervane

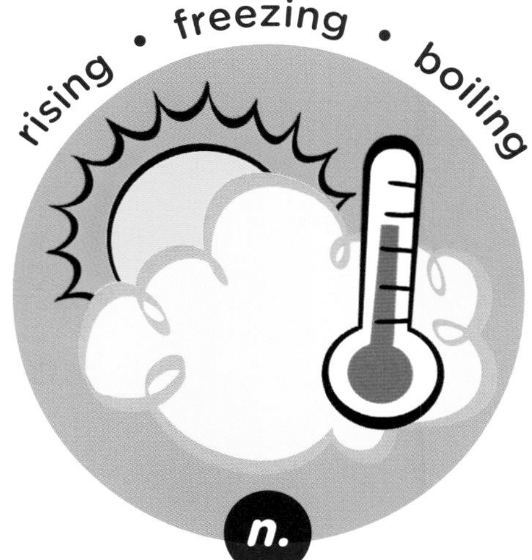

rising • freezing • boiling

n.

temperature

how hot or cold something is;
like the difference in how the air feels between winter and summer

SEASONS > FALL

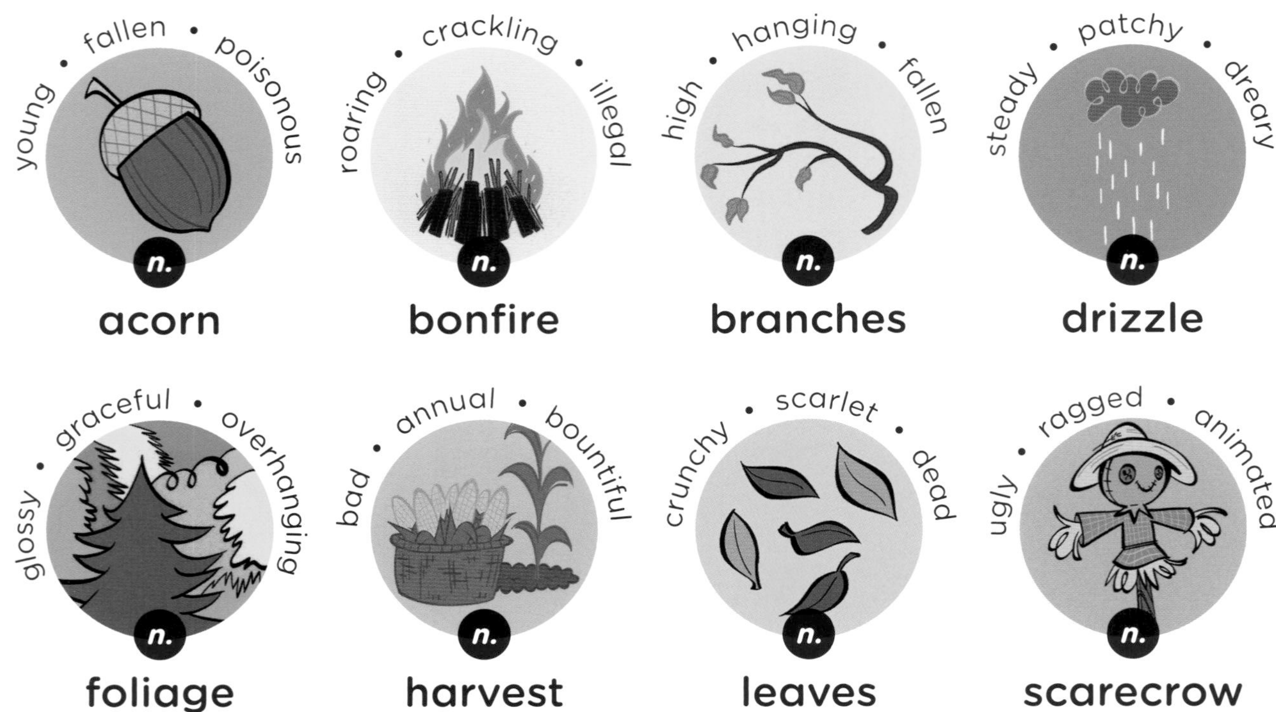
young • fallen • poisonous
n.
acorn
roaring • crackling • illegal
n.
bonfire
high • hanging • fallen
n.
branches
steady • patchy • dreary
n.
drizzle
glossy • graceful • overhanging
n.
foliage
bad • annual • bountiful
n.
harvest
crunchy • scarlet • dead
n.
leaves
ugly • ragged • animated
n.
scarecrow

SEASONS > SPRING

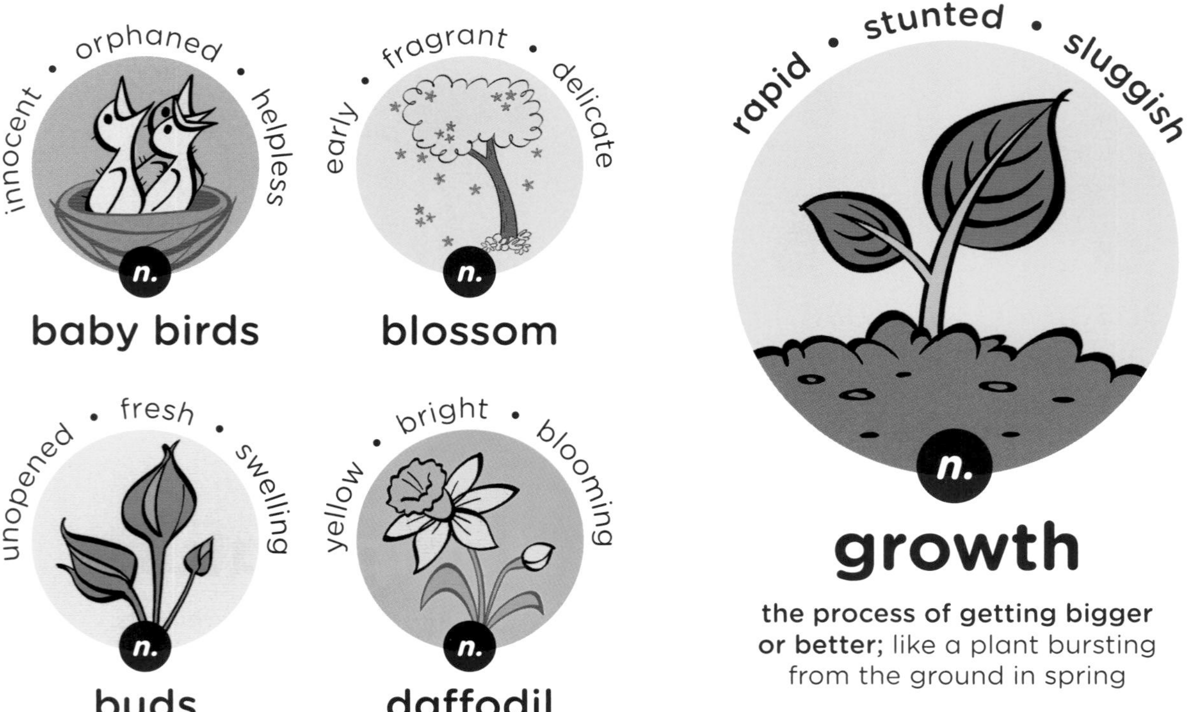
innocent • orphaned • helpless
n.
baby birds
early • fragrant • delicate
n.
blossom
unopened • fresh • swelling
n.
buds
yellow • bright • blooming
n.
daffodil
rapid • stunted • sluggish
n.
growth

the process of getting bigger or better; like a plant bursting from the ground in spring

Action | Character | Emotion | Setting | Taste & Smell | **Weather** nouns

SEASONS > SPRING

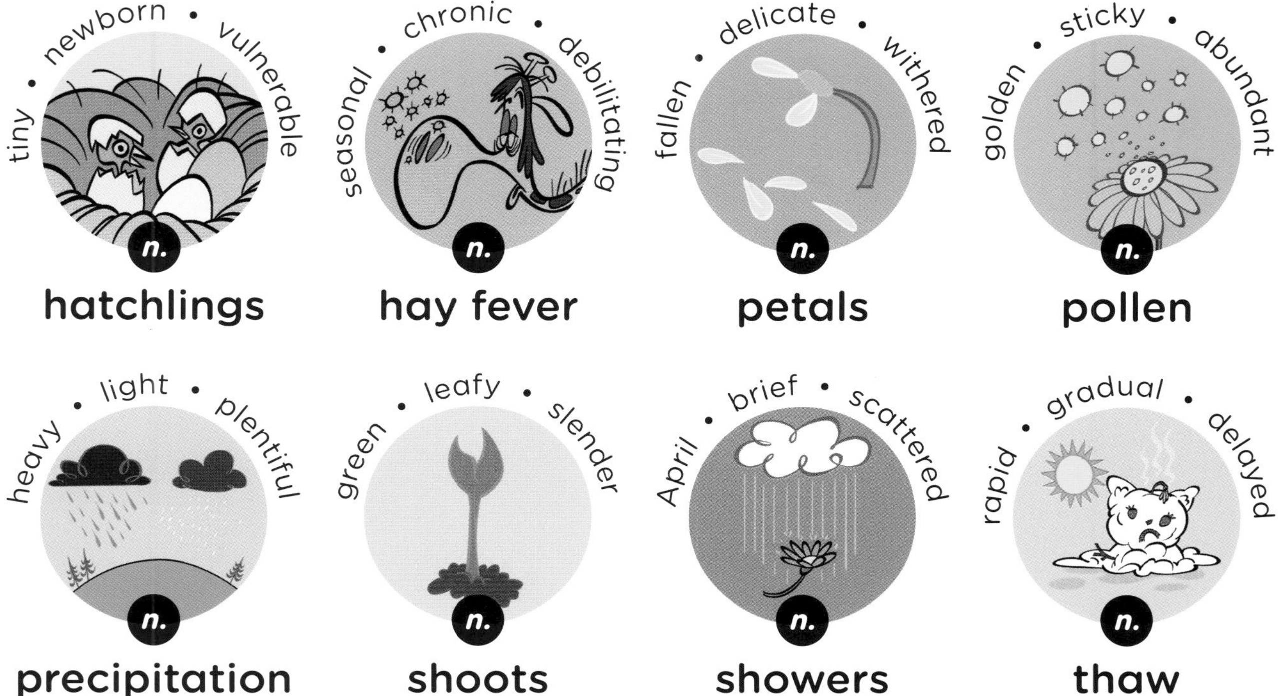
tiny • newborn • vulnerable
n.
hatchlings
seasonal • chronic • debilitating
n.
hay fever
fallen • delicate • withered
n.
petals
golden • sticky • abundant
n.
pollen
heavy • light • plentiful
n.
precipitation
green • leafy • slender
n.
shoots
April • brief • scattered
n.
showers
rapid • gradual • delayed
n.
thaw

SEASONS > SUMMER

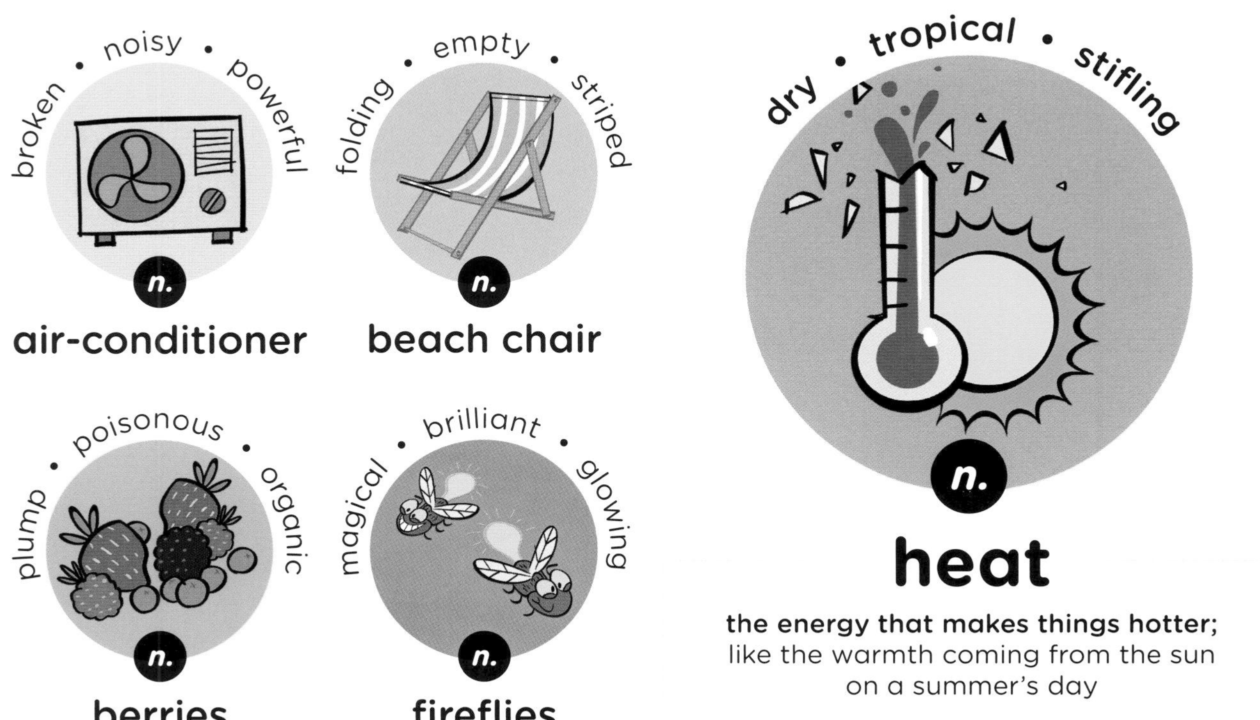
broken • noisy • powerful
n.
air-conditioner
folding • empty • striped
n.
beach chair
plump • poisonous • organic
n.
berries
magical • brilliant • glowing
n.
fireflies
dry • tropical • stifling
n.
heat

the energy that makes things hotter; like the warmth coming from the sun on a summer's day

SEASONS > SUMMER

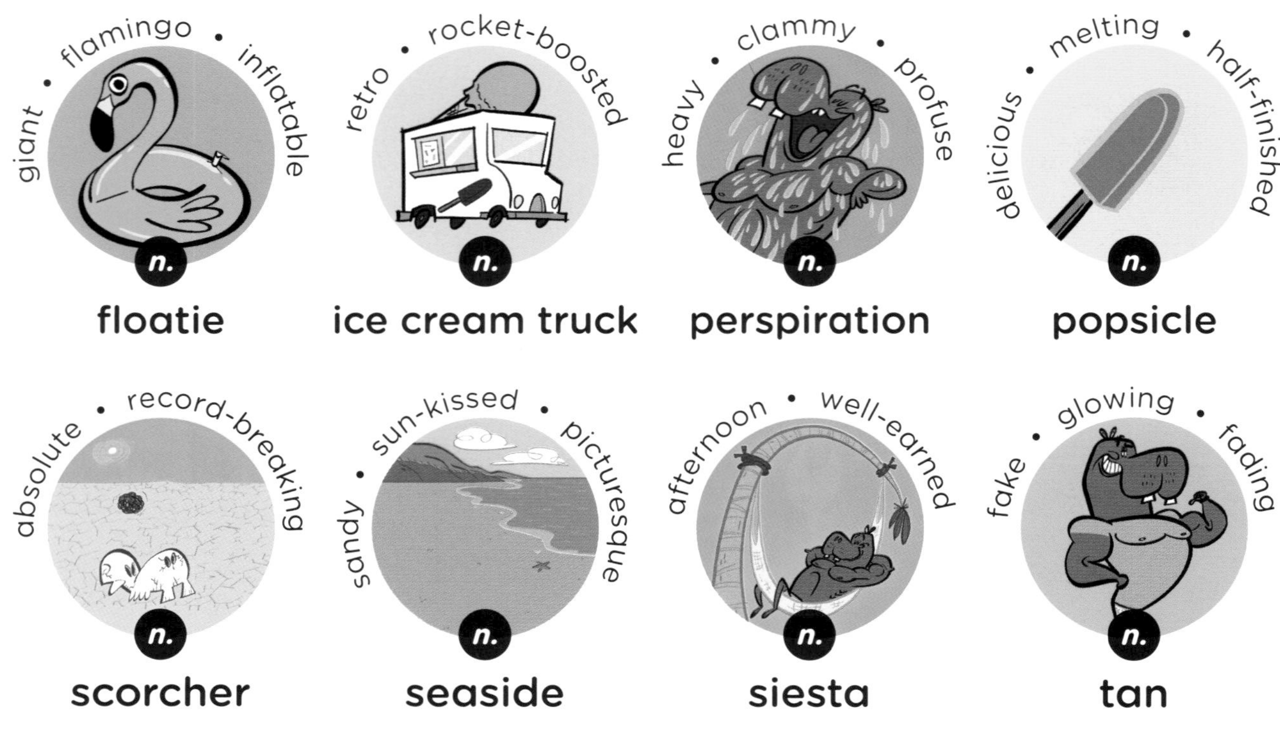
giant • flamingo • inflatable
n.
floatie
retro • rocket-boosted
n.
ice cream truck
heavy • clammy • profuse
n.
perspiration
delicious • melting • half-finished
n.
popsicle
absolute • record-breaking
n.
scorcher
sandy • sun-kissed • picturesque
n.
seaside
afternoon • well-earned
n.
siesta
fake • glowing • fading
n.
tan

SEASONS > WINTER

bitter • widespread • sudden
n.
frost
painful • mild • severe
n.
frostbite
heavy • intense • damaging
n.
hail
slippery • cracked • thawing
n.
ice
glittering • jagged • hazardous
n.
icicles
muddy • ankle-deep • wintry
n.
slush
heavy • fresh • powdery
n.
snow
fluffy • whirling • feathery
n.
snowflakes

WEATHER CONDITIONS > CLOUDY

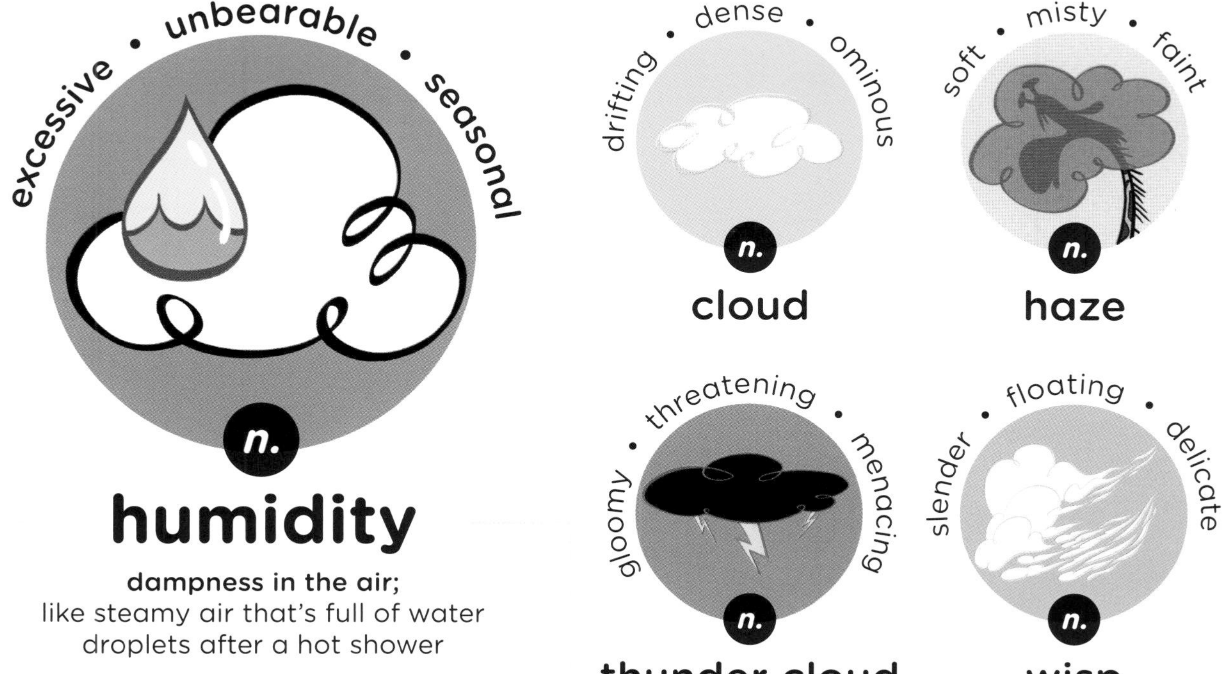
excessive • unbearable • seasonal
n.
humidity
dampness in the air;
like steamy air that's full of water droplets after a hot shower
drifting • dense • ominous
n.
cloud
soft • misty • faint
n.
haze
gloomy • threatening • menacing
n.
thunder cloud
slender • floating • delicate
n.
wisp

WEATHER CONDITIONS > EXTREME

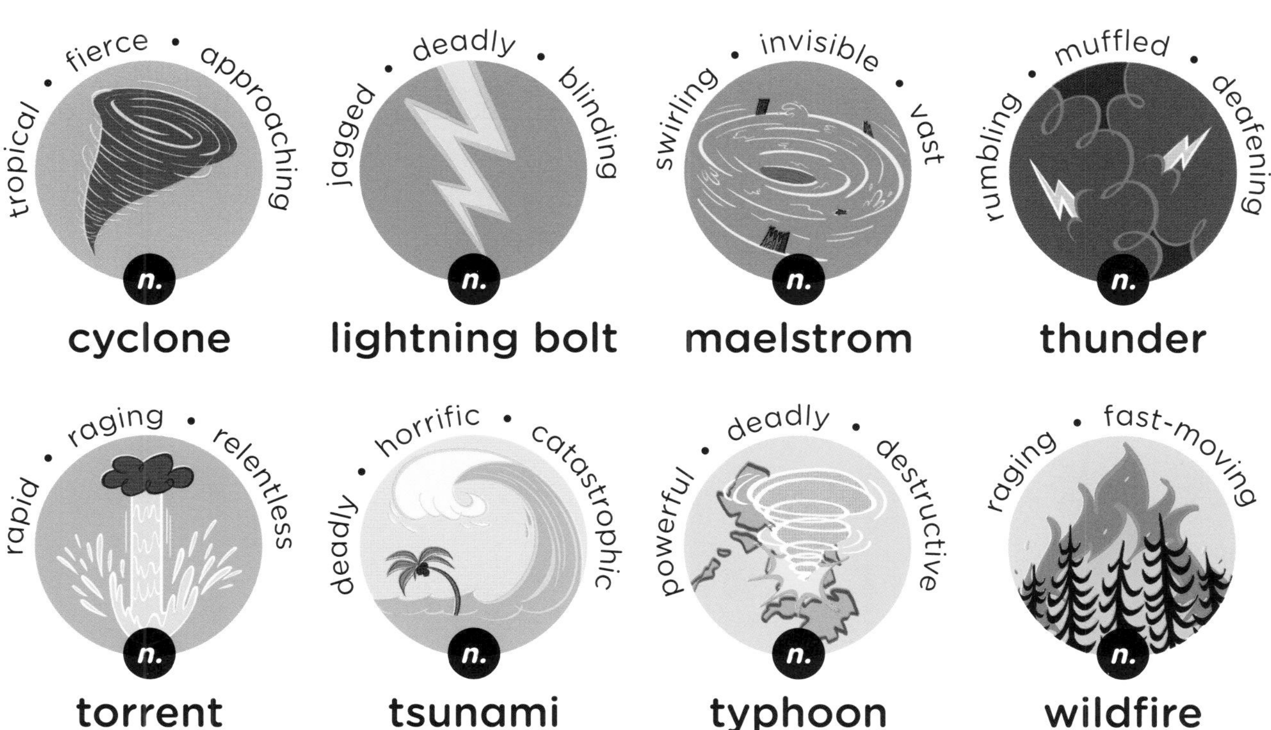
tropical • fierce • approaching
n.
cyclone
jagged • deadly • blinding
n.
lightning bolt
swirling • invisible • vast
n.
maelstrom
rumbling • muffled • deafening
n.
thunder
rapid • raging • relentless
n.
torrent
deadly • horrific • catastrophic
n.
tsunami
powerful • deadly • destructive
n.
typhoon
raging • fast-moving
n.
wildfire

harmful • plastic • industrial
n.
dense • mysterious • luminous
n.
fog
silvery • strange • impenetrable
n.
mist
toxic • suffocating • choking
n.
smog
fine • salty • iridescent
n.
spray

pollution

harmful fumes or dirty waste; like the smoke from a factory that's bad for the environment

WEATHER CONDITIONS > RAINY

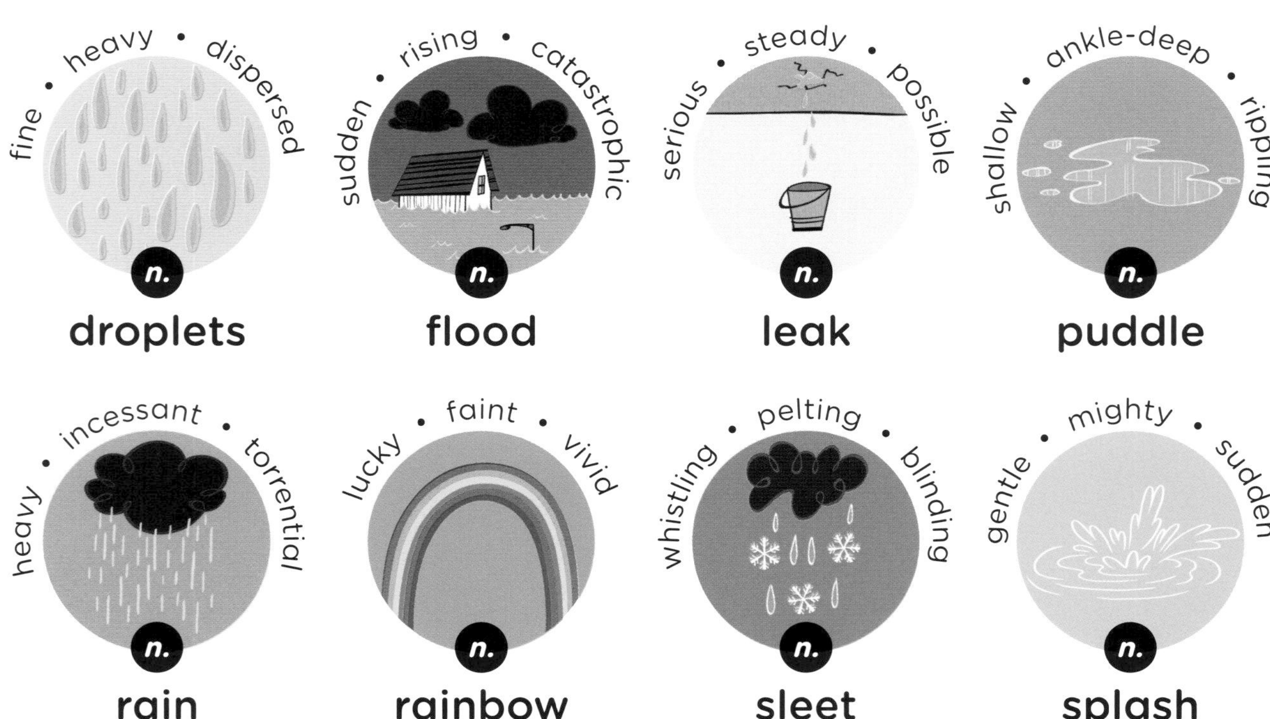
fine • heavy • dispersed
n.
droplets
sudden • rising • catastrophic
n.
flood
serious • steady • possible
n.
leak
shallow • ankle-deep • rippling
n.
puddle
heavy • incessant • torrential
n.
rain
lucky • faint • vivid
n.
rainbow
whistling • pelting • blinding
n.
sleet
gentle • mighty • sudden
n.
splash

WEATHER CONDITIONS > SUNNY

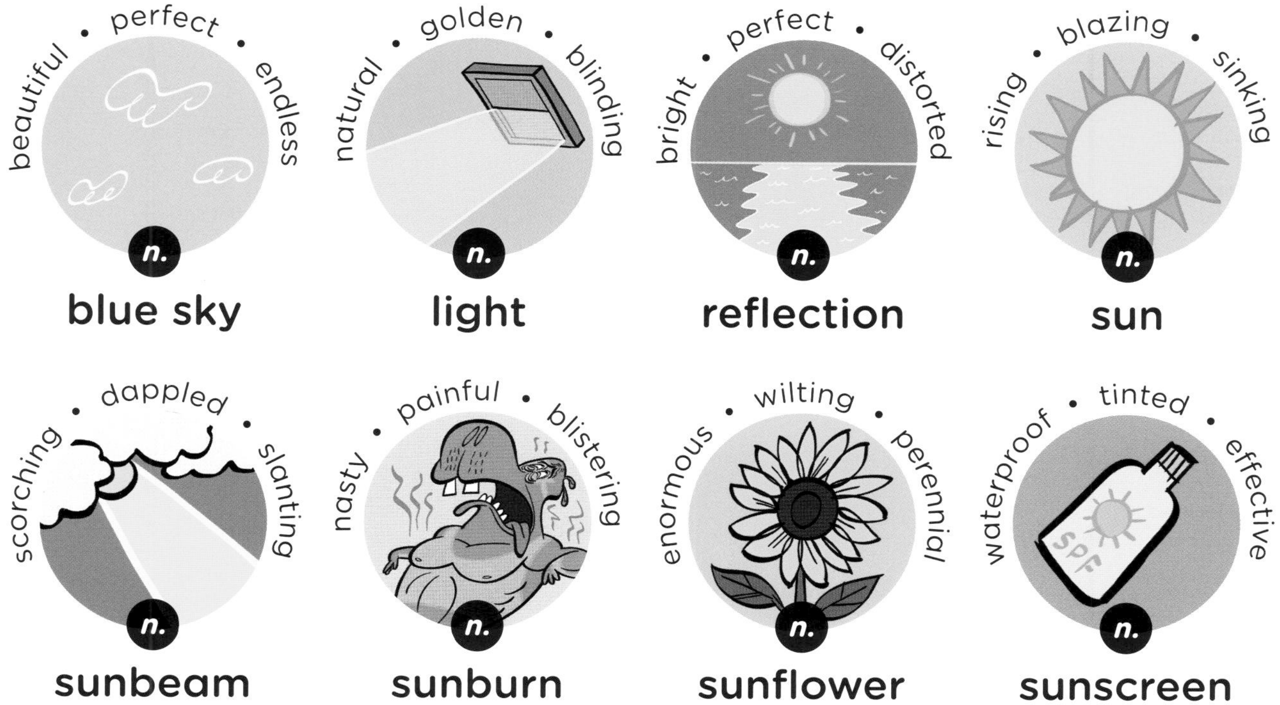
beautiful • perfect • endless
n.
blue sky
natural • golden • blinding
n.
light
bright • perfect • distorted
n.
reflection
rising • blazing • sinking
n.
sun
scorching • dappled • slanting
n.
sunbeam
nasty • painful • blistering
n.
sunburn
enormous • wilting • perennial
n.
sunflower
waterproof • tinted • effective
SPF
n.
sunscreen

WEATHER CONDITIONS > WINDY

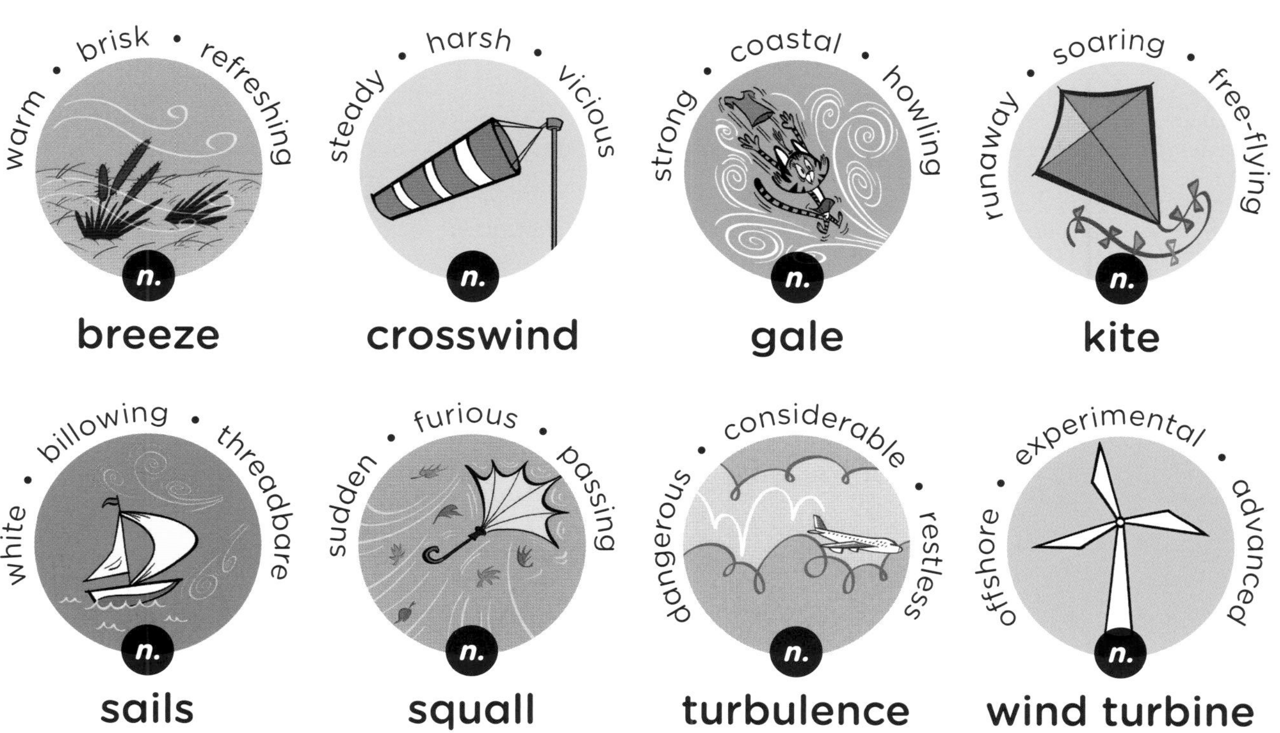
warm • brisk • refreshing
n.
breeze
steady • harsh • vicious
n.
crosswind
strong • coastal • howling
n.
gale
runaway • soaring • free-flying
n.
kite
white • billowing • threadbare
n.
sails
sudden • furious • passing
n.
squall
dangerous • considerable • restless
n.
turbulence
offshore • experimental • advanced
n.
wind turbine

A

abandoned
adj. left or deserted

abnormal
adj. unusual or uncommon

above-average
adj. more than the normal amount

absolute
adj. total or complete

abstract
adj. showing ideas, not real things

abundant
adj. having a large amount or plenty

accelerated
adj. quicker or happening faster

accidental
adj. happening by chance

accomplished
adj. highly trained or skilled

accumulated
adj. piled up over time

accurate
adj. showing correct information

accusing
adj. saying someone is guilty

aching
adj. in constant dull pain

activated
adj. made to start working

addictive
adj. making you want more

adjustable
adj. able to be resized or adjusted

adorable
adj. cute, charming, or lovable

advanced
adj. using the latest technology

advancing
adj. moving forward

afternoon
n. time between noon and evening

aged
adj. allowed to mature

agile
adj. able to move quickly and easily

airborne
adj. in the air or flying

airtight
adj. sealed so that no air gets in

airy
adj. open and full of fresh air

alien
n. a creature from outer space

all-you-can-eat
adj. with unlimited portions

alleged
adj. reported or said without proof

alluring
adj. tempting or drawing you in

alpine
adj. relating to high mountains

amazing
adj. stunning or astonishing

ambushed
adj. suddenly surprised and attacked

amphibious
adj. suited for both land and water

ancient
adj. very old or from long ago

angelic
adj. like an angel

angry
adj. wild, raging, or out of control

ankle-deep
adj. deep enough to cover your feet

annoying
adj. irritating or maddening

annual
adj. every year or in one year

anonymous
adj. unnamed or unknown

antigravity
adj. acting against gravity

antique
adj. old and precious

approaching
adj. coming closer

April
n. the fourth month of the year

arch
adj. main or chief

arched
adj. curved or bent

architectural
adj. to design buildings with

arid
adj. very dry or barren

aristocratic
adj. belonging to a grand family

armed
adj. carrying a weapon

armored
adj. protected or covered by metal

aromatic
adj. having a strong, pleasant smell

artisan
adj. run by a skilled worker

artistic
adj. creative or imaginative

aspiring
adj. ambitious, hopeful, or budding

asthmatic
adj. suffering from asthma

athletic
adj. fit and strong

atomspheric
adj. in the air or atmosphere

atomic
adj. used for looking at atoms

attentive
adj. helpful and paying attention

austere
adj. harsh and bare

authentic
adj. real or made in the proper way

automated
adj. done using machines

automatic
adj. working by itself

available
adj. free to use

average
adj. ordinary or typical

avid
adj. very keen or enthusiastic

avocado
n. a pear-shaped, green fruit

avoidable
adj. unnecessary or needless

award-winning
adj. having won awards or prizes

babbling
adj. making a continuous noise

back-up
adj. used if the original doesn't work

bad
adj. not good or low-quality

baggy
adj. too big or hanging loosely

baked
[1] *adj.* dried in an oven
[2] *adj.* cooked in an oven

bald
adj. without hair

balmy
adj. pleasantly warm or mild

balsamic
adj. dark, sweet, and strong-tasting

bamboo
Go ask a panda!

bandaged
adj. wrapped in protective cloth

barbed wire
n. wire with lots of sharp spikes

bare
adj. naked or not covered

barren
adj. with nothing growing in it

basic
adj. only with the important parts

battered
adj. beaten and damaged

beached
adj. lying stranded on a beach

beachfront
adj. looking out over a beach

beachside
adj. next to a beach

beaded
adj. in small, round drops

beady-eyed
adj. with small, shiny, round eyes

bearskin
adj. made from the skin of a bear

beastly
adj. unkind, savage, or cruel

beaten
adj. whisked into a smooth liquid

beating
adj. pounding or drumming

beautiful
You!

bedraggled
adj. messed up and untidy

bejeweled
adj. decorated with jewels

belching
adj. sending out smoke or flames

beloved
adj. deeply loved or precious

bent
adj. twisted, curved, or crooked

big-bellied
adj. having a large belly

big-city
adj. found in a large city

billionaire
n. a person with billions of dollars

billowing
adj. swelling or bulging in the wind

biodegradable
adj. rotting away naturally in soil

bitter
[1] *adj.* cold or harsh [2] *adj.* sharp or not sweet [3] *adj.* angry or grudging

bittersweet
[1] *adj.* tasting both bitter and sweet
[2] *adj.* making you feel sad and happy

black
adj. the darkest color

blackened
adj. turned black

blank
adj. empty or plain

blaring
adj. loud or booming

blazing
adj. very hot or burning

bleak
adj. gloomy or depressing

bleating
adj. making a crying sound

B

blind
adj. without thinking or judging

blinding
[1] *adj.* so bright that you can't see
[2] *adj.* so thick you can't see through

blinking
adj. quickly turning on and off again

blistered
adj. having sore, swollen bubbles

blistering
adj. so hot that your skin blisters

bloated
adj. full and swollen

blocked
adj. not letting things go through

bloodshot
adj. red, sore, and tired

bloodsucking
adj. blood-drinking

bloody
adj. stained or smeared with blood

blooming
adj. producing a flower

blotchy
adj. uneven or patchy

blueberry
n. a small and sweet berry

Bluetooth
n. wireless, short-range connection

blunt
adj. not having a sharp edge

boiled
adj. cooked in very hot water

boiling
[1] *adj.* very hot or scorching
[2] *adj.* very hot and bubbling

bold
adj. brave or daring

bony
[1] *adj.* skinny or scrawny
[2] *adj.* made of bone or bone-like

booming
adj. loud or thundering

borrowed
adj. taken to be used for a short time

botched
adj. done badly or messed up

bottomless
adj. very deep or endless

bouncing
adj. springing off the ground

bouncy
Like all the best castles.

boundless
adj. never-ending or limitless

bountiful
adj. generous or abundant

bowed
adj. lowered or looking down

branded
adj. stamped or marked with a logo

brave
adj. bold and daring

breathtaking
adj. beautiful or stunning

brief
adj. lasting for a short time

bright
adj. shining, radiant, or colorful

brilliant
adj. bright or shiny

brimming
adj. full to the point of overflowing

brisk
adj. cold and fresh

bristly
adj. short, stiff, and spiky

brittle
adj. fragile or breakable

broad
adj. wide or long from side to side

broken
[1] *adj.* not working or injured [2] *adj.* hurt or despairing [3] *adj.* smashed or shattered

bronzed
adj. tanned or bronze-colored

brooding
adj. looking intense and sad

broody
adj. ready to lay eggs and sit on them

brown
The same color as chocolate - yum!

bruised
adj. bashed and discolored

brutal
adj. violent, cruel, or savage

bubbling
adj. frothing, foaming, or gurgling

bug-eyed
adj. with bulging, sticking-out eyes

built-in
adj. fixed or fitted in

bulging
adj. swollen or sticking out

bulky
adj. big or taking up a lot of space

bulletproof
adj. able to block bullets

bumbling
adj. awkward, clumsy, or useless

buoyant
adj. light and able to float

burning
adj. on fire or very hot

burned
[1] *adj.* spoiled by heat or overcooked
[2] *adj.* charred or destroyed by fire

burned-out
adj. completely ruined by fire

burst
adj. broken, torn, or split open

bursting
adj. breaking or splitting open

bushy
adj. thick and full

bustling
adj. crowded or lively

busy
[1] *adj.* full of people
[2] *adj.* with lots of jobs to do

buttered
adj. covered in butter

buttery
adj. rich and creamy, like butter

buzzing
adj. making a continuous, low noise

caged
adj. kept in a cage

calloused
adj. hardened or roughened

calm
adj. still and peaceful

camouflaged
adj. blending into the background

candied
adj. preserved in sugar syrup

canned
adj. kept in a sealed can

capsized
adj. upside down or flipped

captive
adj. kept prisoner or caged in

captured
adj. caught or taken by force

caramelized
adj. cooked slowly and sweet

carpeted
adj. covered with a carpet

cascading
adj. gushing or falling down quickly

cast-iron
n. easily molded black metal

catastrophic
adj. disastrous or destructive

celebrated
adj. admired or praised

celebrity
No, you can't have my autograph.

ceramic
adj. made of baked clay

challenging
adj. difficult or dangerous

chaotic
adj. wild and confusing

charming
[1] *adj.* attractive or delightful [2] *adj.* attractive or adorable [3] *adj.* attractive and likable

charred
adj. burned or blackened by heat

cheap
adj. low-priced or not expensive

cheesy
adj. with cheese on top or inside

chemical
adj. made of chemicals or man-made

chewy
adj. tough or hard to chew

chic
adj. stylish or fashionable

chicken
n. a bird used in cooking

chilled
adj. cooled in a fridge

chipped
adj. with a small piece broken off

chiseled
adj. perfectly carved or sculpted

choking
adj. making it hard to breathe

chopped
adj. cut or sliced into pieces

choppy
adj. with lots of little waves

chronic
adj. continuous or long-lasting

chubby
adj. a little fat or round

chunky
adj. thick or with big pieces

cinematic
adj. like something from a movie

circling
adj. moving around in circles

citric
adj. acidic, lemony, and sharp

clammy
adj. soggy, moist, and sticky

clandestine
adj. undercover or secret

clanking
adj. rattling, jangling, or clattering

classic
adj. popular since a long time ago

clattering
adj. noisy and rattling

clean
adj. washed or without any dirt

clear
[1] *adj.* easy to hear or understand [2] *adj.* easy to see through [3] *adj.* easy to spot or notice

clenched
adj. grasped or closed tightly

clever
[1] *adj.* skillful and cunning [2] *adj.* smart or cunning [3] *adj.* well-designed or high-tech

clipped
adj. cut short or trimmed

C

clogged
adj. blocked or stuffed

close
[1] *adj.* knowing each other very well
[2] *adj.* only won by a few points

clotted
[1] *adj.* dried or thickened into chunks
[2] *adj.* thickened or mixed until it's stiff

cloudless
adj. clear or without clouds

cluttered
adj. messy or littered

coarse
adj. rough or scratchy

coastal
adj. on the coast or beside the sea

cobbled
adj. made of round stones

cold
Brrrrrrrrr.

collapsed
adj. fallen down or crumpled

collected
adj. picked or brought together

colonized
adj. taken as a new place to live

colossal
adj. massive or gigantic

colorful
adj. brightly colored or not dull

comfortable
[1] *adj.* cozy or snug
[2] *adj.* easy to wear and the right size

comfy
adj. soft or nice to wear

comical
adj. funny or amusing

common
adj. ordinary or usual

communal
adj. used by everyone or shared

compact
adj. small and neat

competitive
[1] *adj.* to do with winning and losing
[2] *adj.* wanting to be the best

complete
adj. having all the parts

composting
adj. rotting to be used as fertilizer

concealed
adj. hidden or secret

concealing
adj. hiding something

concrete
n. a building material made of stone

confusing
Huh?

congested
adj. blocked or too crowded

considerable
adj. big and noticeable

contaminated
[1] *adj.* spoiled or ruined
[2] *adj.* spoiled by dirt or pollution

contemporary
adj. in a modern style

cookie
A heavenly circle of deliciousness.

cool
adj. popular or fashionable

correct
adj. right or in order

corroded
adj. worn down or burned away

corrosive
adj. harmful or burning

corrugated
adj. ridged or wavy

corrupt
[1] *adj.* ruined or full of mistakes
[2] *adj.* dishonest or misusing power

countless
adj. too many to be counted

covert
adj. secret or undercover

coveted
adj. wanted by lots of people

cowardly
adj. afraid or not confident

cowboy
Yee-haw!

cozy
adj. warm and comfortable

cracked
adj. split or with broken lines

crackling
adj. making small, sharp noises

crackly
adj. making short, harsh noises

cramped
adj. small or without enough room

crashed
[1] *adj.* fallen to the ground or smashed
[2] *adj.* smashed into something

crashing
adj. smashing loudly against things

creaky
adj. noisy when stepped on

creamed
adj. blended, smooth, and soft

creamy
adj. as smooth and soft as cream

credible
adj. easy to believe or reliable

creeping
adj. moving slowly over a surface

creepy
adj. scary or spooky

crescent
adj. curved or in a semicircle shape

C - D

crisp
adj. cold and fresh

crispy
adj. thin, dry, and crunchy

crooked
adj. bent or wonky

crowded
adj. full of people or things

crude
adj. made very simply or badly

cruel
adj. mean or unkind

cruising
adj. sailing or traveling

crumbling
adj. falling down little by little

crumpled
adj. crushed out of shape

crunchy
[1] *adj.* making a noise when you bite
[2] *adj.* making a crushing noise

crushed
adj. broken by squeezing or pressing

crushing
adj. squashing or smashing

cuddly
adj. soft and huggable

cunning
adj. clever or crafty

curdled
adj. separated into lumpy bits

cured
adj. dried or smoked to last longer

curious
adj. wanting to find out more

curly
adj. curved or spiraled

curried
adj. flavored with spices

curved
adj. rounded or bent

custom-made
adj. made specially for you

cute
adj. sweet or lovable

cutting-edge
adj. using advanced technology

cynical
adj. negative or full of doubt

daily
adj. for each new day

dairy-free
adj. free from animal milk products

damaging
adj. harmful or destructive

damp
adj. slightly wet or soggy

dangerous
adj. unsafe or likely to cause harm

dapper
adj. neat and stylish

dappled
adj. marked with spots or patches

daring
adj. brave or bold

dark
[1] *adj.* with little or no light
[2] *adj.* any color close to black

dated
adj. old-fashioned or from the past

daunting
adj. seeming scary or intimidating

daytime
adj. while the sun is up

dazzling
adj. very bright or amazing

dead
[1] *adj.* out of energy
[2] *adj.* no longer alive

dead-end
adj. with no way out the other side

deadly
adj. dangerous or life-threatening

deafening
adj. very loud or noisy

debilitating
adj. weakening or holding you back

decadent
adj. very luxurious or indulgent

decisive
adj. answering or settling a problem

decorated
adj. made prettier by adding things

dedicated
adj. committed or devoted

deep
adj. going far down below the top

deep-fried
adj. cooked by being dipped in hot oil

deep-set
adj. fixed or firmly in something

deep-water
adj. growing in very deep water

defective
adj. broken or not working properly

defined
adj. obvious, clear, or outlined

deflated
adj. flat or with the air let out

delayed
adj. later than expected

delectable
adj. very tasty or delicious

delicate
[1] *adj.* fine, elegant, and detailed [2] *adj.* fragile and breakable [3] *adj.* with a mild or subtle flavor

delicious
adj. tasty or enjoyable to eat or drink

D

dense
adj. thick, solid, or heavy

dented
adj. pushed in from being hit

dependable
adj. reliable or always works well

derailed
adj. driven off the tracks

derelict
adj. run-down or left to fall apart

deserted
adj. empty or abandoned

desiccated
adj. completely dried out

desolate
adj. bleak, bare, and empty

desperate
adj. anxious, frantic, or without hope

destructive
adj. damaging or devastating

detached
adj. not joined onto another building

detailed
adj. packed with info and facts

devastating
adj. very damaging and destructive

devious
adj. cheating, sneaky, or sly

dewy
adj. covered in little water droplets

diced
adj. chopped into small cubes

die-hard
adj. unchanging or never giving up

digital
adj. using electronics or computers

dilapidated
adj. ruined, run-down, or shabby

dim
adj. faint or not shining brightly

dim-witted
adj. silly or not clever

dimmed
adj. turned down

dingy
adj. dark or gloomy

direct
adj. straight or uninterrupted

dirty
adj. unclean or mucky

discarded
adj. thrown away or rejected

disgusting
adj. gross or revolting

dismal
adj. dark and depressing

disorganized
adj. messy or cluttered

dispersed
adj. spread out over a big area

disposable
adj. thrown away after it's used

distant
adj. far away or faint

distinctive
adj. easy to identify or recognize

distorted
adj. twisted or bent out of shape

disused
adj. not used any more

doomed
adj. unlucky or headed for disaster

double-breasted
adj. overlapping flaps at the front

double-decker
adj. with two floors or decks

downward
adj. toward the ground

downy
adj. filled with soft feathers

drafty
adj. breezy and cold inside

drained
adj. run-down or empty

drawn
adj. closed or pulled shut

dreadful
adj. really bad or horrible

dreary
adj. dull and miserable

dried
[1] *adj.* dehydrated to make it last
[2] *adj.* dehydrated or sun-baked

drifting
adj. floating gently away

dripping
adj. wet and with droplets falling off

driverless
adj. automatic and without a driver

drizzled
adj. sprinkled or poured carefully

droning
adj. constantly humming or buzzing

drooling
adj. dribbling or slobbering

drooping
adj. hanging down or sagging

dry
adj. not wet or damp

dull
adj. blunt or not sharp

durable
adj. strong and lasting a long time

dusty
adj. full of dust, dried mud, or soot

D - F

dwindling
adj. getting smaller and weaker

eager
adj. keen or enthusiastic

ear-splitting
adj. so loud that it hurts your ears

early
adj. sooner than expected

early-warning
adj. giving a warning ahead of time

eclipsed
adj. blocked out by another thing

edible
adj. safe to eat

eerie
adj. weird, ghostly, or creepy

effective
adj. working well

ejectable
adj. can be sent flying

elaborate
adj. complex, detailed, or fancy

elbow-length
adj. reaching up to your elbows

electric
adj. powered by electricity

electrified
adj. charged with electricity

electronic
adj. powered by electricity

elegant
adj. graceful and grand

elongated
adj. made longer or stretched

elusive
adj. difficult to find or catch

embedded
adj. fixed, lodged, or planted firmly

embroidered
adj. with a stitched design

empty
adj. with nothing inside

enchanted
adj. under a magic spell

encrypted
adj. hidden or protected by a code

endangered
adj. likely to go extinct soon

endless
adj. unlimited or with no end

engraved
adj. with a design carved in

enormous
adj. really big or huge

enraged
adj. very angry or furious

enviable
adj. making other people jealous

environmental
adj. to do with the natural world

epic
adj. heroic or grand

erratic
adj. unpredictable or unreliable

escaped
adj. running free

essential
adj. very important or necessary

eternal
adj. with no end or lasting forever

ethical
adj. moral, honest, and fair

evil
adj. bad or wicked

excess
adj. more than you need

excessive
adj. too much or over the top

excited
adj. lively or enthusiastic

exclusive
adj. only letting a few people in

exhausted
adj. worn-out or very tired

exotic
adj. unusual and from far away

expensive
adj. costing a lot of money

experimental
adj. testing or based on new ideas

exploding
adj. bursting, popping, or blowing up

exposed
adj. bare or not covered

expressive
adj. showing a lot of emotion

exquisite
adj. excellent or magnificent

external
adj. outside or separate

extortionate
adj. too much or overly expensive

extra
adj. more than the usual

extreme
adj. strong, intense, or severe

fabulous
adj. amazing or wonderful

faded
adj. faint or worn-out

fading
adj. slowly losing its color

failing
adj. not working properly

F

faint
adj. slight or barely noticeable

faithful
adj. loyal and devoted

fake
adj. not real or not natural

fallen
adj. having dropped to the ground

falling
adj. dropping to the ground

family-owned
adj. owned by one family

famous
adj. known by lots of people

fancy
adj. decorative or expensive

faraway
adj. distant or not nearby

farmed
adj. produced on a farm or fishery

fast
Blink and you might miss it.

fast-growing
adj. getting bigger quickly

fast-moving
adj. moving or spreading quickly

fat
adj. round or with a lot of flesh

fatty
adj. with a lot of fat

faulty
adj. not working properly

favorite
adj. liked more than all the others

fearless
adj. brave or not showing fear

fearsome
adj. frightening or menacing

feathered
adj. soft and cut at different lengths

feathery
adj. light and soft, like feathers

fenced-in
adj. surrounded by a fence

fermented
adj. gone sour

ferocious
adj. fierce or violent

fertile
adj. fruitful or able to grow things

fierce
adj. violent or savage

fiery
[1] *adj.* very spicy or hot-tasting
[2] *adj.* burning or producing fire

filthy
adj. disgustingly dirty or mucky

fine
[1] *adj.* light, thin, or wispy
[2] *adj.* excellent or top-quality

finest
adj. best or nicest

fireproof
adj. protected against fire

firm
adj. hard or solid

first
adj. at the beginning or before others

first-degree
adj. mild or not very harmful

fishy
adj. tasting or smelling like fish

fitted
adj. made to be the right shape

five-star
adj. of the highest standard

flaky
adj. breaking easily into flakes

flaming
adj. on fire or burning

flamingo
n. a bright pink bird with a long neck

flapping
adj. moving quickly up and down

flared
adj. opened or made wider

flashing
adj. quickly switching on and off

flat
adj. smooth and even

flat-screen
adj. thin and not curved

flattened
adj. squashed or made flat

flattering
adj. making you look better

fleeing
adj. running away or escaping

flesh-eating
adj. eating the meat of humans

flexible
adj. able to bend without breaking

flickering
adj. burning or shining unsteadily

flightless
adj. not able to fly

flimsy
adj. weak, thin, or easy to break

floating
[1] *adj.* sitting on top of the water
[2] *adj.* staying up in the air

flooded
adj. covered with too much water

floppy
adj. limp or hanging loosely

floral
adj. with a flowery pattern

floured
adj. dusted with a layer of flour

flowering
adj. producing flowers

flowing
adj. hanging loosely and smoothly

fluffy
[1] *adj.* wooly, fleecy, and soft
[2] *adj.* light and full of air

fluorescent
[1] *adj.* producing a bright light
[2] *adj.* vividly colorful and bright

fluttering
adj. with wings flapping up and down

flying
adj. moving through the air

foaming
adj. frothing or making tiny bubbles

folded
adj. with one part turned over

folding
adj. able to be made smaller or neater

fond
adj. loving or affectionate

foolish
adj. silly or unwise

foot-long
The length of a grown-up's smelly foot.

forensic
adj. using science to find the truth

formal
adj. right for important occasions

formidable
adj. impressive and intimidating

fortune
n. luck or chance in life

fossilized
adj. preserved in a rock

foul
adj. disgusting or revolting

fragile
adj. easy to break or ruin

fragrant
adj. sweet-smelling or perfumed

frayed
adj. with worn-out edges

free
adj. without any cost or payment

free-flying
adj. able to move easily in the air

free-range
adj. not raised in small cages

freezing
adj. below zero or very cold

frenzied
adj. wildly excited or frantic

fresh
adj. made or created recently

freshly baked
adj. just out of the oven

freshly squeezed
adj. recently pressed from fruit

fried
adj. cooked in a pan with oil

friendly
adj. kind, sociable, and welcoming

frightened
adj. scared or fearful

front
adj. on the side that faces forward

frosty
adj. freezing or icy

frothy
adj. foamy and bubbly

frozen
adj. iced-over or kept in a freezer

fruit
n. a sweet, healthy food from plants

fruity
adj. tasting or smelling like fruit

full
adj. complete or without empty space

full-length
adj. as long as your body

fully stocked
adj. with everything you might need

fur-lined
adj. with a layer of fur inside

furious
adj. wild, angry, and violent

furry
adj. soft, fluffy, and hairy

futuristic
[1] *adj.* using the latest technology
[2] *adj.* with a very modern design

fuzzy
adj. wooly, fluffy, or frizzy

galloping
adj. racing or sprinting

gaping
adj. open very wide

gargantuan
adj. huge or enormous

garish
adj. much too bright and flashy

gaudy
adj. bright, glaring, or flashy

gaunt
adj. far too thin and scrawny

general
adj. common or from all around

genetic
adj. involving DNA or genes

gentle
adj. calm, soft, or mild

geographical
adj. to do with a certain area

G - H

ghostly
[1] *adj.* creepy or scary
[2] *adj.* creepy or like a ghost

giant
Fee, fi, fo, fum!

gifted
adj. talented or skilled

gigantic
adj. huge or enormous

gladiator
n. an armed Roman warrior

glass
adj. made of a clear, hard material

glazed
adj. with a thin layer of icing

gleaming
adj. shining or bright

glimmering
adj. glowing faintly or twinkling

glistening
adj. shining or sparkling

glitching
adj. not working properly

glitchy
adj. often working incorrectly

glittering
adj. shiny or sparkling

global
adj. of the whole world

gloomy
adj. dark and depressing

gloopy
adj. thick and sticky

glorious
adj. beautiful and magnificent

glossy
adj. shiny and smooth

glowing
[1] *adj.* bright or shining
[2] *adj.* bright and healthy-looking

gluten-free
adj. without gluten

glutinous
adj. sticky, gooey, or glue-like

gnarled
adj. knobbly, rough, and twisted

golden
adj. of the color of gold

gooey
adj. with a soft and sticky texture

gossipy
adj. talking about other people

graceful
adj. elegant and beautiful

gracious
adj. polite, kind, and pleasant

gradual
adj. happening slowly

grand
adj. big and impressive

grassy
adj. like grass or covered in grass

grated
adj. cut into thin slices by a grater

grazed
adj. lightly scraped and bleeding

grazing
adj. slowly eating grass

greasy
adj. oily or waxy

greedy
adj. wanting too much

green
You don't need help with this one!

greenish
adj. slightly green

grilled
adj. cooked on a hot grill

grim
adj. serious, gloomy, or unpleasant

grimy
adj. dirty or covered with grime

gristly
adj. with tough bits that are hard to eat

grizzly
adj. with patches of gray

groaning
adj. creaking under heavy weight

groomed
adj. looked after or styled

growling
adj. making noise due to hunger

grubby
adj. a little dirty or grimy

gruesome
adj. horrible or disgusting to look at

grunting
adj. making a short, low sound

gushing
adj. coming out quickly in big amounts

hacked
adj. broken into with a computer

hairy
adj. covered with hairs

half-eaten
adj. only partly eaten

half-finished
adj. only partly finished

halved
adj. cut into two equal pieces

hand-painted
adj. painted by a person

hand-picked
adj. picked by a person

handheld
adj. small enough to hold

H

handmade
adj. made by a person

handwritten
adj. written with a pen or pencil

handy
adj. helpful or convenient

hanging
adj. drooping or dangling

hard
adj. solid or firm

hard-fought
adj. played with lots of effort

hardened
adj. harder than before or not soft

harmful
adj. dangerous or unhealthy

harmless
adj. not causing harm or damage

harnessed
adj. wearing straps for guiding

harsh
adj. sharp or unpleasantly intense

haunted
adj. lived in by ghosts

hazardous
adj. dangerous or unsafe

headless
adj. without a head

healthy
adj. fit and well or good for you

heaped
adj. in a big pile or completely full

heart-shaped
adj. in the shape of a heart

hearty
adj. filling and wholesome

heated
adj. made hot or warm

heavy
[1] *adj.* sad or miserable [2] *adj.* weighty, thick, or hard to lift [3] *adj.* forceful or in big amounts

heavy-duty
adj. not easily worn out

heavyweight
adj. above the normal weight

helpless
adj. weak, powerless, or unprotected

herbal
adj. made using herbs

hidden
adj. secret or kept out of sight

high
adj. tall or near the top

high-end
adj. expensive or luxury

high-powered
adj. with a lot of power or energy

high-rise
adj. in a tall, multi-story building

high-security
adj. strictly guarded or protected

high-tech
adj. using the latest science

hilarious
adj. very funny or hysterical

hilly
adj. with lots of hills

hissing
adj. making a 'sssss' sound

historic
adj. important and famous

holey
adj. full of holes

hollow
adj. empty or with nothing inside

homemade
adj. made at home

homing
adj. able to find and hit a target

honking
adj. beeping or hooting

hooked
adj. curved or bent

hopping
adj. jumping or leaping

horned
adj. with a horn on its head

horrific
adj. terrible and shocking

horse-drawn
adj. pulled by horses

hostile
adj. unfriendly and aggressive

hot
Like warm, but a little warmer.

hovering
adj. floating or fluttering in the air

howling
adj. crying or wailing

huge
adj. very big or enormous

hulking
adj. big and heavy

human
Look in a mirror!

humble
adj. modest, plain, and simple

humid
adj. muggy or with damp air

humming
adj. making a continuous sound

hunched
adj. bent over or arched

hungry
Warning: this dictionary is not edible.

H - I

hurtling
adj. moving very fast or rushing

hydroelectric
adj. using water to make electricity

hypnotic
adj. mesmerizing or captivating

ice-cold
adj. as cold as ice

frosted
[1] *adj.* covered with icing
[2] *adj.* served cold and with ice

iconic
adj. famous and recognizable

icy
adj. with ice or covered in ice

idyllic
adj. ideal or perfect

illegal
adj. against the law

immaculate
adj. perfect or spotless

immense
adj. very large or huge

immersive
adj. making you completely involved

immortal
adj. living forever or never dying

immune
adj. not affected by certain illnesses

impenetrable
adj. dense or inaccessible

important
adj. valuable or significant

imported
adj. brought from another country

imposing
adj. grand or impressive

impractical
adj. not useful or sensible

impregnable
adj. impossible to enter or defeat

impressive
adj. admirably good or big

inadequate
adj. too few or not enough

incessant
adj. constant or never stopping

incoming
adj. approaching or arriving

incompetent
adj. lacking skill or useless

incorrect
adj. wrong or not accurate

incurable
adj. unable to be made better

indestructible
adj. impossible to break or destroy

indulgent
adj. luxurious or pampering

industrial
adj. relating to factories or industry

industrious
adj. hard-working

infected
adj. affected by a virus or disease

infinite
adj. going on forever

inflatable
adj. able to be filled with air

inflated
adj. filled with air

infrared
adj. using invisible light rays

ingenious
adj. clever and inventive

ingrown
adj. growing backwards or sideways

injured
adj. hurt or wounded

innocent
adj. harmless, pure, or not guilty

innovative
adj. new, advanced, and original

inquisitive
adj. wanting to discover things

inspiring
adj. exciting and motivating

instant
adj. immediate or very quick to make

intelligent
adj. clever or able to work things out

intense
adj. strong, powerful, or extreme

interactive
adj. responding to what you do

international
adj. involving different countries

interplanetary
adj. going between planets

interstellar
adj. going between stars

intoxicating
adj. making you feel dizzy

intruding
adj. going where not wanted

intrusive
adj. unwelcome and annoying

intuitive
adj. easy to understand without training

invasive
adj. growing aggressively

invigorating
adj. making you feel lively and alert

invisible
adj. impossible to see

inviting
adj. attractive or tempting

iridescent
adj. colored like a rainbow

isolated
adj. alone or far from others

itchy
adj. making you want to scratch

ivy-covered
adj. covered with a climbing plant

jagged
adj. with sharp or pointy edges

jealous
adj. wanting what someone else has

jittery
adj. nervous, scared, and jumpy

jolly
adj. happy and joyful

jolting
adj. moving suddenly and roughly

juicy
adj. full of juice or moisture

jumbo
adj. especially big or large

key
adj. important or essential

khaki
adj. yellowish brown

killer
adj. deadly or dangerous

kind
adj. friendly, generous, and caring

knee-high
adj. reaching up to your knees

knitted
adj. made by knitting wool

knobbly
adj. with lumps and bumps

lakeside
adj. next to a lake

lanky
adj. tall, thin, and ungraceful

lapping
adj. gently flowing or splashing

large
adj. big or great in size

late-night
adj. staying open late at night

latest
adj. newest or most recent

lazy
adj. not working hard

leafless
adj. bare and without leaves

leafy
adj. with lots of leaves

leaky
adj. letting water in through holes

leather
adj. made of animal skin

leather-clad
adj. covered in leather

leering
adj. gazing, ogling, or gawking

leftover
adj. uneaten by the end of a meal

legendary
adj. famous or told of in stories

lethal
adj. deadly or very harmful

life-saving
adj. able to cure people

life-size
adj. full-size or the actual size

lifelike
adj. very like a living thing

lifelong
adj. for your whole life

light
adj. not thick or heavy

lightweight
adj. thin or not weighing much

limited
adj. not very good or poor

lingering
adj. lasting or not ending

lit
adj. on fire or burning

littered
adj. covered in trash or messy

little
adj. small or tiny

live
adj. not dead

livid
adj. raging or furious

loaded
adj. full or carrying a lot

loathsome
adj. making you feel hatred

local
adj. in or from a nearby area

locked
adj. sealed shut with a lock and key

lofty
adj. very tall or high up

lone
adj. on its own or solitary

lonely
adj. alone or isolated

long
[1] *adj.* lasting a while or not fast
[2] *adj.* far from beginning to end

long-lasting
adj. not ending quickly

L - M

long-time
adj. for many years

loose
adj. baggy or not tight

loose-leaf
adj. made using loose tea leaves

lopsided
adj. drooping or leaning to one side

lost
W-w-where am I? HELP!

loud
adj. noisy or easy to hear

lovable
adj. adorable or sweet

low
adj. less than the normal amount

low-fat
adj. not containing much fat

low-flying
adj. flying low in the sky

low-sodium
adj. not containing much sodium

loyal
adj. faithful and reliable

lucky
adj. bringing good luck

lukewarm
adj. a little warm

luminous
adj. bright, shining, or glowing

lumpy
adj. uneven or with lots of bumps

lurking
adj. hiding and waiting to attack

luscious
adj. rich, sweet, and delicious

lush
adj. rich and growing healthily

luxurious
adj. very comfortable and expensive

luxury
n. richness or comfort

magic
n. mysterious or unexplained power

magical
[1] *adj.* with mysterious power
[2] *adj.* wonderful or special

magnificent
adj. very beautiful or impressive

majestic
adj. beautiful or powerful

makeshift
adj. temporary and not very good

malfunctioning
adj. not working properly

malicious
adj. spiteful or meaning harm

mammoth
adj. very large or giant

man-eating
adj. likes feeding on human flesh

man-made
adj. created by humans

manicured
adj. tidy and well looked after

marauding
adj. looking for things to kill or steal

marbled
adj. streaky like marble

marinated
adj. soaked in spices or flavors

marine
adj. used at sea

marshy
adj. wet and boggy

mashed
adj. crushed or blended into a pulp

masked
adj. disguised or covered

massive
adj. very large or giant

matted
adj. tangled or knotted

meandering
adj. wandering or taking a bendy path

meaty
adj. large, weighty, or fleshy

mechanical
adj. controlled by a machine

meddling
adj. getting involved or interfering

medical
adj. relating to medicine or doctors

medieval
adj. from the Middle Ages

mellow
adj. soft and soothing

melted
adj. turned from solid to liquid

melting
adj. turning from solid to liquid

menacing
adj. threatening to do harm

mesmerizing
adj. very attractive or bewitching

messy
adj. untidy or dirty

metal
n. a hard, shiny material

metallic
adj. looking like metal

mighty
adj. big, strong, and powerful

migrating
adj. moving from one place to another

M - O

mild
adj. not very strong or not spicy

military
adj. to do with the army or soldiers

mindless
adj. foolish or senseless

mini
adj. smaller than usual

mint
n. a plant used in cooking

minted
adj. flavored with mint

miraculous
adj. wonderful or magical

mirrored
[1] *adj.* reflective or with a mirror
[2] *adj.* shiny or mirror-like

mischievous
adj. naughty and playful

mismatched
adj. not the same color or pattern

misplaced
adj. in the wrong place

missing
adj. lost or gone

mistreated
adj. treated badly or cruelly

misty
adj. like a thin fog

misunderstood
adj. not understood or appreciated

mixing
adj. combining things together

mobile
adj. able to be carried around

modern
adj. in the latest or current style

moist
adj. damp or not dry

monstrous
adj. horrible or like a monster

moonlit
adj. lit up by the moon

moored
adj. tied up with a rope or anchor

moth-eaten
adj. full of holes made by insects

motionless
adj. still or not moving

motorized
adj. powered by a motor

moldy
adj. rotten or covered with mold

mounted
adj. on horseback

mournful
adj. very sad or full of regret

much-needed
adj. very important and necessary

mud
n. a mixture of water and soil

muddled
adj. confused or mixed-up

muddy
adj. covered in mud

muffled
adj. quiet and not heard properly

murky
adj. dark, muddy, or cloudy

muscular
adj. strong and powerful

mushy
adj. mashed or pulpy

musty
adj. stuffy, moldy, or stale

mutated
adj. changed into something else

mysterious
adj. strange, eerie, or unexplained

mythical
adj. existing only in stories

narrow
adj. small or not far from side to side

nasty
adj. very bad or unpleasant

natural
adj. made by nature

neglected
adj. not well looked after

nesting
adj. building a home or nest

network
n. a system of connected things

new
adj. just made or just bought

nimble
adj. moving quickly and skillfully

nocturnal
adj. active at night

noise-canceling
adj. blocking out other sounds

noisy
WHAT? I CAN'T HEAR YOU.

non-stick
adj. not letting food stick

nondescript
adj. not unusual or not memorable

number-one
adj. the best or highest-rated

nutty
adj. tasting of nuts or with nuts in

oaty
adj. made with oats

obscure
adj. hidden or unclear

O - P

obsessive
adj. too interested or addicted

obvious
adj. easy to see or notice

odd-looking
adj. looking unusual or strange

offshore
adj. out at sea

old
adj. having existed for a long time

ominous
adj. scary, threatening, or menacing

oncoming
adj. moving toward you

oozing
adj. slowly trickling or leaking

open
[1] *adj.* not shut or not closed
[2] *adj.* wide and exposed

open-air
adj. outside or not walled in

open-plan
adj. with no dividing walls

oppressive
adj. cruel, harsh, and overpowering

optical
adj. relating to eyes and sight

opulent
adj. rich and luxurious

orbiting
adj. circling or moving around

organic
adj. made without using chemicals

ornamental
adj. fancy or decorative

ornate
adj. detailed and decorated

orphaned
adj. without a mother or father

outdoor
adj. not inside

outer
adj. on the outside

outspread
adj. spread open or wide apart

overcast
adj. cloudy or gray

overcrowded
adj. full of too many people

overflowing
adj. too full and spilling over

overgrown
adj. grown too big or thick

overhanging
adj. above or hanging over

overhead
adj. above your head or in the sky

overloaded
adj. carrying too much stuff

overnight
adj. during the night

overripe
adj. too ripe or past its best

oversized
adj. bigger than normal

overstocked
adj. filled with too many things

overstuffed
adj. stuffed with too many things

overturned
adj. tipped upside down

packed
adj. full or overcrowded

padded
adj. stuffed with a soft material

painful
adj. causing pain or distress

painted
adj. covered with paint

palatial
adj. vast or splendid

paper
n. thin sheets made from trees

parboiled
adj. boiled until partly cooked

parked
adj. left somewhere without moving

passing
adj. moving or going past

passing
adj. not lasting long

patchy
adj. uneven or not everywhere

patterned
adj. with a repeated design

peaceful
adj. calm and tranquil

pebbly
adj. with a lot of pebbles

peeled
adj. with the outer peel removed

peeling
adj. coming off or shedding

peep
adj. showing or poking out

pelting
adj. bombarding or battering

perennial
adj. living for many years

perfect
adj. ideal or flawless

perilous
adj. dangerous and full of risk

personal
adj. belonging to you or for you

P

pesky
adj. causing trouble or annoying

pessimistic
adj. gloomy or negative

phenomenal
adj. fantastic or extraordinary

photographic
adj. using photos or in photos

pickled
adj. preserved in a vinegary liquid

picturesque
adj. attractive or scenic

pink
adj. the color of red and white mixed

pinstripe
adj. with very thin stripes

pioneering
adj. new and innovative

piped
adj. applied in thin stripes

piping-hot
adj. extremely hot

pirate
Ahoy, matey!

pitted
adj. with the pits removed

pivotal
adj. very important or critical

plastic
n. an easily molded material

platform
n. a raised level or surface

playful
adj. fun-loving and lively

pleasant
adj. enjoyable or nice

plentiful
adj. in large amounts

plowed
adj. with the soil turned over

plucked
adj. with feathers or hairs pulled off

plump
adj. round and fat

plush
adj. rich, soft, and luxurious

poached
adj. cooked in a hot liquid

pointed
adj. ending in a sharp point

pointy
adj. with a pointed tip

poisoned
adj. made toxic with poison

poisonous
adj. deadly or toxic

poky
adj. tiny or cramped

polar
adj. near the North or South Pole

polished
adj. made shiny by being rubbed

polluted
adj. dirty or full of waste

poor
adj. low-quality or not very good

pop-up
adj. spring-loaded

popular
adj. liked by many people

porous
adj. with lots of tiny holes

portable
adj. easy to carry or move

possible
adj. likely or able to happen

potted
adj. grown in a pot

powdery
adj. fine and powder-like

powerful
adj. strong, mighty, or effective

precious
adj. loved, valued, or expensive

precipitous
adj. steep or dangerously high

precise
adj. exact or accurate

predatory
adj. hunting other creatures

preening
adj. grooming itself with its beak

pregnant
adj. going to have a baby soon

preserved
adj. protected from going bad

pressed
adj. flattened to get rid of creases

prestigious
adj. important and respected

prickly
adj. covered in sharp spikes

primitive
adj. basic, rough, or crude

princely
adj. good enough for a prince

pristine
adj. brand-new or spotless

private
adj. for one person or not for everyone

prize-winning
adj. good enough to get an award

prized
adj. valued very highly

P - R

professional
adj. trained or expert

profitable
adj. making money

profuse
adj. a lot of or abundant

projectile
adj. pushed forward forcefully

prolific
adj. producing a lot

prominent
adj. easy to see or noticeable

promising
adj. hopeful or having potential

prosthetic
adj. made to replace the real thing

protected
adj. kept safe from harm

protective
adj. keeping you safe from harm

protruding
adj. sticking out or bulging

proud
adj. feeling important and confident

prowling
adj. roaming and looking for prey

pruned
adj. with the branches cut back

public
adj. for everyone to use

puffed
adj. swollen or bigger than before

puffed-up
adj. sticking out proudly

punctured
adj. damaged by making a hole

pungent
adj. strong-smelling or tasting

pure
adj. not mixed with anything else

purple
Color you turn if you hold your breath.

purring
adj. making a low and happy hum

quaint
adj. charming and picturesque

quaking
adj. shaking or trembling

queasy
adj. feeling sick or nauseous

quick
adj. able to learn in a short time

quiet
Shhhh!

quilted
adj. with a layer of soft padding

quirky
adj. in an unusual or eccentric style

rabid
adj. wild and violent

radiant
adj. bright, brilliant, or glowing

radioactive
adj. sending out toxic waves

ragged
adj. old and torn

raging
adj. furious or uncontrollable

rainbow-billed
adj. with a beak full of colors

ramshackle
adj. falling to pieces

random
[1] *adj.* odd or irregular
[2] *adj.* chosen without a reason

ransacked
adj. damaged and robbed

rapid
adj. very fast or quick

rapid-fire
adj. firing quickly one after another

rare
[1] *adj.* very few or not often seen
[2] *adj.* very lightly cooked

raucous
adj. making a harsh, loud noise

ravenous
adj. hungry or starving

raw
adj. uncooked or unprocessed

razor-sharp
adj. able to cut things very easily

reborn
adj. made new again

rechargeable
adj. able to be refilled with energy

reclining
adj. able to be tilted backwards

record-breaking
adj. more than ever before

recycled
adj. reused for something new

red-brick
adj. made with red-colored bricks

red-hot
adj. so hot that it glows red

reduced
adj. lowered or lessened

reedy
adj. with tall grass everywhere

refreshing
adj. making you feel energized

refurbished
adj. repaired, fixed, or revamped

regular
adj. always at the same time

R

reinforced
adj. made stronger or tougher

rejuvenating
adj. making you feel better or younger

relentless
adj. constant or nonstop

reliable
adj. trusted and dependable

remote
adj. far away or distant

renowned
adj. well-known and respected

rented
adj. paid to be used for a short time

replenished
adj. refilled or topped up

reputable
adj. well-respected and reliable

rescued
adj. saved from danger

respected
adj. admired or thought highly of

responsible
adj. sensible and trusted

restless
adj. unsettled or constantly moving

restored
adj. repaired or fixed

retired
adj. not working anymore

retractable
adj. able to be drawn back in

retro
adj. old-fashioned and cool

reusable
adj. working more than once

revolutionary
adj. bringing about a big change

revolving
adj. moving in a circle

rich
[1] *adj.* creamy, heavy, and delicious
[2] *adj.* lush, fertile, and full of life

rickety
adj. wobbly, shaky, or poorly made

ridiculous
adj. funny, silly, or absurd

ripe
adj. soft and ready to eat

ripped
adj. torn or pulled apart

rippling
adj. flowing in small waves

rising
adj. getting higher or moving up

roaring
[1] *adj.* making a loud and deep noise
[2] *adj.* full of loud and powerful flames

roasted
adj. cooked for a long time

roasting
adj. used to roast

robotic
adj. mechanical or like a robot

robust
adj. strong and tough

rocket-boosted
adj. made faster using rockets

rocky
adj. made of rock or stone

rogue
adj. rebellious and different

rolled
adj. turned over and flattened

rolling
[1] *adj.* rippling, wavy, or tumbling
[2] *adj.* turning round and round

romantic
adj. showing love and passion

roof-mounted
adj. fixed to the top of a roof

rotating
adj. spinning or turning

rotten
adj. decayed, old, and stinking

rotting
adj. going bad or decaying

rough
adj. carelessly made or badly made

rounded
adj. smooth and curved

royal
adj. for the family of a king or queen

rubber
n. a soft, bendy material

rubbery
adj. flexible and tough

rude
You smell.

ruffled
adj. scrunched up in a design

rugged
adj. rough, uneven, or craggy

rumbling
adj. deep, muffled, and continuous

rumpled
adj. wrinkled or creased

run-down
adj. old and needing repairs

runaway
adj. escaped or out of control

running
n. moving quickly on foot

runny
adj. liquid or flowing easily

ruptured
adj. broken open or burst

R - S

rustic
adj. typical of the countryside

rusty
adj. covered in rust or red flakes

sabotaged
adj. broken or ruined on purpose

sacred
adj. holy, religious, or spiritual

sad
Turn that frown upside down!

safari
n. a trip to look at or hunt animals

sagging
adj. drooping or hanging loosely

salted
adj. containing or covered in salt

saltwater
adj. containing salty water

salty
adj. tasting like salt

salvaged
adj. saved or rescued

sandy
adj. covered with sand

satin
n. a smooth, glossy fabric

savage
adj. cruel, violent, and uncontrolled

scalding
adj. extremely hot or burning

scaly
adj. covered in scales

scampering
adj. scurrying or dashing

scarlet
adj. vivid red in color

scattered
adj. spread randomly

scenic
adj. with beautiful views

scented
adj. with a nice smell

scheming
adj. plotting devious tricks

scientific
adj. to do with science

scorching
adj. red-hot or blazing

scraped
adj. grazed or scratched

scrappy
adj. determined and feisty

scrawny
adj. thin and bony

screeching
adj. squawking or squealing

scruffy
adj. shabby or untidy

scrumptious
adj. tasty or delicious

scuffed
adj. lightly damaged from scraping

sculpted
adj. beautifully shaped or carved

scuttling
adj. running with short steps

sea
Why is the sea friendly? It waves.

sealed
adj. shut tightly

seared
adj. quickly cooked on the surface

seaside
adj. by the sea

seasonal
adj. happening in certain seasons

seasoned
adj. with salt, pepper, or spices

secluded
adj. quiet or kept hidden

secret
My lips are sealed.

secure
adj. safe against danger or attacks

seedless
adj. without seeds

self-service
adj. letting people serve themselves

sensible
adj. wise and responsible

sensitive
adj. able to notice small changes

sentient
adj. able to feel things

serene
adj. peaceful or calm

serious
adj. important or not to be ignored

serrated
adj. sharp, rough, and jagged

serving
adj. used for giving out portions

severe
adj. very serious or harsh

shabby
adj. scruffy and worn

shaded
adj. sheltered from the sun

shady
adj. giving shelter from the sun

shaggy
adj. long, thick, and messy

shallow
adj. not deep

S

sharp
[1] *adj.* able to cut or pierce things easily
[2] *adj.* quick, clear, and noticeable

sharp-eyed
adj. quick to spot things

sharpened
adj. made more pointy

shattered
adj. smashed into small pieces

shaved
adj. shredded into thin flakes

sheltering
adj. protecting or covering

shifting
adj. moving in different directions

shimmering
adj. glinting and flickering

shocking
adj. surprising and distressing

shooting
adj. moving very fast

shorn
adj. with its fleece cut off

short
adj. not very long

shredded
adj. cut or torn into thin pieces

shrill
adj. sharp or very high-pitched

shriveled
adj. wrinkled or shrunken

shuttered
adj. closed with shutters

shy
adj. nervous, timid, or hiding

sifted
adj. put through a sieve

silk
n. a strong, soft, and thin fabric

silver
adj. pale gray and shiny

silvery
adj. light gray and reflective

simple
adj. basic and plain

single
adj. only one or with no others

sinking
adj. moving slowly downwards

sizzling
adj. very hot or hissing with heat

sizzling-hot
adj. hot or extremely spicy

skillful
adj. talented or expert

skilled
adj. trained or experienced

skimpy
adj. small and revealing

skinny
[1] *adj.* thin or scrawny [2] *adj.* made with less fat [3] *adj.* slim and tight-fitting

sky-high
adj. very tall or very high

sky-piercing
adj. taller than the sky

slanting
adj. sloping at an angle

slathered
adj. spread on thickly or heavily

sleek
adj. smooth and shiny

sleeping
adj. asleep or not awake

sleepy
adj. quiet and peaceful

slender
adj. slim and graceful

sliced
adj. cut into thin pieces

slimy
adj. slippery, wet, and gooey

slippery
adj. smooth, wet, or difficult to grip

slithering
adj. sliding or moving smoothly

slivered
adj. cut into very thin pieces

slobbering
adj. drooling or dripping saliva

slow
adj. taking a long time or not fast

slow-moving
adj. moving slowly or barely moving

sluggish
adj. slow, lazy, or lifeless

sly
adj. clever and dishonest

small
adj. little in size or not big

smart
[1] *adj.* using computers to work
[2] *adj.* looking good or neat

smashed
adj. broken or shattered

smelly
You smelt it, you dealt it.

smoked
adj. preserved using smoke

smoky
adj. sending out smoke

smudged
adj. blurred, rubbed, or smeared

snarling
adj. making a growling noise

sneaky
adj. good at lying and hiding

S

snooty
adj. rudely looking down on others

snow-capped
adj. covered with snow at the top

snowy
adj. covered with snow

snug
adj. cozy and comfortable

soaked
adj. extremely wet

soaring
adj. high, flying, or gliding

sodden
adj. soaked or completely wet

soft
[1] *adj.* faint or dim [2] *adj.* mild and mellow
[3] *adj.* mushy or not hard

soggy
adj. wet and soft

solar
adj. powered by sunlight

solemn
adj. serious and formal

solid
[1] *adj.* hard and thick
[2] *adj.* firm and reliable

solitary
adj. living or spending time alone

somber
adj. sad, gloomy, or dark

soothing
adj. comforting and calming

sore
[1] *adj.* painful or aching
[2] *adj.* angry or annoyed

soundproofed
adj. not letting sound in or out

sour
adj. bitter, sharp, and acidic

sourdough
n. a sour or bitter type of dough

spacious
adj. big or with a lot of room inside

spare
adj. extra or back-up

sparkling
adj. shining or glimmering

sparkly
adj. shiny or glittery

spattered
adj. splashed, stained, or speckled

special
adj. important or unique

speckled
adj. marked with small dots

speeding
adj. moving too fast

speedy
adj. fast or quick

spelt
n. a healthy type of flour

spewing
adj. gushing, spitting, or oozing

spiced
adj. with added flavor from spice

spicy
adj. tasting hot and fiery

spiked
adj. with sharp points or spikes

spilled
adj. fallen out or overflowing

spiral
adj. coiled, twisted, or curved

spiraling
adj. winding around and around

spirited
adj. lively and determined

spiritual
adj. religious and emotional

splendid
adj. bright, glorious, or impressive

splintered
adj. broken into thin, sharp pieces

spooked
adj. scared, frightened, and jumpy

spoon-bending
adj. so stiff it can bend metal

spotless
adj. completely clean

spouting
adj. sending out a jet of water

sprawling
adj. stretching over a large area

spray-painted
adj. painted using a spray

springy
adj. bouncy or moving like elastic

square
Like a circle, but with corners.

squashed
adj. crushed or squeezed

squat
adj. short and stubby

squawking
adj. harshly screeching or shrieking

squeaky
adj. making a high-pitched noise

squealing
adj. making a loud, high noise

squeezed
adj. with the juice pressed out

squirming
adj. wriggling uncomfortably

stacked
adj. piled up, one on top of the other

stagnant
adj. still and stale

S

stained
adj. marked or discolored

stale
adj. old, hard, and crusty

stampeding
adj. rushing wildly in a group

startled
adj. surprised or frightened

steady
adj. constant and unchanging

steak
n. a thick slice of meat

stealthy
adj. sneaky or secretive

steamed
adj. cooked with heat from steam

steaming
adj. giving off misty fumes

steamy
adj. clouded by misty fumes

steep
adj. going sharply up or down

sterile
adj. completely free from germs

stewed
adj. cooked slowly in liquid

sticky
adj. gluey or fixing to things

stiff
[1] *adj.* unbending or hard to move
[2] *adj.* straight and severe

stifling
adj. so hot you can barely breathe

stinging
adj. painful to touch

stinking
adj. smelling nasty

stolen
adj. taken illegally or without asking

stone-ground
adj. crushed up finely using stones

stony
[1] *adj.* unfriendly or unfeeling
[2] *adj.* covered in small rocks

stormy
adj. rainy, thundery, and windy

strained
adj. tense, tired, or painful

stranded
adj. left, stuck, or abandoned

strange
adj. odd or unusual

strapless
adj. without straps

strappy
adj. held together with straps

stray
adj. escaped or without an owner

streaky
adj. marked with stripes

streamlined
adj. made simple and easy to use

stretched
adj. pulled tight and not loose

strict
adj. sticking to the rules

striped
adj. patterned with lines

strong
[1] *adj.* intense and full of flavor [2] *adj.* powerful, tough, and mighty [3] *adj.* firm and muscular

strutting
adj. walking upright and confidently

stubborn
adj. difficult to get rid of or move

stubby
adj. short and thick

studded
adj. decorated with pieces of metal

stuffed
adj. filled or packed with something

stumpy
adj. short, thick, and squat

stunning
adj. beautiful and impressive

stunted
adj. stopped from growing fully

sturdy
adj. strong and solidly built

stylish
adj. fashionable or elegant

submerged
adj. completely underwater

subtle
adj. faint and delicate

succulent
adj. juicy, fresh, and tasty

sudden
adj. unexpected or without warning

sufficient
adj. enough or plenty

suffocating
adj. making it hard to breathe

sugar-loaded
adj. full of sugar

sugary
adj. very sticky and sweet

sulfurous
adj. smelling like rotten eggs

sun-kissed
adj. warmed or browned by the sun

sunken
[1] *adj.* lower or beneath a surface
[2] *adj.* under water or submerged

sunny
adj. lit up by the sun

super-strong
adj. very powerful

S - T

supercharged
adj. very powerful or lasting longer

superfast
adj. extremely speedy

surfacing
adj. coming up above the water

surgical
adj. used in surgery

suspected
adj. thought to be guilty

sustainable
adj. caught safely and responsibly

swarming
adj. moving together in a big group

swaying
adj. moving gently from side to side

sweet
adj. pleasant and sugary

sweetened
adj. made to taste sugary

swelling
adj. growing bigger or expanding

sweltering
adj. very hot or baking

swimming
adj. moving through water

swirling
adj. spiraling or twirling

swollen
adj. bulging, expanded, or inflamed

swooping
adj. flying downwards quickly

sympathetic
adj. understanding and comforting

table
n. a surface for eating or working

tailored
adj. specially made to fit you

tainted
adj. spoiled or contaminated

talented
adj. skilled and gifted

talkative
adj. chatty or talking a lot

talking
adj. saying words out loud

tall
adj. high off the ground

tame
adj. well-trained and obedient

tangled
adj. twisted, knotted, or messy

tart
adj. sharp and sour

tasty
adj. delicious or yummy

tattered
adj. old, torn, and worn-out

teeming
adj. full or crowded

teen
n. a person aged 13 to 19

telepathic
adj. reading thoughts

televised
adj. shown on the television

temperamental
adj. emotional, moody, or fiery

tempestuous
adj. wild, stormy, and unpredictable

temporary
adj. lasting for a short time

tempting
adj. attractive or hard to say no to

terrible
adj. very bad or awful

tethered
adj. tied up or chained

thatched
adj. made with straw or hay

thawing
adj. melting into water

therapeutic
adj. healing or making you feel better

thick
[1] *adj.* not very runny [2] *adj.* chunky, wide, and heavy [3] *adj.* closely packed in or dense

thieving
adj. robbing or stealing

thirsty
adj. in need of water

thorny
adj. having lots of thorns

threadbare
adj. old and worn thin

threatening
adj. ominous or scary

three-legged
adj. with three legs

thriving
adj. growing and doing very well

throbbing
adj. pulsing in pain

thundering
adj. making a sound like thunder

thunderous
adj. very loud or like thunder

ticking
adj. making a repetitive sound

ticklish
adj. making you wriggle and giggle

tie-dyed
adj. with round color patterns

tiered
adj. with one row on top of another

tight
[1] *adj.* dense or pressed firmly together
[2] *adj.* close-fitting or figure-hugging

tiled
adj. covered in flat stone slabs

timid
adj. shy or fearful

tinted
adj. with a faint color

tiny
adj. very small

tired
adj. worn out and sleepy

toasted
adj. heated until crispy and brown

toasty
adj. keeping you warm

top
adj. best or of the highest standard

toppling
adj. tumbling or about to fall over

torn
adj. cut or split

torrential
adj. falling heavily and forcefully

total
adj. complete or absolute

touchscreen
adj. controlled by pressing a screen

tough
[1] *adj.* difficult to cut or chew
[2] *adj.* strong and resilient

towering
adj. extremely tall

toxic
adj. poisonous or deadly

trained
adj. prepared and practiced

trampled
adj. walked over and crushed

trampling
adj. stomping and crushing

tranquil
adj. peaceful or blissfully quiet

tranquilized
adj. made sleepy or calm with a drug

translucent
adj. letting light through

transplanted
adj. moved from another body

trapped
adj. stuck or caught

treacherous
[1] *adj.* dangerous or unsafe
[2] *adj.* lying and not to be trusted

treasured
adj. loved and valued

trembling
adj. shaking with nerves or fear

trendy
adj. fashionable or in style

trophy
n. a prize given to winners

tropical
adj. in or from a hot country

trusted
adj. loyal, reliable, and honest

trusty
adj. tried and tested, or reliable

turbocharged
adj. made extra fast or strong

turbulent
adj. violent and unpredictable

twinkling
adj. sparkling and flickering

twirling
adj. spinning or swirling

twisting
adj. bending or curling around

twitching
adj. fluttering or jerking

two-headed
adj. with two heads

two-person
adj. with space for two people

two-pronged
adj. with just two sharp points

two-time
adj. having happened twice before

ugly
adj. unattractive or hideous

unattended
adj. left alone or not watched

unbearable
adj. impossible to take or put up with

unbeatable
adj. impossible to trick or beat

unbreakable
adj. very strong or not easily broken

unbuttoned
adj. with the buttons undone

uncharted
adj. unexplored or not mapped

uncomfortable
adj. unpleasant or not comfortable

unconvincing
adj. not very believable

undeciphered
adj. impossible to read or understand

undefeated
adj. never beaten before

undercover
adj. working secretly or in disguise

underground
adj. under the surface of the ground

undetectable
adj. impossible for others to see

U - V

undrinkable
adj. too disgusting to drink

uneven
adj. bumpy or not level

unexpected
adj. surprising or without warning

unfeeling
adj. without emotions

unflushed
adj. left full of gross waste

unforgiving
adj. showing no mercy

unicorn
n. a magical horse with a single horn

unidentified
adj. unknown or unrecognized

uninflated
adj. not filled with air

uninhabitable
adj. not possible to live in

unique
adj. the only one of its kind

unkempt
adj. messy or untidy

unknowable
adj. impossible to know about

unlikely
adj. unexpected or not probable

unlit
adj. dark and without lights

unlocked
adj. not shut with a lock

unlucky
adj. unfortunate or out of luck

unmade
adj. not arranged neatly

unmanned
adj. without people on board

unopened
adj. closed or not opened

unpaid
adj. still needing to be paid

unpatrolled
adj. not checked by inspectors

unplugged
adj. not plugged into electricity

unripe
adj. not ready to be eaten

unscooped
adj. left or not picked up

unseen
adj. hidden or out of sight

unsightly
adj. ugly or not pleasant to look at

unsinkable
adj. unable to stop floating

unstoppable
adj. impossible to stop

unsuccessful
adj. failed or giving bad results

unsung
adj. uncelebrated or not praised

unsuspecting
adj. not realizing what is going on

unswept
adj. unchecked or uncleared

unswerving
adj. steady or constant

untidy
adj. messy or cluttered

untuned
adj. sounding wrong

unwanted
adj. rejected or not wanted

unwieldy
adj. large and difficult to use

unwitting
adj. not aware of the facts

upcoming
adj. happening soon

upright
adj. standing up straight

upscale
adj. fashionable and expensive

upturned
adj. tipped over or upside down

useful
adj. handy or helpful

useless
adj. pointless or without use

user-friendly
adj. easy for anyone to use

vacant
adj. empty or not lived in

valiant
adj. brave or fearless

varicose
adj. painfully swollen or twisted

vast
adj. very large or enormous

vegan
adj. avoiding all food from animals

vegetable
What grown-ups make you eat.

velvety
adj. soft, smooth, and silky

vengeful
adj. wanting revenge

venomous
adj. poisonous or toxic

versatile
adj. able to do lots of different things

vicious
adj. cruel, brutal, and violent

V - W

vintage
adj. old, high-quality, and stylish

visceral
adj. deeply felt and uncontrolled

viscous
adj. thick and sticky

vivid
adj. full of bright colors

volcanic
adj. made by volcanoes

voluminous
adj. large and full

waddling
adj. walking in short, wobbly steps

wagging
adj. shaking or waving up and down

wailing
adj. moaning or howling

walk-in
adj. big enough to walk into

warm
[1] *adj.* keeps in the heat
[2] *adj.* hot, but not too hot

wary
adj. careful or cautious

washed-up
adj. dumped on a beach by the tide

watchful
adj. alert or observant

waterproof
[1] *adj.* won't stop working in water
[2] *adj.* not letting water through

weak
adj. watery or not very strong

weekly
adj. happens every week

weightless
adj. not held down by gravity

welcome
adj. wanted or pleasing

welcoming
adj. making people want to go in

well-cut
adj. well-made and of high quality

well-done
adj. cooked for longer than normal

well-earned
adj. deserved after hard work

well-lit
adj. covered in light and easy to see

well-run
adj. efficient and organized

well-worn
adj. old and worn-out

wet
adj. covered in water or full of water

wheezy
adj. panting, gasping, and hissing

whipped
adj. thickened using a whisk

whirling
adj. moving around in quick circles

whirring
adj. making a continuous, low sound

whistling
adj. making a high-pitched sound

white
adj. of the color of snow

whitewashed
adj. painted with a thin, white liquid

whole
adj. in one piece or not cut up

whole-grain
adj. made using complete grains

wicked
adj. evil or bad

wide
adj. broad or with the sides far apart

widespread
adj. covering a large area

wild
[1] *adj.* violent or uncontrolled
[2] *adj.* not grown on a farm

willing
adj. eager or happy to agree

wilted
adj. cooked until slightly soft

wilting
adj. dying from lack of water

winding
adj. bending or moving in a curve

windowless
adj. without any windows

windswept
adj. windblown or beaten by winds

winged
adj. with wings attached

winning
You have to be in it to win it.

wintry
adj. looking or feeling like winter

wire-framed
adj. with thin metal frames

wireless
adj. without any wires

wise
adj. clever and sensible

wispy
adj. thin or fine

withered
adj. wilted, dried-up, and drooping

wobbly
adj. shaky or unsteady

wood-burning
adj. using wood as fuel

wood-fired
adj. burning wood for heat

W - Z

wooden
adj. made of wood

wooly
adj. made of wool

world-class
adj. one of the best in the world

worn-out
adj. damaged from being used a lot

worthy
adj. respectable and deserving

wounded
adj. hurt or injured

wriggling
adj. twisting and turning

wrinkled
adj. with lots of little creases

writhing
adj. wriggling or squirming

yellow
adj. of the color of bananas

young
adj. not having lived for long

zesty
adj. fruity and sharp-tasting

zingy
adj. lively and sharp-tasting

zooming
adj. moving very quickly

A

C

D

F

A B C D E F G H I J K L M N O P Q R S T U V W X Y Z

G

H

I

J

K

L

M

N

O

L
M

Q

R

R

S

S

T

U

V

W

X

Y

Z

Credits to...

Editor-in-Chief
Sofia Fenichell

Art Director
Craig Kellman

Artists
Aghnia Mardiyah
Brett Coulson
Daniel Permutt
Holly Jones
Joan Varitek
Nicolò Mereu
Phillip Mamuyac
Wendell Luebbe

Senior Writers
Tatiana Barnes
Mark Holland

Editors & Lexicographers
Ian Brookes
Nicole Le Vine
Penny Hands

Academic Advisors
Emma Madden
Prof. Susan Neuman

Graphic Designers
Lady San Pedro
James Sales
Fabrice Gourdel

Machine Learning
Benjamin Pettit
Rob Koeling
Stanislaw Pstrokonski

Producers
Leon Welters
Eva Schumacher Payne

Mrs Wordsmith is an independent publisher of illustrated materials that teach children better vocabulary. It combines creativity and data science to produce content that is relevant, entertaining, and effective.

First hardback edition February 2019

ISBN 978-1-9996107-8-4

FSC
www.fsc.org
MIX
Paper from
responsible sources
FSC® C016379

mrswordsmith.com